THE DIETER'S DILEMMA

Eating Less
and Weighing More

WILLIAM BENNETT, M.D.

&

JOEL GURIN

Basic Books, Inc., Publishers   New York

Library of Congress Cataloging in Publication Data

Bennett, William, 1941–
   The dieter's dilemma.
   Includes index.
   1. Reducing diets. 2. Obesity. 3. Body image.
4. Body, Human—Social aspects. I. Gurin, Joel, 1953–
II. Title.
RM222.2.B443   613.2'5'019   81-68403
ISBN: 0–465–01652–9 (cloth)
ISBN: 0–465–01653–7 (paper)

The Dieter's Dilemma

For Alan, Carol, and Sarah

CONTENTS

ACKNOWLEDGMENTS

In the three years that we have been working on this book, we have incurred debts to many people.

Marion Nestle and Margaret Mackenzie saw our prospectus in its early stages and helped us focus on the most promising areas. Arthur Rosenthal gave us encouragement and valuable criticism at this stage. George Cahill offered guidance and source material as we began our research.

Ethan Sims was generous with time and information; he and Dorothea Sims gave us hospitality at the beginning, and with equal graciousness criticized the final manuscript. Hospitality, encouragement, and information were also provided by Victor De Gruttola and by Jonathan and Bilgé Friedlaender. Jerry and Pat Gurin's interest, encouragement, and support at every stage of this undertaking were terrifically helpful.

Jules Hirsch first called our attention to the concept of a setpoint for body fat, and he pointed out the role that exercise might play in regulating it. Albert Stunkard helped us to refine our understanding of the concept, cautiously egged us on as we began to take it seriously, and commented on our manuscript. Susan and O. Wayne Wooley gave us valuable insight into the clinical aspects of weight regulation. Reubin Andres educated us about the epidemiology of fatness.

Stuart Agras, James Ferguson, Peter Herman, Richard Nisbett, and Stanley Schachter shared their perceptions of the psychological aspects of fatness and eating behavior.

Elliot Danforth, Jeffrey Flier, Joel Grinker, Jerome Knittle, Sheldon Margen, Stephen Phinney, Jesse Roth, Lester Salans, Judith Wurtman, and James Young all took more time than they could easily afford to discuss their work with us. M. Nagulesparan, James Reitman, Barbara Howard, and David Mott of the Phoenix Indian Medical Center introduced us to their work with the Pima Indians.

Glynn Isaac, Barbara Smuts, Peter Ellison, John Seger, Daniel Hrdy, Sarah Blaffer Hrdy, and other members of the "Simian Seminar" at Harvard University challenged our ideas about the evolution of fatness, led us to sources, and paid us the high compliment of taking us seriously. Sarah Hrdy, who read an early draft of chapter 6, was characteristically generous with ideas, criticism, and moral support. Wilma Wetterstrom and Adrienne Zihlman were most helpful with information and suggestions on evolution.

Harriet Ritvo and Barbara Sicherman led us to sources that were used for chapter 7, discussed the ideas with us, and criticized a draft.

George Blackburn, George Bray, Anthony Gualtieri, James Naughton, Randall Lee, and Peter Lindner, as well as several members of the American Society of Bariatric Physicians, helped us to evaluate a wide range of weight reduction systems.

Gail Butterfield, Judith Stern, Joan Ullyot, and Peter Wood explained the effects of physical activity on body composition and body size.

Sarah Finkelhor, Judy Freespirit, Melody Marks, Marcia Millman, and Louise Wolfe talked with us about the experience of being fat in America.

Lois Banner, Stacey Corcoran FitzSimmons, Margaret Mackenzie, Linda Nochlin, Peter Wood, Ethan Sims, and Albert Stunkard kindly gave us access to unpublished material.

The magnificent libraries of Harvard University often made our research not merely possible but a pleasure and an adventure as well. The librarians at Harvard's Baker, Countway, Museum of Comparative Zoology, Tozzer, and Widener libraries were ever patient and resourceful.

Linda Stewart, who typed the manuscript, was not only fast,

accurate, and accommodating, but, as our first reader, wonderfully supportive. Frank Fox of Marcella's Sandwich & Espresso Store supplied encouragement along with many cups of coffee, croissants, and his excellent sandwiches.

We are grateful to Martin Kessler and the others at Basic Books who gave this book a high priority, for their unflagging attention to this project.

We are also conscious of an indebtedness to many people other than those we have named—family, friends, and acquaintances who have not only put up with endless conversations about fat but have offered ideas and criticisms that we may, unconsciously, have incorporated as our own.

We are, of course, wholly responsible for any errors of fact and interpretation that may appear in this book, and we are aware that everyone we have thanked will probably find something in it to disagree with.

PREFACE

People who are fatter than the average may find it difficult to talk about their state, and we have had to think about the best way to describe them in this book. The conventional euphemisms for fatness are inaccurate and contain hidden value judgments. Calling someone "overweight" implies that he exceeds an ideal standard, but, as we show, the commonly applied standards are quite arbitrary. A "heavy" person's weight can represent muscle or fluid rather than fat. "Obesity" sounds like a medical condition (and its etymology implies that an unnaturally large appetite is the cause of fatness); yet fatness in and of itself may have little consequence for health and there is no evidence that fat people consistently eat more than the lean. There is, of course, a whole host of adjectives—chubby, chunky, husky, plump, zaftig, stout, portly, fleshy—which are variously used as insults or euphemisms as the occasion arises. Both of the authors, who were fat as children, had to put up with such descriptions. One was identified as "that chubby kid down the block," and the other remembers wearing "husky" sizes and enduring a summer at camp under the nickname "Flab Lad."

The terms "fat" and "lean" really indicate a continuum, but it is awkward always to specify where a person belongs in that scale, and often it is not necessary. In this book we generally refer to people who are fatter than average as "fat," and we use the term "fatness" when we need to talk about the amount of adipose tissue on the body, or the state of being fat. We use "overweight" when discussing people in relation to some explicit standard of "desirable" or "ideal" weight.

And we use the term "obese" when we wish to acknowledge that someone is so fat that his health is threatened or impaired by his fatness. We occasionally resort to synonyms just to avoid repetition.

The word "fat" has the virtue of simplicity and reasonable accuracy. Moreover, it has become the choice of various "fat pride" groups, such as the Fat Underground and the National Association to Aid Fat Americans. Their reasoning is that any effort to use a different word implies that there is something about fatness to be concealed (even though the physical reality cannot be disguised). Our belief is that fatness is not a shameful condition. To use a word other than "fat," then, would be as inappropriate and unwieldy as calling a lean person "small-framed" or describing shortness as "underheight."

The Dieter's Dilemma

1

FAT AND FATE

Y OU probably want to lose weight. Most Americans do, especially if they are in the upper-middle class, or are moving in that direction. Mainly you want to look thinner, but you also think reducing would make you healthier.

You may put off the effort and live with the persistent, faintly miserable sensation that you ought to be a better person. But if you decide to take yourself in hand, you know what to do. You will go on a diet. You will use artificial sweeteners. You will probably spend money—to buy a diet book, to join a weight-loss club, to seek therapy, to fill your grocery bag with low-calorie foods, or to purchase appetite suppressants at the drugstore. You will not bother with exercise because you know that physical activity burns disappointingly few calories and it makes you feel hungrier.

Chances are, you're in for a nasty struggle, some short-lived success, and an inexorable return to your old weight. In the long run, diet failures outnumber the successes by a very wide margin.

The failure, however, does not lie in your weak will. It lies

3

in the misconceptions about weight and weight control that dominate our belief system. Most of what we are routinely told about how fat is gained or lost is either wrong, misleading, or meaningless. It is not just *The Beverly Hills Diet*, sauna suits, or Maxi-Slim pills—bizarre and lucrative gimmicks that exploit the customer's good faith and lack of good sense. The standard, "sensible" recommendations to change eating habits and diligently use calorie charts are also no more than elaborate folklore, expressions of faith in a world that ought to exist, but in fact does not.

Although the reducing diet is not an effective means of weight control, it has become our modern ritual of self-improvement and self-purification. And like any ritual, dieting needs a myth to give it meaning. The central tenet of the diet mythology is that thin people are *better* than fat people—more beautiful, healthier, stronger of will. To validate this invidious comparison, it is argued that virtually anybody can, with a reasonable amount of conscious effort, control how fat he or she becomes. But the best evidence and common experience both contradict this rationalization. With rare exceptions, dieters lose weight temporarily and then, despite great determination, gradually regain it. The mere fact that one diet program after another appears on the best-seller list is proof, if proof were needed, that none works for very long. National statistics also demonstrate the failure of dieting. All told, Americans now eat about 10 percent less than they did fifteen years ago. So they ought to weigh less. But they do not. Since the mid-sixties, the typical American has grown as much as four or five pounds heavier—almost certainly because the effects of a drop in activity level have outweighed those of lower intake.[1]

In this book we present the case that the amount of fat a person carries is automatically regulated and that some people are naturally fatter than others. Being fat reflects neither weakness of character nor neurotic conflict; it is a biological fact of life, an aspect of the human species' inherent variability.

4

We suggest that, while there are ways of lowering the body's demand for fat, dieting by itself is not effective. Of the known methods, frequent physical activity is probably the most effective and the safest. Moreover, certain common practices—such as the use of appetite suppressants and artificial sweeteners—are futile or self-defeating approaches to weight control.

We also challenge the most common reasons people give for wanting to reduce. The idea that health automatically benefits from weight loss is dubious at best. Nobody has ever proved that losing weight prolongs the life of moderately fat people, much less those of average weight. On the contrary, fatness itself appears not to be a major cause of disease, as we have been told it is.

If the warnings issued in the past few decades by life insurance companies and health educators had been true, the rise in average weight since the 1960s would be reflected in increasing death rates from heart attacks, strokes, and other kinds of degenerative diseases. But the death rate from cardiovascular disease has been falling since 1965, and overall life expectancy has increased by a couple of years. Careful scientific investigations reported in the last ten years, moreover, have repeatedly failed to show that moderate amounts of body fat are harmful to health.[2]

In about 30 percent of fat people, their fatness is a warning, a signal that diabetes or high blood pressure is developing. Anyone who tends to gain weight easily, especially one with a family history of either disease, should have relatively frequent medical checkups. Weight control can be an important element in the treatment of both diabetes and high blood pressure when they do appear. But without a commitment to exercise, pure dieting is usually a poor means of weight control.

For most people the real motivation to lose weight is to achieve not better health but a more desirable physique. There is no disputing taste, but it can be analyzed. We argue that current standards of beauty prizing extreme slenderness are historically very recent and primarily reflect ambivalence toward the sexual liberation of women.

We hope that, when they finish this book, many of our readers will like themselves a little better. We also hope that all our readers will come to be not only more tolerant of human variety but also more respectful of the body's ability to take care of itself.

The common conception of weight control is based on three assumptions. First, the body doesn't really "care" how much fat it has; it merely stores the energy leftovers from each meal. Second, eating is the significant behavior; fat people obviously eat more than people of normal weight. Third, the conscious mind is capable of balancing intake and expenditure of energy and thus achieving any desired weight. It is quite easy to show that these assumptions are false.

An alternative theory—and, we think, the correct one—holds that the body does "care." Built into every person is a control system dictating how much fat he or she should carry. We'll speak of this control system as determining a *setpoint* for body fat, a term now appearing in the scientific literature.

A thermostat is an example of a common setpoint mechanism: It determines the temperature of a room by turning the furnace on or off to maintain the temperature at which it is set. The mechanism controlling the setpoint for body fat is far more complicated: It receives more information than a thermostat does, and it has more than one way to produce results. But its function is similar; it actively seeks to maintain a given "set" amount of fat on the body. Some individuals come with a high setting, others with a low one. Some are therefore naturally fat and others thin. The difference is not between the weak and the strong or the impulsive and the abstemious, but between internal (quite probably innate) controls that are set differently in different people.

Going on a diet is an attempt to overpower the body's setpoint. (For that matter, the skinny person who overeats in order to gain weight is fighting a similar battle.) It is not a fair contest. The setpoint is a tireless opponent. At any given time it has a single goal, and it has effective ways of making the dieter miserable until he or she desists. The dieter's only allies are will power and whatever incentives serve to make chronic physical discomfort worthwhile. But will power is subject to fatigue and incentives often lose their value after a time, whereas the setpoint seldom wavers.

The ideal means to weight control would be a safe method that lowers an individual's setting rather than simply resisting it. So far, our knowledge of ways to influence the setpoint is exceedingly primitive, but there are some leads. Of these, as we have mentioned, physical activity is the most promising: Exercise seems to function as a handle to crank down the setting.

Much of the rest of this book develops and, unavoidably, complicates this introductory description of the setpoint mechanism. But at this juncture the reader might ask, "If everybody has a setpoint, how can I find out what my own setting is?" The answer is bound to be somewhat unsatisfactory: Your setting is the weight you normally maintain, give or take a few pounds, when you are not thinking about it.

This answer is, to be sure, crude and circular. And chronic dieters may find it difficult to apply; a lifetime of eating by the calorie charts can put one out of touch with one's own comfortable weight. But even many dieters can identify a weight to which they spontaneously return. Young people who have been experimentally starved or overfed return rapidly to their previous weight. And many who make no conscious effort whatever to change will maintain the same weight for years on end.

As a case in point, one of the authors is within two pounds of his weight when he graduated from high school twenty-four years ago. With some fluctuation, he has maintained that weight for most of the intervening period. Assuming that he has consumed about twenty-four million calories since 1958, the two-pound gain represents a net caloric surplus of less than 0.03 percent, or about 0.8 calories a day—roughly the amount in a single carrot stick. He has never counted calories for even one of the 8,766 days in question, although, during periodic efforts at self-improvement, he has skipped an occasional dessert, and he has taken up jogging in order to remain about as active as he was in June 1958.

Not everyone, of course, holds to such a stable weight. Most people gain weight as they get older, perhaps because they exercise less, perhaps because they are genetically programmed to gain weight with age. Some fluctuate, perhaps because they have relatively lax setpoints. And rare, very unhappy individuals seem to lack a functioning setpoint altogether. One such was Robert Earl Hughes of Monticello, Missouri, who died, in July 1958, at the age of thirty-two. According to the *Guinness Book of World Records,* Hughes weighed 1,041 pounds when he was buried—just a few short of the all-time maximum, 1,069 pounds, that he had achieved the preceding February.[3]

If we all depended solely on conscious management of our food intake instead of an internal control system, it would be incredibly easy to suffer Hughes's fate. Innumerable diet manuals have presented weight control as purely a matter of measuring calories consumed against calories expended. Fat has been described as the bottom line on a caloric balance sheet: CREDIT —breakfast, lunch, dinner, snacks; DEBIT—the effort of breathing, running up and down the back steps, having sex, playing tennis or pinball; NET—an ounce of adipose tissue, one way or the other. Anyone who could pass a high-school bookkeeping course should be able to do the sums. It looks easy enough on paper, but let's examine the arithmetic more closely.

Consider what it would take, theoretically, to gain ten pounds in one year—the fastest rate at which most normal adults ever gain weight, except for those just coming off a diet. This gain requires no more than 100 "extra" calories a day. The excess amounts to one tablespoon of butter *or* a plain muffin without butter *or* a pear *or* a cup of minestrone *or* a biscuit of shredded wheat. And the caloric mistake is not being made at a single meal. It is spread out over an entire day in which 2,000 to 3,000 calories are being consumed and burned away. A few extra flakes of cereal at breakfast, three more bites of cheese at lunch, a couple of Life Savers in the afternoon, a chicken breast instead of a drumstick at dinner—and the jig is up. Indeed, this error is so subtle that a trained nutritionist, shadowing someone all day long, could not guess to within 300 or 400 calories how much the subject had eaten.

Even Hughes, according to the standard charts, needed to make only a small daily error to become the "heaviest medically weighed human" on record: He presumably ate 265 calories more than his maintenance requirement every day, about the equivalent of an apple, a tablespoon of butter, and a small glass of orange juice. At this rate he could, theoretically, have gained the 523 pounds that he added in the nineteen years before his death. (Granted, his maintenance requirement would have increased as he gained weight, so that eventually he must have been eating a lot.)

Measuring caloric intake is only half the task. To know whether food is a necessity or a luxury, you need to know how much energy you are expending in the course of a day. For example, scrubbing the floor for approximately fifteen minutes will use up the caloric equivalent of a biscuit of shredded wheat. So will spending fifty minutes cooking dinner or swimming a fast crawl for about thirteen minutes. But these estimates are even less accurate than the assessment of intake.

And for each of us to keep a running total of our own intake and exertion would require an inordinate amount of mental effort. Imagine having to subtract accordion playing from apples in the course of your day. (One apple equals about thirty minutes of playing the instrument, as opposed to about fifty minutes of just sitting and listening.) The chance of coming out within 500 calories of the right count is ridiculously small.[4]

The alternative is to let your body do the subtraction (which it does anyway) and measure the difference (namely, fat) on your bathroom scale. But because the scale registers fluctuations in body fluids and feces as well, it cannot be very precise about changes in fat accumulation. Indeed, a dietary indiscretion showing up on the scale as a couple of pounds may have added only ounces of fat; the rest of the two-pound gain could be extra fluid, which is retained only temporarily. Someone who gains ten pounds in a year does so at the rate of three ounces a week, an amount that defies the precision of even the best scales in common use. (Hughes himself gained little more than an ounce a day.)

It strains belief to think that people—even those who lead very well regulated lives—can supervise their own weight with anything like the precision commonly achieved by nondieters. Consciously making the necessary fine adjustments in food intake simply cannot be done, short of curtailing the variety of foods consumed and weighing every portion. This point was nicely illustrated by a group of dieters in an experimental program. They were instructed to cut their habitual daily intake by a modest, sensible 400 calories. In the belief that they were complying, the dieters went ahead to eliminate a full 1,000 calories. Only at that level did they actually feel they were dieting; they were appropriately uncomfortable, and they could soon detect the results on their bathroom scales.[5]

All in all, it is no wonder that dieters typically go through periods of relatively rapid weight loss and then a longer phase of insidious gain, punctuated by eating binges. Unless they do something to lower their setpoint—for example, by increasing their activity levels—this is precisely the pattern that resisting a setpoint can be expected to produce. Of course, there are rare individuals who manage, with extraordinary and obsessive effort, to remake themselves by dieting. There are others who can starve themselves to death by an act of will, and there have been saints who could sit for decades at the top of a pillar. These examples have little to teach the majority of people, who have other things to do with their lives.

Unhindered, the setpoint mechanism manages to keep the body's weight fairly constant, presumably because it has more accurate information about the body's stores of fat than the conscious mind can obtain. Critics of the setpoint concept have joked that we would all have to have scales in the soles of our feet to make it work. More likely, at least one chemical substance, such as a hormone, is released by the cells responsible for storing fat. The blood level of this substance, which is proportional to the amount of fat being stored, is monitored by the brain. If it falls too low, the setpoint device, a complex structure within the brain, begins to pressure the conscious mind—at first almost imperceptibly—to change behavior. This pressure may be experienced initially as a kind of agitation— a "noshy" feeling, a restless inclination to eat between meals and to eat a little more at each meal. Later on, as dieting proceeds, the feeling hardens into voracious hunger, and restlessness gives way to energy-conserving lethargy. This succession of events was vividly recorded during an artificial famine that was staged nearly forty years ago.

In the rainy November of 1944, thirty-six conscientious objectors to military service took up residence in dormitories at the University of Minnesota. They came with the intention of dieting very strictly for twenty-four weeks. Predominantly members of the Church of the Brethren or of the Society of Friends, they had been assigned to alternative service in institutions around the country. Because many of them felt guilty at not sharing the suffering of soldiers in battle, they were actually eager to join when they saw a brochure offering the opportunity to participate as subjects in a study of semistarvation. The investigation for which they became guinea pigs, as they called themselves, was led by Ancel Keys, who was then at the beginning of a research career that would be typified by large and ambitious projects. Keys was initiating the most detailed study of experimental starvation ever conducted on human beings. His hope was that information from the study would help rehabilitate starved populations in the war zones.

The volunteers were physically as unremarkable as any group of draftees. They were in their mid-twenties, of average height and weight for their age. They were mentally bright and emotionally stable, according to psychological tests administered by the experimenters. They had already demonstrated strength of character by refusing to serve in a popular war. By any common definition of the term, they had will power.

During the first three months of their stay at the university, the volunteers ate normally—about 3,500 calories a day—and established a regimen intended to carry them through the ensuing six months of semistarvation and several more of recovery. They were required to walk about three miles a day, engage in other physical activity several times a week, and carry out various maintenance jobs around their living quarters. They also had the opportunity to attend courses and to form their own study group on problems of rehabilitation, a subject many of them found interesting. No plans were made to restrict the men's freedom of movement; they were on their honor to stick with the assigned diet. Indeed, they approached the experience with such high spirits, idealism, and energy that it would have been insulting to propose restraints.

On February 12, 1945, the experiment began. The men were put on half their usual ration, while they continued to work, exercise, and play as before. The new diet was primarily whole-wheat bread, potatoes, grains, turnips, and cabbage—foods intended to resemble those available in European famine areas—offered on a schedule of three rotating daily menus. Token amounts of meat and dairy products were added, and low-calorie "picnics" were held at infrequent intervals to help break the monotony.

In the early phases of their diet the men were cheerful, if

uncomfortable, and they sometimes even experienced euphoria
—perhaps akin to the feeling of transcendence reported by
people who fast. But hunger never left them, as it is said to do
after about a week of total fasting, and their highs were always
followed by depressions. They began losing weight rapidly—
most of it from their stores of fat plus a far smaller proportion
of protein. After a couple of months, the men had lost about
half their total body fat. Virtually all the fat stored under their
skin and in their abdomens was gone; what remained was built
into the structure of their cells. By now the men were irritable
and quarrelsome—very much out of character for them. The
strain was so great that their regular group meetings had to be
canceled. After that, the volunteers lived in an atmosphere of
restrained and artificial politeness.

They also began to conserve energy. Although they continued their required walks and exercise, lethargy led them to
avoid as much work, study, or play as they could. Small chores
around the dormitory were neglected, hair went uncombed,
teeth unbrushed. Their clothing, which now fitted them poorly,
was disheveled.

About halfway through the experiment, the men could no
longer guarantee that they would abide by the diet. Because
they were afraid they would cheat when they left the dormitory, a "buddy" system was instituted to protect them from the
culinary enticements of the outside world. There was almost no
cheating, and such episodes as occurred were followed by
guilty, half-crazed confessions to the experimenters. Two
volunteers suffered emotional breakdowns severe enough to
excuse them from completing the full six months of deprivation. Another, as the experimental famine was nearing its end,
chopped off the tip of a finger, evidently hoping, if not intend-
ing, that he would be dismissed as a result.

Keys and his colleagues never really asked themselves precisely what it was that made the men so miserable, perhaps
because the answer seemed obvious. They were starving. But

what is it about starvation that the body finds so hard to endure? These men were deprived of calories only. They had an adequate intake of vitamins and minerals, and they were given enough protein to meet their calculated need for it. (Yet they lost reserves of body protein as it was broken down to provide energy.)

In general, one of three things could have brought on their discomfort. First, their bodies could have been calculating each day's caloric balance and saying in some biochemical language, "This isn't enough." Second, the loss of protein reserves could have been producing the men's malaise. Third, and, as we shall see, the most probable explanation, a decrease in body fat could have been the main cause of their distress. While the men were starving, there was no effective way to differentiate between these possibilities. The only clear fact was that prolonged deprivation of food was sufficient to produce extreme misery.

By the end of their sixth month of semistarvation, virtually all the men were deeply apathetic. They had lost interest in sex and had ceased masturbating. They were indifferent to their visitors. Although their intellectual abilities never declined (scores on standardized tests held constant), their mental activity narrowed to thinking about food.

Mealtimes, which came at half-past eight in the morning and five in the evening, were the focus of their lives. The men were impatient before each meal was served but would then toy with it for as long as two hours. They were far from indifferent to flavor, and many experimented with unorthodox combinations, or covered their food with salt and spices to intensify its taste. Although starving people are often forced to eat unappetizing food, they do not typically lose their sensitivity to flavor, as the "guinea pigs" demonstrated. On the contrary, they may become rather finicky.

At the end of the volunteers' starvation period, three months of gradual refeeding began. The men had all lost a quarter of their starting weight, and on their new, but still restricted, diets they all began to gain. Even so, they remained miserable. This fact alone suggests that daily energy balance was not the secret of morale because, even though the men were now consuming more calories than they were burning each day, they were far from content.

Near the end of the third month of recovery, it became clear that the men could no longer tolerate their restriction. As the experimenters reported:

The urgent desire for dietary freedom expressed by the men was extreme; postponement for another week could have produced severe emotional crises and possibly open rebellion. All the men were counting the hours until they could have more food, and this intense concern was scarcely less in those who had been on the most liberal rehabilitation diet.[6]

This amounted to some *4,000* calories a day.

At their farewell banquet to mark the end of dietary restriction, on October 20, 1945, the men were still ravenous; many of them became ill from overeating. Thereafter, they ate steadily, some of them as much as breakfast, three lunches, and dinner in a single day. They consumed a daily average of 5,000 calories and said they were still hungry, even at the end of a very large meal. The overriding sense of hunger these men felt was not appeased even by a large daily excess of food. Thus, even though their bodies were taking in considerable food energy, the profound psychological alteration that semistarvation had produced remained with them.

As Thanksgiving of 1945 approached, a year after the "guinea pigs" had convened for their experiment—and some fifteen weeks after they had begun to regain the weight they had lost —the men were still obsessed with food, although for some it was decreasing in importance. They were also, at last, recovering their old personalities.

By the time they sat down for the Thanksgiving meal, only about half the men felt their interest in food had returned to normal. At the same time, something else had returned to normal: their weights. Once allowed to eat what they wished, the men had gorged steadily while remaining incessantly hungry. But as the scales returned to the readings of a year before, the men began to feel released from the compulsion to eat. Other measurements made at the same time revealed that the men were only then recovering all their original fat, though muscle tissue was still significantly depleted. This observation suggests that the missing fat was what made them feel deprived, that their bodies had some means of recognizing the deficiency and were striving to restore it as quickly as possible. Once it was recovered, they no longer had a caloric monkey on their backs.

People who have dieted long enough to lose weight, only to succumb to a binge of guilty eating, may recognize their own experience in this story. They will recall the ceaseless hunger that a single indulgence cannot relieve and the internal pressure to continue eating until all the pounds so triumphantly shed have returned. Like the "guinea pigs," fat people evidently have setpoints. What differs is the setting. It is important to understand that the fat person is by nature no more a binge eater than the "guinea pigs" were. What a fat person is, by nature, is fat.

For nine months after recovering their original weights, the conscientious objectors were not truly normal. It took that long to rebuild the muscle they had lost. In the process, they also grew fatter for a time, but eventually they returned to their original balance of muscle and fat.[7]

Keys's experiment provides some of the clearest evidence that the human body itself demands a certain amount of adipose tissue. Severe disruption can alter the body's balance of fat and muscle, but it is restored with adequate time and food. The psychological distress that accompanies starvation appears to come principally from reducing the body's store of fat to an amount below its setpoint, and the distress is relieved only when the full amount is replenished, *not* by just eating a few big meals.

If everyone's body really determines on its own how fat it is to be—if there is a setpoint—then gaining appreciable amounts of weight should be as difficult as losing. For obvious reasons, Keys did not attempt to test this possibility during his experiments on starvation. Such a project was initiated two decades later by a wiry, soft-spoken New Englander, Ethan Allen Sims. Sims was interested in the metabolic factors that connect obesity and diabetes. In the mid-sixties, after experimenting for a while with hamsters, he realized that nobody really knew whether the metabolic differences between fat and thin people were the result of their different quantities of fat or were, instead, the cause. He resolved, therefore, to find a group of thin people whom he could make temporarily fat while he studied them intensively.

Sims began with four university students who volunteered to see whether they could gain 20 percent over their normal body weight by deliberately overeating. The students ate huge amounts of food, meanwhile keeping up with their courses and their usual extracurricular activities. Surprisingly, many found it difficult to add even 10 percent to their normal weight. As Sims has written, "This was the first finding which made us realize that obesity in young people may not be a simple behavioral problem of overeating. . . . It became clear to us that for normal young people, gaining weight would have to be a full-time job."[8]

Sims's abortive experience with the students, as his later studies confirmed, made it clear from the start that a weight gain or loss cannot be explained simply by the number of calories consumed. Despite what we've often been told in recent years (but consistent with folk wisdom of long standing), it is perfectly possible for some people to eat a lot and gain very little, whereas others gain weight while eating abstemiously. This fact was interesting in and of itself, but it also posed a problem for Sims. Where could he find a group of people whom he could make experimentally fat in order to compare them with the spontaneously obese?

17

He needed a group of lean young men with no obesity in their family backgrounds and a lifestyle sufficiently quiet and restricted to keep them relatively inactive while overeating. Monks or prisoners might have served, but prisons are easier to find than monasteries in the modern world. In 1964 Sims approached Robert G. Smith, warden of the Vermont State Prison, with his proposal for an experiment in voluntary overeating. Smith, concluding that the prisoners might actually benefit from the experience of participating in Sims's research, consented to the experiment. A small research unit, including a recreation room, dining room, and kitchen, was set aside in the prison's hospital area.

Groups of prisoner-volunteers entered the project committed to gaining twenty to thirty pounds. For 200 days they ate heroically. In the early weeks of the experiment they continued with their usual prison regimen, but to achieve the maximum weight gain they also temporarily limited their activity. They did not all succeed in reaching the goal, but eventually twenty prisoners managed to do so. All had virtually doubled the amount of food they normally ate. Only two men found it easy to gain; the others had to struggle. And, once they had added 20 to 25 percent to their starting weights, the prisoners could retain it only by dint of continued overeating—on average, two thousand extra calories a day, not the mere couple of hundred that might seem theoretically necessary. Even though the men were only moderately active, they were obliged to eat the equivalent of five meals a day to remain fat. One prisoner, who gained relatively easily, went from 110 to 138 pounds, but he had to consume seven thousand calories a day during the last two months of the experiment to acquire and maintain his adipose baggage.

The prisoners evidently did not suffer from their experience in quite the way that Keys's conscientious objectors had. But they all found it trying, and many of them considered dropping out at one time or another. Breakfast became the major hurdle.

Most of the men found the meal at least unpleasant, and a few would regurgitate after taking the first food of the day. At the peak of their obesity, the men were lethargic, disinclined to take initiative, and neglectful of their prison tasks, an observation suggesting that the weight at setpoint is optimal for activity and mood—much above or below, and apathy sets in.

Once the experiment was over, weight loss came readily to all the men, except for the two who had gained most easily. Along with two others, they were found to have an unrevealed family history of obesity or diabetes. The prisoner who gained twenty-eight pounds by eating seven thousand calories a day began to lose weight the day he stopped force-feeding himself. In this phase of the study, he was urged to exercise vigorously but allowed to eat whatever he chose. Of his own accord, he consumed about half his normal daily diet and, in seventy-five days, had stabilized at only four pounds above his starting weight. His experience was typical, except that most of the prisoners left the experiment with no weight increase at all. "Essentially all of the subjects to date have lost weight readily," Sims summarized, "with the same alacrity, in fact, as that with which most of our obese patients return to their usual and customary weight after weight loss."9

If we lived in a world that prized being fat instead of thin, Sims's results might be attributed to the prisoners' lack of character. One of his volunteers, for example, began at 132 pounds. He struggled resolutely for more than thirty weeks to gain weight, ate great amounts of food, and reduced his activity to less than half its former level, but was never able to push above 144 pounds. He simply didn't have the "will power" to get fat.

Both Keys and Sims, in their attempts to understand the nature of eating, such a fundamental human activity, resorted to experimenting with social deviants—people who for one reason or another could live abnormally for long periods. Perhaps it was appropriate that, for the ascetic's trial, Keys used conscientious objectors, whose strength of will was hardly open to question, while Sims used prisoners for an exercise in gluttony. The members of each group were asked to follow what one might suppose were their natural inclinations. The difficulties and even failures both groups experienced are some indication of the irrelevance of character to fatness.

Sims's experiments demonstrated a remarkable tenacity in human physiology. Even in the face of extreme overload, the prisoners' bodies grew fatter very slowly. Exactly how they were prevented from getting fat is unclear, although it seems probable that they had a biochemical means for literally burning off the surfeit of food. (Recently, Sims and others have begun to study the nature of the metabolic safety valve; their work is described in chapter 3.)

Most of the time, no such sleight-of-hand is needed. From week to week, though not from day to day, appetite spontaneously balances the amount we eat against the amount of energy we burn in activity. The ability of appetite to compensate for changes in physical activity has been demonstrated repeatedly.

In one such study, a dozen British military cadets were followed, during the first two weeks of July 1953, by physiologist O. G. Edholm and his colleagues from Cambridge University. They attempted to play out the scenario we dismissed as impossible at the beginning of this chapter: to record everything the cadets ate and everything they did, compare the two, and see how the books balanced. Life in a military academy was sufficiently regimented for the investigators to make a pretty good stab at obtaining accurate figures. Most of what the cadets ate was weighed when it was served to them—as were the leftovers on their plates—and careful estimates were made of the number of calories in anything else they ate, such as "chocolate and biscuits" purchased at the canteen. The energy actually expended by the cadets in various typical activities—lying down, standing, sitting, drilling—was measured in a series of brief tests. The cadets then kept a record of everything they did throughout the day, on a sheet of paper designed for the purpose. The upshot of the study was that, over the two-week period, these twenty-year-old men of normal weight managed to eat precisely what they needed to account for all the energy they had used—even though they gave no conscious thought to balancing their energy budgets (and were not restricted in what they ate). (In fact, the figures show a slight excess of calories consumed over calories expended, but since no mention was made of sexual activity, the discrepancy is probably explainable.)

Edholm and his group were curious to see whether they could find a pattern in the cadets' eating habits: Did they eat a lot on the days when they were most active? They did not; rather, it appeared, they were consistently eating to compensate for energy they had used two days earlier. Later the scientists attempted to replicate their study of the cadets with a population of army recruits. The two-day lag could not be demonstrated in the recruits, who seemed far more variable. (But there were also variations in their situation—the recruits were living at six different centers and were not all following an identical routine.) A lag between exertion and intake could be expected if increased appetite is a response to depleted fat stores. Although Edholm could not confirm his initial finding, the two-day lag has appeared in other experiments.[10]

At the University of Pennsylvania, another group of normal volunteers demonstrated that they could balance their energy budgets without giving it conscious thought, but only after a few days had passed. They also proved that they could do their caloric arithmetic without referring to a calorie chart, without seeing what they were eating, and without weighing themselves.

These men and women agreed to subsist entirely on Metrecal, the dietary drink, dispensed to them from a contraption designed by Henry Jordan, a psychiatrist at the university. A volunteer would enter Jordan's laboratory and sit down at a desk from which a wooden arm jutted up to mouth level. Emerging from this support was a stainless-steel nipple connected by tubing to refrigerated reservoirs of the liquid flavored with Dutch chocolate, vanilla, strawberry, or coffee. The volunteer would take the metal spout in his mouth and, by pushing a button, start a pump to deliver his meal. When he felt "full" he would stop.

From a series of experiments with this device, Jordan had concluded that people who received a single liquid meal were scarcely influenced by the number of calories in the liquid. Feeling full was mainly a reaction to tasting the fluid and perceiving its volume in their stomachs. Theresa Spiegel, a psychologist working with Jordan, then set out to learn whether the same would hold true if the subjects were to depend on the machine for all their nourishment for a period of several weeks.

Her volunteers were instructed to consume nothing but black coffee, tea, or water outside the laboratory and not to weigh themselves. They could come to the laboratory at any time to take as much or as little as they wanted. Their only cue for eating was hunger, their only cue to stop was feeling full.

Most of her nine subjects took a few days to adapt to their new way of life. At first they ate too little, but within two to six days they had returned to their normal intake (about 3,000 calories a day). A week after the experiment began, without telling the volunteers, Spiegel reduced the concentration of calories in the Metrecal to half the former amount. The fluid was doctored to keep about the same taste and texture, and few of the subjects even guessed that it had changed. Again, for about two days they took in too little but then, by doubling the amount of fluid they swallowed, they brought themselves back up to the mark—the amount they needed to hold a reasonably steady weight. Now, to feel full they had to suck in twice as much fluid as before.

Spiegel then returned two subjects to the original formula. Neither was aware of the change, but after about two days each volunteer dropped back to his or her earlier rate of consumption. Somehow, each body was counting calories and adjusting intake accordingly. As had the English cadets, Spiegel's volunteers usually took about two days to adjust to a changed formula, but over a longer time span they met their caloric needs without any conscious effort.[11]

We have described four groups of people, widely separated in time and place: One starved. One stuffed. One lived a more-or-less normal life but kept meticulous records. And one was reduced to eating everything from a metal teat. What happened to them tells us a lot about everyday experience, about such things as appetite, hunger, satiety, and the substance—fat— that seems to bind these states of mind together in a working system. The moral of these four little narratives is that certain kinds of behavior—the quest for food, the choice of how much to eat, and so forth—are directed by forces beyond conscious awareness. But the forces in question are not the familiar denizens of the Freudian unconscious—repressed conflict, displaced anger, infantile deprivation. They are, instead, physiological pressures to keep a foreordained amount of fat on the body. In this case, anatomy is indeed destiny.

2

THE MIND-BODY PROBLEM: THE PSYCHOLOGY OF DIETING

T HE NOTION that some people are fatter than others merely because they are made that way—because they come equipped with bodies that call for a certain supply of fat—should have an intrinsic appeal. Why not? Some of us can grow very long hair, others cannot. A few can become coloratura sopranos or run a marathon in little more than two hours—most, even with effort, cannot. Myriad physical attributes are taken as facts of life; nature distributes her endowments unequally.

But when it comes to fat, the straightforward explanation has met with much resistance. Instead, psychological theories have been invoked to account for physical differences between people. This tendency seems to reflect a prejudice; we are a nation of psychologizers. Asked to explain a "spare tire" or an ample figure, our first inclination is to find a psychic conflict: "I stay fat because, deep down, I'm afraid of being too attractive." "I eat when I'm lonely, nervous, or depressed." "When things go well, I celebrate with a hot fudge sundae." "My mother always pushed food on me; it was her only way to show love." "My mother was cold and ungiving; she never fed me enough."

Perhaps because they have an all-purpose flexibility, such explanations are remarkably tenacious among the lay public, even though they are mutually contradictory and based on precious little evidence. The pop psychology of fatness plays into a hoary moralistic belief that there is something defective in the character of fat people—or of their mothers. And, to be sure, there are people who overeat in a desperate attempt to handle inner conflicts. But although these unhappy gorgers are prominent in the psychological literature on obesity, they are probably a small fraction of fat people.

In fact, fat people as a group are mentally quite healthy, considering what they must put up with. Stigmatized, badgered to go hungry for weeks, months, or years on end, denied access to schooling, employment, and becoming clothes—they are entitled to their share of psychological problems. And yet, as a group, they are no more neurotic than thin people and, in some ways, even less so. They have maintained their mental health through decades of well-intentioned but ineffective efforts to explain and "improve" them.

Sigmund Freud never asked, "What do fat people want?," but his psychoanalytic heirs did, and they easily concocted an answer. In the halcyon years of psychoanalysis, obesity was generally interpreted as stemming from oral eroticism—the infantile form of sexuality in which sensual gratification comes from sucking and swallowing.

The case of "Nancy," a teen-age girl treated by New York analyst Susan Deri, has often been cited as an example of orality leading to obesity. Deri's report of the case, published in 1955, reflects the analyst's empathy with her patient and a relatively nondogmatic approach to treatment. But dogma was highly visible in the interpretation: "The fact of obesity alone, after all organic causal factors are ruled out, is enough to diagnose the presence of serious emotional disturbance in which oral fixation and a conflictual mother-child relationship are of essential causal importance." Thus, for example, Nancy's taste ran to cupcakes, pies, and other "whole, round pieces of sweet food . . . round, sweet things symbolized mother's breasts—devouring them was a perfect symbolic expression of destructive oral aggression as well as the need to be united with mother."[1]

Because they so emphatically identified fatness with oral sexuality, the analysts had to assume that fat people were sexual cripples who did not experience the fullness of adult, genital gratification. Unable to cope with mature sex, it was claimed, they retreated to search, through food, for what one analyst termed the "alimentary orgasm."[2] This singularly odd concept eventually disappeared from psychiatric discourse, but the basic notion that fat people are afraid of sex did not.

In 1954, psychiatrist Stanley Conrad reviewed his profession's current position on weight. "Obesity may serve for some women," he wrote, "as a *protection against sexual temptation.*" As a case in point, he cited a Mrs. C. O.:

[She] would become panicky and immediately overeat whenever she discovered she had lost some weight. . . . One day, while waiting on a corner for a bus, a truck passed by and the driver whistled at her. She had an acute anxiety attack, ran home, and immediately gorged herself with food. She thus attempted to regain her fat and make herself once more unattractive to men.[3]

This rather Pavlovian example may seem laughable now, but the image of fat as a psychological battlement, protecting its possessor from sex, has survived the last three decades all too well. Spared the expense of an analysis, fat women today proclaim, with self-analyzed assurance, their neurotic need to protect themselves behind "walls of fat." Ironically, women who are not even obese—whose bodies would have been called "voluptuous" during the first fifty years of Freud's life—now see their own bodies as an expression of sexual inadequacy.

The fear-of-sex theme has been given a modern twist by Susie Orbach, a psychotherapist and author of *Fat is a Feminist Issue.* Orbach believes that many women become fat, and thus sexually unattractive, because it is the only way to get men to take them seriously. "It is almost as though, through the protective aspects of the fat, women are saying they must deny their own sexuality in order to be seen as a person. *To expose their sexuality means that others will deny them their personhood.*" This interpretation at least presents fatness as more than a psychological problem; Orbach believes it is a social problem as well. But she still argues that fat must have some psychic meaning, that it cannot be a simple biological fact. For that reason, ironically, her book has infuriated some groups of self-described fat feminists.[4]

Despite all the semiofficial folklore, there is really no evidence that fat people as a group are sexually incapacitated. Even very fat people, according to psychologist Colleen Rand, have the usual desires, although they may be limited in their ability to attract partners. In 1979, Rand reviewed psychiatric evaluations of both massively obese patients awaiting intestinal surgery for weight control and others in psychoanalysis. Warning against the "psychosocial stereotype" of the obese, she concluded: "There are no data which indicate that the obese individual has significantly greater or fewer sexual problems than nonobese individuals." The same conclusion emerged from a 1977 study of morbidly obese candidates for intestinal surgery at Johns Hopkins Hospital: All of them showed "a general level of adequate sexual functioning," although they were hampered by social isolation and, occasionally, by physical obstacles to intercourse, according to Thomas Wise and Jacqueline Gordon. In sum, disturbance of sexual functioning is more likely the result of fatness than the cause. As psychiatrist Henry Jordan and psychologist Leonard Levitz summarize their findings: "Obese individuals are not lacking in normal sexual responsiveness. Although their desire for sex may be high, their fear of rejection because of their body size may be the inhibiting factor."[5]

Women who have lost a large amount of fat after intestinal bypass surgery (a procedure devised to limit their ability to absorb food) often do experience difficulty in their sexual relationships. But this finding seems to refute rather than support the sexual-defense theory. Their new attractiveness and increasing self-confidence in sexual matters often makes these women threatening to their *partners*, who evidently have preferred the relatively asexual status quo.[6]

Psychological approaches to fatness have, in general, suffered from two major flaws: the willingness to generalize from only a few case reports, and the inclination to assume that the individual actively, if unconsciously, wants to be fat, presumably as a reflection of disordered sexuality. It is probably true that a few people are neurotically motivated to eat themselves into protective cocoons of fat, despite the physical discomfort and stigmatization they encounter. But no scientific psychological study has warranted the nearly universal assumption that this is the usual state of affairs. Unfortunately, a minority of cases has been made conspicuous because the subjects were interesting to psychoanalysts and conformed to their preconceptions. The popularity of analytic ideas in America in the middle of this century helped to turn concepts of limited validity into the common coin of pop psychology.

By the late 1950s, professional psychologists had to admit that they really could not explain why fat people were fat, notwithstanding the abundance of analytic studies. Fat people were still regarded as neurotic; that much was taken for granted. But what, precisely, was their conflict? In 1957, psychiatrist Harold Kaplan and Helen Singer Kaplan, a clinical psychologist, wrote: "Almost all conceivable psychological impulses and conflicts have been accused of causing overeating, and many symbolic meanings have been assigned to food." Their inventory, culled from the psychological literature, reads like the packing list for Pandora's box. They summarized the available reports thus:

Overeating may be:
· A means of diminishing anxiety, insecurity, tension, worry, indecision.
· A means of achieving pleasure, gratification, success. . . .
· A means of expressing hostility, which hostility may be conscious, unconscious, denied, or repressed. . . .
· A means of rewarding oneself for some task accomplished. . . .
· A means of diminishing guilt, which guilt may itself be due to overeating.

And on and on, through some twenty-three more sets of mutually contradictory examples. Ideas about the deeper symbolism of overeating were equally diverse, and more colorful:

Overeating or food may be symbolically:
· Representative of pre-Oedipal mother conflict.
· A type of alimentary orgasm. [This again.]
· Expression of an unsatisfied sexual craving.
· Expression of destructive sadistic impulses.
· Expression of penis envy and a wish to deprive the male of his penis, i.e., an unconscious association between food and phallus.
· Expression of a fantasy where overeating results in impregnation.

The Kaplans' sensible, and rather devastating, review made it clear that no specific psychological pattern could be identified as the cause of fatness. Yet they could not discard the idea that overeating must somehow have emotional roots: "The present authors believe . . . that *any* emotional conflict may eventually result in the symptom of overeating. . . . The only psychopathological generalization that can be made with confidence about obese patients is that they are individuals whose life pattern is conflictual and anxiety ridden." They concluded: "The people affected by obesity typically have some degree of personality disturbance and/or emotional conflict which may be of *any* type or severity." In their view, fat people had one thing in common: Eating to allay anxiety, they used food as a kind of pacifier.[7]

Lame as this conclusion sounds, it raised certain important questions. Were fat people more anxious than thin people? More depressed? Less happy? When these issues were systematically examined, fat and thin people proved to be psychologically fairly similar—except that the fat suffered from social disapproval and the stress of dieting.

Albert Stunkard was one of the first psychological investigators to study fat people in the population at large—not just those who entered psychotherapy. A psychiatrist working primarily at the University of Pennsylvania, Stunkard has been one of the most original thinkers in obesity research through almost three decades; his ideas permeate the field. Known universally as "Mickey" to friends and colleagues, he is both informal and animated when discussing theories of fatness or characterizing data as "nifty" and "neat." Throughout his career, Stunkard—who is himself tall and lanky—has stressed the great difficulty fat people have in losing weight. Today, he has come to believe that the persistence of obesity may have a physiological basis, and has lately argued for the role of a set-point.

A few years after the Kaplans' summary appeared, Stunkard and his colleagues set out to establish whether fat people really were more neurotic than thin ones. The clear answer, from their first study, was no. Eighteen obese men, and an equal number of normal weight, were given a battery of psychological tests. The two groups produced roughly the same results.[8]

Reasoning that a larger sample might show some differences between the fat and the thin, Stunkard turned next to data that had been collected in the famous "Midtown" study. This survey had examined the mental health of 1,660 adults from Manhattan's East Side during the 1950s. Although virtually all were white, the subjects belonged to a variety of ethnic groups and all social classes. The study was already famous for correlating low social status with psychological disorders when Stunkard returned to the data. Because height and weight had been recorded for each subject, Stunkard could inquire whether obesity had affected their mental health.[9]

"The answer, when it finally came after all these years, was an anticlimax," Stunkard writes in *The Pain of Obesity,* his engaging professional autobiography. Fat people did appear to be more neurotic than thin people of the same age and social class, but the difference was statistically significant in only three of nine psychological measures: "immaturity," "suspiciousness," and "rigidity." Even here, recalls Stunkard, "the problem was that the differences were really very small. Although they were statistically significant, largely because they were based on such a large sample, they were quite insignificant from a practical point of view."[10]

The results were puzzling, too, in light of the then prevailing psychological theories. "Immaturity," is understandable; but "rigidity" or "suspiciousness"? In retrospect, the high scores on these two scales could be seen as the result of the fat person's experience, not the cause of his fatness. If the fat people of midtown Manhattan were constantly straining to diet, they could not have escaped becoming rigid; one of life's most frequent and casual activities, eating, would have been subject to continual monitoring. And the pervasive medical condemnation of fatness, which was bordering on frenzy in the mid-fifties, could easily have made them suspicious, if not downright paranoid.

Negative findings from Stunkard's analysis were as revealing as the positive ones. "Tension-anxiety," widely believed to be a major cause of overeating, was not significantly correlated with obesity. Indeed, fat people showed slightly *less* "childhood anxiety" than did those of normal weight. As Stunkard later summarized his study: "It would be difficult to find in these data much support for the theory that neurosis was the cause of obesity."[11]

Stunkard's results from the Midtown Manhattan Study have been supported by other data, some of it fragmentary or hard to interpret but, on the whole, persuasive. For decades, an odd yet consistent feature of mortality data is the fact that fat people commit suicide less frequently than those of normal weight. Periodically in the 1960s, fat people attending medical clinics were evaluated for evidence of mental pathology or emotional disturbance—and were regularly found to be no more neurotic than whatever control population was used. And in 1976, a random survey of suburbanites near London supported the conclusion. Of 700 subjects, those who were fat were found to be less anxious than those of normal weight; moreover, the fat men were also found to be less depressed.[12]

It has been easy enough, of course, for investigators to rationalize these results with their durable belief that fatness is a sign of emotional conflict. It has only been necessary to assume that overeating is a *successful* defense mechanism. Thus, in 1963, an Air Force clinician found that overweight airmen were very rarely depressed. He concluded that obesity was a "depressive equivalent, that is, . . . that certain individuals ward off and allay depressive feelings by increasing the amount and frequency of their food consumption."[13] With this sort of reasoning, absolutely any data could be used as evidence for an emotional cause of obesity.

Today, obesity is not officially recognized as a sign of emotional distress. The 1980 edition of the *Diagnostic and Statistical Manual of Mental Disorders*—the American Psychiatric Association's classification scheme—describes it thus: "Simple obesity is . . . a physical disorder . . . not generally associated with any distinct psychological or behavioral syndrome." Although they have tried for several decades, theorists have been unable to come up with a plausible psychodynamic explanation for fatness. This failure became embarrassingly clear when the American Academy of Psychoanalysis undertook to study some eighty-four obese analysands. As part of their protocol, Colleen Rand and her colleagues tried to determine how psychoanalytic theories affected the actual treatment of obese patients. "To our surprise," Rand reported in 1978, "we were unable to find any clearly articulated statement of a psychoanalytic theory of obesity and believe that none such exists in the literature."[14]

But, officially or not, obesity is still seen as presumptive evidence of an emotional conflict—albeit unspecified and perhaps unspecifiable. The academy's study of patients in psychoanalysis was used to support this belief, though in a rather confusing way. As Rand reports, a whopping 94 percent of obese patients "were reported to eat in association with feelings of depression, anxiety, boredom, guilt, high spirits, anger, and feelings of accomplishment and satisfaction"—in short, almost any strong emotion at all. This is a far cry from the view that fat people overeat exclusively to deal with such *negative* feelings as depression and anger. What are we to make of it?

One possibility, of course, is that the figures are simply wrong. Since these findings are based on analysts' reports of their patients, they must be assumed to reflect biased reporting. Moreover, people in analysis are an infinitesimally small fraction of the population; they may have an unusual emotional makeup; and they are themselves committed to the psychoanalytic worldview. But suppose for a moment that fat people do eat for emotional reasons as diverse as boredom and high spirits. Can the apparent paradox be explained?

It can, with a hypothesis that requires something of a conceptual leap. The fat person's peculiar response to emotion may be not the cause of fatness, but rather an effect of dieting. Fat people, for obvious reasons, are far more likely than thin people to diet, and dieting is always a difficult feat of self-control. If one is constantly counting calories—perhaps in a "rigid" way, as Stunkard's data suggest—then any strong emotion could disturb the balance. Eating bouts could be triggered by either sadness or celebration.

Reinterpreting fat people as chronic dieters puts the psychology of obesity in a whole new light. If dieting is the crucial variable, then the fat do not eat because they hurt inside; rather, they hurt because they are trying not to eat, to make their bodies conform to social norms. The struggle is constant, but lapses are inevitable, especially when emotions are taxed.

Radical though the idea is, it is not at all far-fetched. In fact, this view of fatness is the logical outcome of a decade of psychological research that began when psychoanalytic approaches had clearly failed.

In the early 1960s, most psychologists still believed that fat people and thin people thought and ate differently. They were having a hard time proving it, however. Psychodynamic theories of obesity had become almost metaphysical. By the end of the decade, a new theory had emerged—one that was simple, testable, and persuasive.

The "externality" hypothesis, as it came to be called, was not concerned with the psychic conflicts of fat people, but only with their behavior. According to this formulation, fat people are unable to recognize true hunger signals within their bodies. Rather than eating out of an "internal" physiological need, they eat in response to "external" cues—primarily, the presence of tasty food. In an environment filled with appetizing dishes, as is modern America, they would gain weight.

The idea has become a staple of popular psychology, and it has provided much of the rationale for behavior therapy of obesity. However, recent experiments have led to drastic revision of the externality hypothesis. It now appears that fat people do not necessarily eat according to external cues. Dieters, however, probably do. To diet, a person is forced to ignore the body's physiological demands. When hunger is denied, only external cues remain to shape eating behavior.

An early inspiration for the externality hypothesis was Hilde Bruch, a psychiatrist now at Baylor University, in Texas. Bruch, who has probably had greater influence than anyone else on psychological theories of obesity, began her medical career as a pediatrician with a special interest in fat children. When she began her practice in the 1930s, glandular explanations of obesity were popular—and, in Bruch's view, singularly unhelpful. "The error," she later recalled, "lay in the application of mere endocrine labels which were simply repeated from one doctor to another, without being put to the test of objective validation."[15]

Coming from a different field, Bruch brought a clear-headed iconoclasm to her psychoanalytic studies. In a key paper published in 1961, she explains her "deliberate avoidance of psychoanalytic terminology," observing that "Freud's style, even when translated into English, reminds me of Victorian 'gingerbread' architecture, in contrast to modern functional design and usage."[16] Bruch freed herself not only from the psychoanalysts' jargon but also from their obsession with orality. Instead, she began to interpret the struggle with weight control as a reflection of developmental difficulties with autonomy and the sense of self. According to Bruch, many (though not all) of her obese patients came from homes in which certain of their most basic rights—deciding whether to eat and how much to eat—had been denied. Parents had given or withheld food for all sorts of reasons that were completely irrelevant to the child's experience of hunger. Food, for example, could have been given as a sign of love in an otherwise cold household, or simply as a pacifier to occupy the child of a busy, distracted parent. The specific circumstances were less important than the central experience: The children were never able to decide for themselves whether they were really hungry.

As a result, children grew up with two basic deficiencies: "the inability to recognize hunger and other bodily sensations, and the lacking of awareness of living one's own life." Thus, Bruch concluded, "these people are unable to recognize when they are hungry or satiated, nor do they differentiate need for food from other sensations and feelings of discomfort. They need signals from the outside to know when to eat and when to stop; their own inner awareness has not been programmed correctly."[17]

Often the problem surfaced in adolescence. A teen-ager might grow fat because he literally could not control his eating; he had never learned the internal hunger cues that make eating controllable. Curiously, similar psychodynamic factors could push an adolescent to the opposite, even more desperate, path: the self-starvation of anorexia nervosa. For anorexics, primarily young women, food can become a tool in a power struggle with parents. Self-starvation can be a desperate, paradoxical attempt to gain the independence and self-assertion that has always been quashed.

Bruch herself has been careful to point out that her analysis applies only to a small group of fat people—namely, those who, having sought psychiatric help, have become her patients. She notes that many people, perhaps the majority, may be constitutionally predisposed to fatness, although our culture has denied this possibility. "As long as we insist that being fat is ugly and undesirable and should not be permitted, we force a great many people to fight or to disregard the individual endowment of their own physique," she writes in *Eating Disorders*. But as an analyst, Bruch paid relatively little attention to the naturally overweight, focusing instead on those who grew fat for psychological reasons. Her work was persuasive, and its influence extended well beyond the analytic community.[18]

A crucial aspect of Bruch's formulation was its testability. Whatever their individual problems, many obese people, she suggested, had one thing in common: They were unable to recognize true, physiological feelings of hunger. This idea was dramatically supported by an experiment of Stunkard's, reported in 1959. His subjects swallowed balloons attached with tubes to a device for recording pressure. This contraption showed that obese women had normal stomach contractions; but, unlike thin women, they did not recognize the contractions as signs of hunger. Attempts to replicate these elegant findings were made, and they failed; stomach contractions proved to be a poor measure of hunger in the first place.[19] Even so, Stunkard's experiments and Bruch's theories inspired Stanley Schachter, a social psychologist.

Following their lead, Schachter carried out a series of clever, and now classic, experiments that have done much to shape current, popular conceptions of fatness. Schachter is an owlish, witty man, whose charisma and original intellect attracted many students to his laboratory at Columbia University. At first a somewhat revolutionary cadre in the psychology of obesity research, within a decade they virtually became its establishment.

In the early 1960s, Schachter's group was studying the ways in which people interpret various internal states. For example, adrenaline is a hormone that is naturally released in response to stress and produces a complex of physiological responses, such as speeding of the heart rate and slowing of intestinal contractions. The investigators found that, far from producing a stereotyped psychological response, an injection of the drug could provoke euphoria, anger, or anxiety—or no emotion at all —depending on the subject's situation at the time of the injection. Further, Stunkard's work at that time was implying that hunger signals, another kind of internal stimulus, could be interpreted differently by different people. Most important, Schachter found that fat people seemed to ignore the bodily signals altogether.[20]

In the first—and perhaps the most striking—of their series

of experiments, Schachter and his colleagues found that internal signals were, in fact, largely irrelevant to the way their fat subjects ate. Groups of fat and thin people were asked to rate five different kinds of cracker according to taste. This was a ruse. In fact, the experimenters were not interested in how the crackers tasted but only in how many were eaten. By disguising the purpose of the experiment as a "taste test," they hoped to let the volunteers eat without self-consciousness. Before passing out the crackers, however, the experimenters tried to make some of their subjects less hungry—in a physiological sense—to see how their eating patterns might be affected.

One procedure was straightforward. Some of the subjects were allowed to eat roast beef sandwiches "till you're full," while others simply filled out a questionnaire about food. As one would expect, the thin people who had sandwiches first ate fewer crackers than did those who filled out the questionnaire. But the fat subjects ate about the same number of crackers, no matter what—as Schachter had predicted.

The second part of this experiment was more clever, in a rather nasty way. Physiological studies had shown that fear could inhibit stomach contractions and thus, presumably, dull internal hunger signals. So the researchers decided to frighten some of their subjects before they let them eat. All were told that they would receive electric shocks to measure "the effect of tactile stimulation on taste." Some were told that the shock would be barely perceptible. But for others,

the experimenter pointed to an 8-foot high, jet-black console loaded with electrical junk and said, "That machine is the one we will be using. I am afraid that these shocks will be painful. For them to have any effect on your taste sensations, they must be of a rather high voltage. There will, of course, be no permanent damage." The subject was then connected to the console by attaching a very large electrode to each ankle. While doing this, the experimenter looked up at the subject and asked, "You don't have a heart condition, do you?"

Before the shocks came—and, of course, they never did—subjects were asked to taste the crackers. As expected, frightened thin people ate considerably less than those who were not scared. But fat people did not eat significantly more or less when faced with the mock shock-box. Fat people's stomachs seemed to be insensitive to another internal state—anxiety. Even so, the fat subjects did not eat significantly more, as a group, than the thin ones.

This finding seemed to dispose of the idea that fat people overeat to cope with unpleasant feelings—such as the fear of impending electrocution. As Schachter and his colleagues wrote, "the single most pervasive theme in psychosomatic theorizing about obesity [is the assumption] that overeating by the obese represents an attempt to cope with anxiety or fear or emotional disturbance of some kind. . . . We have found no evidence to support it." The Columbia experiments were seriously undercutting the theory that obesity results from inner conflicts—or, indeed, from any internal psychological state at all.[21]

On the contrary, according to other experiments also published in 1968, *external* cues were what caused fat people to eat. For example, subjects were taken to an isolated room in which a clock was prominently located. They were asked to remain for a series of make-work tasks and were offered crackers to snack on. The clock, in fact, could be made to run fast or slow, so that at 6:00—which the experimenters assumed was the standard dinnertime—the clock would read 6:30 or 5:45. The fat subjects in this experiment noshed by the clock, eating more if they thought it was past their dinnertime; the thin subjects, heeding a different, internal timepiece, did not.[22]

Richard Nisbett, who later would advance a hypothesis to replace Schachter's "externality" theory, conducted one of the most elegant, and famous, of the Columbia experiments at this time. Quite simply, he offered his subjects roast beef sandwiches and counted how many were eaten. Some sandwiches were offered on a plate, but others were nearby in a refrigerator. In general, Nisbett found that fat subjects tended to eat what was put before them—whether it was a skimpy half sandwich or three whole ones—but would not go to the refrigerator for more. Thin subjects, in contrast, predictably ate about a sandwich and a half under either experimental condition; they would leave food on the plate if served too much or go to the refrigerator if they were unsatisfied.[23]

A series of ingenious "naturalistic" experiments also supported the hypothesis. Fat Columbia freshmen, it was found, were more likely than their thin classmates to cancel their college meal plans, presumably because their concern with the quality of food—an "external" variable—made institutional meals especially unappealing. A study of Air France personnel showed that fatter pilots were less likely to have their eating patterns disrupted by jet lag. This was as expected; people insensitive to internal hunger cues should not be bothered by the shift from an old time zone to a new one. And fat Jewish students who fasted on Yom Kippur had an easier time of it the longer they stayed in the synagogue, where food was simply unavailable. Eventually, the Schachter group offered its summary of their diverse results: "Fasting, fat, French freshmen fly farther for fine food."[24]

The "externality" hypothesis looked splendid—for a while. But attempts to replicate the results from Columbia demonstrated that the picture was not as clear-cut as Schachter's original interpretation made it seem. In recent years, the chief exponent of externality as a characteristic of fat people has been Yale psychologist Judith Rodin, originally a member of the Columbia group. Her view has been considerably modified over the past decade.

Rodin still believes that responsiveness to external cues may help predispose a person to overweight, but she thinks that many other factors must also determine obesity. In a 1980 review, "The Externality Theory Today," she wrote:

The role of external responsiveness in the development of obesity has not received extensive confirmation. . . . *Most* people are responsive to some external food cues. Indeed, *there are people in all weight categories who are highly responsive to these external cues.* . . . The internal versus external concept is far too simple a description of, or explanation for, differences between obese and normal-weight individuals.[25]

In its simplest form—fat people follow external cues, thin people obey internal commands—Schachter's hypothesis did not survive attempts to replicate the earliest experiments. Then the theory took a somewhat new form, whereupon both the original experiments and the failures at replication began to make sense.

In essence, the revisionist version went, most fat people did not respond to an inner voice saying "now you are hungry" because, quite simply, they were *always* hungry. And they were always hungry because they were dieting. Dieting puts a person in a state of almost constant hunger, and therefore renders internal signals useless as a guide to meal time or meal size. Dieters are left with only "external" evidence (the clock, a memorized calorie chart, the amount of food on the plate) or enticements (the odor and sight of food) to guide them. Because, in North America, many thin people are also on self-imposed diets, performance in a Schachterian experiment should be determined more by a history of dieting than by body weight.

In 1972, a few years after his sandwich experiment was published, Richard Nisbett (currently at the University of Michigan) proposed a startling explanation for the behavior of fat people. They might be chronically "starved," he said; in a physiological sense, fat people could actually be underweight. Nisbett found many similarities between obese people, starving people (notably Keys's volunteers), and rats that overate because of brain damage (as described in chapter 3). In all three cases, finicky eating habits, irritability, and emotional lability were prominent characteristics, as Nisbett interpreted the evidence. These and some other parallels are still being debated, but his insight was fruitful and probably correct.

Nisbett took the idea of a setpoint for fatness—which had been established in experiments with rats—and applied it to human behavior. When fat people dieted, eating too little to keep them at their natural setpoint, he argued, they were bound to suffer, even if they remained fatter than average. The unusual eating patterns of fat people, he reasoned, could be caused by the stress of rebelling against their natural weights.[26]

The idea begged to be tested, and it soon was, by another of Schachter's former students. Peter Herman had completed a dissertation on smoking behavior, and he intended to pursue the subject when he left Columbia to join the faculty at Northwestern University. His research accidentally took a different turn, however. "A student at Northwestern named Debbie Mack, a sorority girl, came along; she wanted to study compulsive eating, and why it is that girls go on binges," he recalls. As they were beginning to study the question, Nisbett's paper came out. "I was just captivated by it. I was struck by the paradoxical implication that fat people were underweight. Could there be a more enchanting notion?"

I was having a lot of insomnia at that time, and late one evening it all fell together. I decided that these sorority girls were really below setpoint because of their dieting. Nisbett kept talking about *obese* people being dieters. I guess the contribution I made was talking about *normal-weight* people being dieters—which is obvious when you think about it, but nobody had thought about it that way before.[27]

Herman thought of dieters as "restrained eaters"—people who, through an effort of will, were forcing themselves to eat less than they wanted. (The concept came in part from his earlier work with smokers, many of whom forced themselves to limit their tobacco consumption.) To identify restrained eaters, Herman and Mack administered a simple questionnaire.

The "restraint scale," which has since been changed, contains the following questions in its revised form:

1. How often are you dieting?
2. What is the maximum amount of weight (in pounds) that you have ever lost within one month?
3. What is your maximum weight gain within a week?
4. In a typical week, how much does your weight fluctuate?
5. Would a weight fluctuation of 5 lbs. affect the way you live your life?
6. Do you eat sensibly in front of others and splurge alone?
7. Do you give too much time and thought to food?
8. Do you have feelings of guilt after overeating?
9. How conscious are you of what you are eating?
10. How many pounds over your desired weight were you at your maximum weight?[28]

The questionnaire provides a quick, simple means to gauge a person's dieting behavior. With it, Herman and Mack were able to divide their subjects into groups of restrained and unrestrained eaters. The two groups, it turned out, had dramatically different styles of eating.

In a replay of Schachter's earlier experiments, Herman and Mack decided to see how people would eat when they were full —only this time, instead of comparing fat and thin people, they compared restrained and unrestrained eaters. Women in each group were given either one cup of milkshake, two cups, or none at all. Since they were always tested after lunch or dinner, those who drank two cups of milkshake were likely to be stuffed indeed. Following the "preload"—or overload—they were asked to eat as much ice cream as they wanted. In true Schachterian style, they were told that this was a "taste test."

The unrestrained eaters behaved as Schachter's "thin" subjects had—that is, as one would expect normal people to behave. The more milkshake they had received as a preload, the less ice cream they ate during the experiment. But the restrained group, as a whole, ate in an altogether bizarre fashion. They ate *more* ice cream if they had had one cup of milkshake, and still more—over a third of a pound—if they had had two cups.[29]

Clearly, the study had pointed up an important difference between restrained and unrestrained eaters; but what could it possibly mean? "We had all sorts of trouble with that first study," Herman recalls. "It was barely accepted as a senior thesis at Northwestern because nobody believed the data—they were too crazy. And we had all sorts of trouble getting it published."[30] But the study has now been well replicated, and further evidence has supported his and Mack's interpretation. They reasoned that restrained eaters use tremendous will power to restrict their caloric intake, and that drinking a sweet, high-calorie milkshake could simply destroy their resolve. It was as though, prior to the experiment, a spring had been held in place by a tight clamp. Loosened during the preload, the clamp gave way during the experiment, and appetites sprang forth with a vengeance. In common parlance, the subjects had blown their diets.

Over the last several years, Herman and his colleagues have found increasing evidence that restraint is a major determinant of eating behavior. Much of the work has been done by Janet Polivy, to whom Herman is married; she and Herman are now both at the University of Toronto. The dichotomy of restrained and unrestrained eating has largely replaced Schachter's model of external versus internal, as the older psychologist graciously admits. Herman's and Polivy's ideas, says Schachter, are "really closer to the way God see things. . . . They can incorporate far more data than any scheme that I know of, including my own." But, he adds with a laugh, "Dick Nisbett and Peter Herman were both my students, and if somebody had to top me I'm certainly pleased it was they."[31]

Polivy's and Herman's experiments have shown that several factors can "break" restraint and lead to an eating bout. If they are given alcohol beforehand (and are aware of the fact), restrained eaters, but not unrestrained ones, eat more ice cream.

Alcohol, of course, has long been thought of as a potent destroyer of inhibitions. Do the notorious marijuana "munchies" affect mostly restrained eaters? We wonder.[32]

The concept of restraint may also explain the commonplace observation that anxiety, or depression, leads some people to gain weight, whereas others lose. There is some evidence that people eat in response to these emotional states if they have been restrained, and react with a fast if they have not been. In essence, then, the eating is not a way of handling bad feelings; rather, feeling bad has merely broken the dieter's resolve.[33]

The restraint questionnaire, in itself, does not as yet tell whether someone is holding his or her weight below its natural setpoint. What it does reveal is whether the respondent is constantly resisting an urge to eat. People with a high score—indicating that they are restrained eaters—react in a highly stereotyped fashion to psychological experiments designed to fool them into temporarily abandoning their diets. Given a milkshake to consume, the serious dieter's predictable mental process is, "I broke my diet because I couldn't help it. Oh well, today's a loss. I may as well go ahead and pig out. Tomorrow is another day."

The questionnaire would be far more powerful if there were some way to correlate it with a physiological measure of setpoint. It could then be used to separate fat people into three classes: those who are holding themselves below their setpoint, those who are above it, and those who are, in a physiological sense, "just right." Approaches to treating the three groups would be quite different. Stunkard has developed an expanded version of Herman's instrument, and he has some evidence that it identifies people who are below setpoint. One physiological indicator of setpoint is the size of fat cells; people whose fat cells are unusually small, for reasons given in chapter 3, are likely to be below their "natural" weight. They also appear to score high on Stunkard's restraint scale.[34]

Herman himself is no longer convinced that restrained eaters are necessarily below setpoint, though he notes that Polivy still believes it, "and she usually ends up being right." But he does believe that physiological factors, including the metabolic changes described in chapter 3, make weight loss difficult, and ensure that dieting will be a source of frustration. Restrained eaters manifestly suffer from this chronic frustration, he believes, whether or not a setpoint really exists.

With or without setpoint theory, restrained eaters face certain inevitable hazards. They may, for example, be setting themselves up for eating binges. If they really are below their setpoints, bingers are like Keys's volunteers at the end of their starvation regimen; they are actually experiencing constant, intense hunger to which the binge is a natural reaction. Their usual effort to eat modestly is artificial as long as they are below setpoint—a fragile state of affairs maintained at the cost of great effort. Herman, without fully accepting the existence of setpoints, acknowledges that dieting creates a pressure to eat, and that binges occur when frustration mounts to intolerable levels. Whichever interpretation is correct, the observation holds true that binge eating generally does not begin spontaneously in someone who is fat; rather, it is a reaction to dieting.

Similarly, dieters are often emotionally labile. Why? Setpoint theory holds that, like starving people, they become irritable as a reaction to a physiologically abnormal state. Herman thinks that dieters become hyperemotional for psychological reasons. "Could there be a worse way to get yourself into an emotional frazzle," he asks, "than to put yourself on a diet?"[35] Whether for physiological or psychological reasons, restrained eaters are likely to be tense and unhappy.

The psychological dangers of dieting have been apparent since the 1950s. In 1957, Stunkard described the "dieting depression" that afflicted many of his patients when they tried to lose weight. At the time, Stunkard thought these emotional problems reflected unresolved conflicts. Similarly, Hilde Bruch warned that some fat people might even become psychotic when they could no longer use overeating as a psychological defense.[36]

From later studies, conducted at the Rockefeller University and elsewhere, we can infer that the physical strain of being below setpoint in itself produces psychological misery. At Rockefeller in the mid-sixties, six severely obese men and women were hospitalized for eight months and put on a low-calorie liquid diet. Successful weight loss brought anxiety and depression, as well as persistent dreams and fantasies of food. (These symptoms were similar to those experienced by people of normal weight on starvation regimens—a fact that Nisbett noted.) Moreover, the symptoms persisted even *after* the subjects had successfully lost weight and stabilized at the lower level—a finding consistent with the notion that simply being below setpoint is stressful, not just the process of losing weight. People who have been fat since childhood—and are most likely to have naturally high setpoints—are most likely to experience psychic distress when they diet. (They are also more likely than other fat people to be restrained eaters.)[37]

Anyone can experience these problems, whatever his weight, if he diets persistently enough. In *Eating Disorders,* Hilde Bruch points out the existence of "thin fat people." These individuals of normal weight—mostly women—are obsessed with being fashionably slim and, though not truly suffering from anorexia nervosa, restrict themselves desperately. She writes:

Many women make a fetish of being thin and follow reducing diets without awareness of or regard for the fact that they can do so only at the price of continuous strain and tension and some degree of ill health. . . . They come to medical attention only when the weight preoccupation interferes with their living, or when malnutrition gives rise to complaints of fatigue, listlessness, irritability, difficulties in concentration, or chronic depression. It has become customary to prescribe tranquilizers for them; three square meals a day would be a more logical treatment.[38]

The saddest examples, of course, are those—again, mostly young women—who develop true anorexia nervosa. Although they manage to eat next to nothing, they are not free of hunger; far from it. Anorexic girls override their bodies' normal demands for food through a sheer effort of the will, fueled by a morbid fear of being fat. Using the restraint questionnaire, Polivy has found that anorexics score significantly higher than typical, dieting college students. Interestingly, the most restrained of all are the "bulimics," patients who periodically (often quite frequently) go on binges of eating, then force themselves to vomit, and return to starving. Other studies have shown that bulimics are more impulsive than the anorexics, who fast more successfully; they are more likely, for example, to have experimented with sex and drugs. Evidently they go on binges because they are simply unable to endure the extreme discomfort of self-starvation—and then, out of guilt, they return to even more stringent dieting.[39]

Anorexia nervosa is only the dogged extreme of a mania for thinness that affects most of us to some degree. In their studies, Herman and Polivy have found that "virtually all individuals diet to some extent," with women showing generally more self-restraint than men.[40] The emotional toll of compulsive slimness is only now becoming clear. As Bruch wrote of her "thin fat people":

It is impossible to assess the cost in serenity, relaxation, and efficiency of this abnormal, overslim, fashionable appearance. It produces serious psychological tensions to feel compelled to be thinner than one's natural make-up and style of living demand. There is a great deal of talk about the weakness and self-indulgence of overweight people who eat "too much." Very little is said about the selfishness and self-indulgence involved in a life which makes one's appearance the center of all values, and subordinates all other considerations to it.[41]

In the last thirty years or so, psychological theories of obesity have been turned completely around. Emotional problems are now construed as the result of dieting, not the cause of fatness. This new view provides one of the strongest arguments against conventional dieting.

Changing attitudes have also been accompanied by major shifts in the psychological treatment of obesity. Three decades ago, it still seemed advisable to help people lose weight through conventional Freudian psychotherapy. If underlying conflicts could be resolved, the theory went, then people would no longer feel compelled to overeat. Then, in the late 1960s, an alternative approach—behavior modification—came on the scene.

For the next decade, it became the treatment of choice, for several reasons. Behaviorists were becoming more powerful in the psychological community, while orthodox forms of therapy were increasingly challenged as too expensive and relatively ineffective. Some of the behaviorists' assumptions about obesity meshed nicely with Schachter's ideas, which were being developed at about the same time. And, most important, early published reports showed that behavior therapy—unlike conventional psychotherapy—was effective in helping people lose weight.

But behavior therapy for obesity now appears to have had its day. Schachter's theories have been left behind, and the treatment itself has proved less powerful than was originally hoped. At best, behavior modification may help people adjust to a style of eating that is unnatural for them, but which they must follow to maintain a low weight. Like all adjuncts to will power, behavioral techniques eventually lose their effectiveness.

When behavior modification was first tried in the treatment of obesity, in 1962, it was largely ignored. The trial was reported by Charles Ferster and his colleagues at Indiana University Medical Center in an obscure publication, the *Journal of Mathetics.* The approach was based on good behaviorist principles, primarily the notion of "stimulus control." This concept came from experiments showing that animals could be trained to perform certain actions in response to specific stimuli. In Ferster's example, a pigeon was taught that pecking at a green key would deliver a food pellet, while pecking at a red key had no effect. Thereafter, the pigeon would peck at the key and eat the pellet only when presented with a *green* key. Eating became tightly linked to the stimulus color.

Ferster and his colleagues reasoned that fat people had learned to eat in response to all sorts of stimuli, from such situations as watching television to the presence of tasty food itself. They taught their subjects to eat only under certain conditions and to eliminate tempting food from their environments. In addition, the researchers tried to make eating less pleasurable by stressing the unpleasant consequences of being fat. Finally, they believed that obese people ate differently from those of normal weight—specifically, that they ate too fast to be able to control their intake—and the psychologists tried to teach their subjects new eating habits.[42]

Ferster's paper was flawed by circular logic; the theory never explained why *all* people, thin as well as fat, don't become stimulus-bound. It suffered, too, from an even worse omission: Ferster and his colleagues did not say how well their approach worked. It later turned out that the subjects in their program had only lost between five and twenty pounds.[43] These were respectable results, to be sure, but they were not inspiring. Thus, the real rise of behavior therapy for obesity began only five years later, when a young behaviorist at the University of Michigan reported stunning success.

Richard Stuart had refined Ferster's approach and assembled a clear therapeutic package, including many elements still used today. The women in his program began by keeping careful records of exactly what they ate, where, when, and under what circumstances. The goal was to identify stimuli—such as cleaning the living room, watching television, or feeling depressed—that triggered the act of eating. The women were then instructed to remove food from every part of the house except the kitchen, to prepare food only one portion at a time, to do nothing else (no TV) while eating, and to chew carefully—in short, to become fully conscious of eating. At the same time, they learned to replace between-meal snacks with enjoyable activities, to take up new hobbies if necessary. One woman began cultivating African violets. Another started keeping caged birds, a choice that her non-Freudian therapists presumably did not interpret to her.

Stuart's program was clear, and, more important, it worked remarkably well. Only two of his ten patients dropped out, and those who stayed with it for a year each lost an average of forty pounds. This gave Stuart a therapeutic batting average that was, quite simply, the best of any outpatient treatment for obesity hitherto reported in the literature.[44]

Unfortunately, Stuart's results also proved far better than those of the behavior therapists who followed in his footsteps. Why this should be remains a puzzle. In part, Stuart may have been successful because he saw each patient individually and spent a lot of time with each one. (Many later behavior therapy programs have been conducted in groups.) In addition, Stuart could tell his patients that they were going to try the newest, most experimental method of weight control, information that alone must have raised their interest and motivation. Whatever the explanation, Stuart's findings made his career—he even became a psychological consultant to Weight Watchers—and they established behavior therapy as *the* approach to obesity.

From a theoretical standpoint, Stuart's results could not have come at a better time. In 1968, just a year after his first paper on treatment was published, Schachter brought out the theory of externality. Though the two men had been working independently, their ideas meshed nicely. Schachter proposed that fat people eat because of external cues, such as a handy bowl of popcorn in the TV room. In teaching people to control the stimuli that triggered eating, Stuart had been working on a similar assumption. Schachter provided theoretical support for Stuart's practical efforts.

Over the next few years, well-controlled studies showed that behavior therapy indeed worked better than other kinds of counseling for weight loss, although subsequent patients responded less magnificently than Stuart's. A crucial test was carried out by Albert Stunkard in collaboration with Sydnor Penick. Penick treated one group of subjects with traditional psychotherapy—in which he was well versed—while a young psychologist who had done very little therapy treated another group with the behavioral methods. Experience was on Penick's side, but the group in behavior therapy lost significantly more weight.[45]

The behavioral treatment of obesity blossomed. More than a hundred papers on the subject had been published by 1975, and the number was still increasing.[46] Much of the attention came from honest excitement at the potential of this technique, even though Stuart's early results were never quite equaled. But the very nature of the approach also helped turn behavior therapy into a weight-reduction fad. Behaviorists in droves turned to obesity because weight was something they could measure; the pounds lost were a clear index of success. (Previously, behavior therapists had focused on people with well-defined but obscure problems; patients with snake phobias were especially popular.) And behaviorism gave clear prescriptions for action instead of the woolier formulations of psychotherapy. By the late 1970s, many features of behavior modification had been transformed into gimmicks by alert entrepreneurs.

Some of their commercial programs were merely silly. The makers of Water Pik came out with something called the "Countdown," an electronic timer about the size of a pocket calculator. The device is supposed to help people eat more slowly. As the instruction manual says, "You eat too much because you eat too quickly." Mealtime on this program goes like this: You take a bite of food and press a button on the

Countdown; it responds by flashing a red light. You chew along with the pulses until, twenty-four chews later, you may finally swallow. Then take the next bite, press the button, and begin again. As you proceed, the machine records the number of mouthfuls you've eaten. Instead of inculcating better eating habits, the device seemed certain to make people dread every meal. An anonymous staff member at *Consumer Reports* gave the Countdown this pithy review: "If I found that thing on the table in front of me at dinner, I'd stick a fork in it."[47]

Water Pik's foolish implement seems, as of this writing, to have gone down for the count. More durable—and more disturbing—are methods that, as their form of behavior therapy, punish fat people for eating. The Schick Clinics, which originated in the western United States, turn punishment into profit.

This bad idea derives from work begun by well-respected behaviorists. Starting in the 1950s, several behaviorists tried to help their patients abandon tempting, high-calorie treats by creating particularly unpleasant associations with them. In one especially revolting procedure, subjects were instructed to imagine sitting in a pizza parlor with some friends, feeling sick, and vomiting all over the pizza. Stuart initially used a variant of this technique with some subjects; one woman was told to imagine eating her favorite cookie, then to switch to an image of her husband seducing another woman. Sometimes the unpleasant consequences of snacking were not imaginary, but real. Patients were instructed to taste their favorite doughnuts, or whatever, and were then given electric shocks or made to smell nauseating odors. Although behavioral psychologists have not abandoned this approach, known technically as "aversion therapy," they have greatly deemphasized it, inasmuch as it adds little or nothing to the success of treatment. In 1977, a review of the field concluded that "the results of aversion therapy with obesity have been poor. . . . "[48]

Around the time this review came out, we visited a Schick

Center in San Jose, California, and found that aversion therapy was still being promoted as a scientific approach to weight control. Schick couches its techniques in pop-psychology slogans. One proclaims: "The instinctive (subconscious) mind is like a cassette recorder. . . . The reasoning mind is like a calculator. Habits are in the memory, not in the reasoning mind." Schick promises to free people from "compulsive cravings" for food by erasing unwanted memory tapes.

The treatment, we think, focuses on cruel and unnecessary punishment for heavy clients. At the center we visited, we stood behind a one-way mirror to watch a moderately plump blonde teen-ager being treated. Seated before a mirror and a small plastic bowl, with electrodes strapped to her forearm, she gobbled chocolate cake. "Stuff it in!" shouted the Schick attendant seated behind her. "It's slimy, like shortening, isn't it? Chew as fast you can! You make yourself fat, you make yourself really fat." The attendant pressed a button to deliver repeated electric shocks to the poor client. "Now spit it out into the bowl," she commanded. "Stick your tongue out at yourself. You wouldn't eat that stuff in the bowl, would you?"[49]

Most appalling about this scene, to us, is that so many clients are willing to pay large sums of money for abuse. The Schick Centers may be a monument to the self-hatred of fat people in our society—and to their desperation. The commercialization of self-torture has done little to enhance the reputation of behavior therapy.

The behavioral treatment of obesity has, however, run into deeper problems. After more than a decade, several of the most basic assumptions of this approach have come into question. Worse, recent studies show that behavior therapy, in the long term, may actually be no more effective than other methods of inducing weight loss.

Ferster's original paper, and those that followed it, accepted several untested assumptions about the factors that make people fat. There was virtually no evidence that fat people ate faster than thin ones, or, indeed, that there was any identifiable "obese eating style." Stunkard sounded a cautionary note in a 1974 address, when he was still quite optimistic about the potential of behavior therapy. "Some of the more enthusiastic behavior modifiers," he warned, "are saying that because obese persons can lose weight by modifying their eating behavior, disordered eating behavior must have been the cause of their obesity. There is just no evidence for such a contention. It is equally plausible that *behavior modification may simply be helping someone who biologically should be obese to live in a semi-starved condition."* (Our italics.) In fact, as Hilde Bruch has pointed out, "the tricks and strategies that anorexic patients use to adhere to their starvation regimen"—such as elaborate chewing—"are exactly the same as those taught as behavior modification."[50]

Over the next few years, several experiments showed that the assumptions of behavior therapy had probably been wrong. At the University of Pennsylvania, Michael Mahoney found that fat and thin people ate at the same speed in a laboratory "taste test." To study the problem in a more naturalistic setting, Stunkard and his colleagues observed obese women and women of normal weight in a fast-food restaurant. They cleverly made sure that each group would eat the same, standard meals by giving out free meal coupons at the door. Like Mahoney, they found that fat and thin women did not differ in their rates of eating, or in the amounts of food they left on their plates.[51]

In addition, K. S. Kissileff and others at the University of Pennsylvania found that fat and thin people ate under similar circumstances at home. Their subjects kept food diaries recording the times and places of eating, other things they were doing at the time, how hungry they were—in short, all the things that are changed in behavior therapy. The investigators found that fat and lean people differed in none of these eating habits. Moreover, people of all weights often ate when they were only mildly hungry—something that only fat people are theoretically supposed to do.[52]

It seemed that behavior therapists were not teaching their subjects to eat as thin people do, but were teaching them to eat as no normal person would. A study at Western Washington University, for example, found that women who had been through a behavioral program ate far more slowly than anyone else, fat or thin. But if behavior therapy was not "normalizing" eating styles, then why was it effective?[53]

This question was embarrassing for behaviorists. At the same time, Schachter's externality theory was also coming into question and could no longer offer much support for the behaviorist approach. James Ferguson, a prominent California behavior therapist, told us early in 1979 that "the theoretical basis for behavioral programs is gone. . . . Although people lose weight, it's not entirely clear *why* they're losing weight." According to Ferguson, a host of hard-to-measure variables—such as the patient's expectation that the treatment will work—could play the major role in its success.[54]

In point of fact, though, behavior therapy has also turned out to work nowhere nearly so well as had originally been hoped. A reassessment of the results, made by Rena Wing and Robert Jeffrey, has shown that people lose an average of about twelve pounds in behavior therapy programs—very close to the average for weight-loss programs in general. Like other slimming methods, behavior therapy can be modestly successful, but its results are hardly dramatic, considering that many people starting the programs want to lose fifty pounds or more. Moreover, people vary widely in their response to behavior therapy, and no one has yet figured out why some succeed where others fail.[55]

Graduates of behavioral programs, unlike dieters, tend to keep their weight down for as long as a year or two, according to Wing and Jeffery. But in the long run the weight is usually regained—just like weight lost through dieting. In 1979, Stunkard and Penick reported on a five-year follow-up of the patients treated in their first major behavior therapy program. The results, they wrote, were "disappointing"; on average, people gained back half the weight they had lost. Significantly, those with the greatest loss were most likely to regain it. This observation, like so many other observations of dieters' behavior, suggests that there is a comfortable range of weight below which it is very difficult to remain. Stunkard and Penick's review of other follow-up studies showed, in general, that "clinically important weight losses achieved by behavioral treatments for obesity are not well maintained."[56]

Behavior therapy does have one advantage over other common methods of weight loss: It is relatively benign. This kind of therapy does avoid the self-defeating insanity of crash diets and the obsessive rigidity of calorie counting. Many behavioral programs have also begun to focus on another crucial aspect of behavior—physical activity—which may prove more important than all the rituals of timing and bite-counting that have been so prominent. But behavior therapy works only some of the time, for some people—and even when it is successful, no one really knows why. Many people lose weight in these programs without changing their behavior as prescribed, and many who do change their eating habits do not lose weight.[57] Behavior therapy could turn out to be little more than an elaborate placebo.

Certainly it is not the sure cure for obesity that it once almost promised to be. "I think behavior therapy has run its course, I really do," says Stunkard. "I just don't think its clinical usefulness is going to improve much at all; it's leveled off at a point of giving modest improvement. As an analogy, if we're on a journey of a hundred miles, and we had gone five miles, then behavior therapy goes another five miles. That doubles the effectiveness, but we've still got a long ways to go."[58]

Behavioral approaches and other, supportive styles of psychotherapy may help fat people, even if they cannot "cure" them. A good therapist can help someone cope with the stigma of being fat or with the strain of dieting. It now appears that even psychoanalysis may make weight loss easier, after all, although it is far less cost-effective than behavior therapy. An American Academy of Psychoanalysis study found that nearly half of obese analysands lost more than twenty pounds, and a fifth lost more than forty pounds, in the course of treatment—which had lasted, on average, for three and a half years.[59]

Fat people generally have a hard lot in life, and they certainly deserve all the psychological help they want (and can afford). But therapy can't help much unless the nature of the problem is absolutely clear. Fatness, in most cases, is *not* the result of deep-seated psychological conflicts or maladaptive "eating behaviors"; usually, it is just a biological fact. Fat people suffer because they live in a culture that derides their bodies, encourages them to starve themselves, and declares that character flaws have made them fat. Pat psychological explanations of overweight have contributed to the cultural mythology, and have been far more hurtful than helpful.

In *Illness as Metaphor*, Susan Sontag bemoans the fact that mysterious diseases are blamed on the psyche. As she writes, "Every illness can be considered psychologically. Illness is interpreted as, basically, a psychological event, and people are encouraged to believe that they get sick because they (unconsciously) want to, and that they can cure themselves by the mobilization of will. . . ." According to Sontag, the psychological interpretation is possible only when the true, physical cause of the disease is unknown. Tuberculosis was seen in the last century as a reflection of personality, but such notions faded when the germ that caused the illness was found. Sontag predicts that cancer—the main subject of her book—will lose its grim mystique when it is understood scientifically.[60]

Fatness is usually not a disease, but we have come to treat it as one, and Sontag's analysis applies beautifully. Fat people have been taught to seek all kinds of unconscious motivations for the way they look, and they have been told they can save themselves—that is, become thin—through a combination of psychological insight and will power. The psychological view of fatness has been fueled by ignorance of the physiological factors that make it so difficult for many people to lose weight.

3

SETPOINT AND CELLS

FOOD is a red herring. That must be understood. No one gets fat solely by satisfying a big appetite.

According to tradition and common wisdom, a fat body must belong to a big eater. This simplistic belief is also, as we have seen, the point of departure for nearly every psychological theory of obesity. But in the usual sense—that fat people eat appreciably more than lean ones—the idea is unsupported by the evidence.

It's not easy to be sure how much someone is eating in the course of daily life. The very fact of being observed may distort a person's behavior, and self-reporting is subject to self-censorship. But even allowing for these difficulties, indications are that fat people eat about the same amount as thin ones.

This point has been made most emphatically by psychologists Susan and Wayne Wooley, who direct a weight-control program at the University of Cincinnati College of Medicine. Because of their theoretical orientation, the Wooleys do not express moral judgments about fatness. Thus, they are more likely than many investigators to receive candid replies to their questions about food intake. Several years ago, the two psychologists asked each of their clients to record every morsel of food she ate (the majority are women, as in most weight-control programs). The women duly turned in records of literally every bite they had taken, and the results were a revelation. "Either all our patients were lying," Wayne Wooley summarized, "or they weren't eating very much." Granted, a few of them may have been outrageously deceptive about what they had eaten, and the majority of them, as would most people of any weight, probably underestimated their intake. Still, the Wooleys' clients were far from gluttonous. Two women who each weighed more than 260 pounds, for example, appeared to be maintaining their weight on just 1,000 calories a day.[1]

To overcome the inherent uncertainty of self-reporting, the psychiatrist Albert Stunkard devised a way to watch fat people eat in a natural setting. He and his colleagues undertook to observe patrons at fast-food restaurants, snack bars, and ice-cream parlors—places where portions are so standardized that it is relatively easy to calculate the number of calories on any tray served. The investigators stationed themselves in locations from which they could unobtrusively monitor virtually everyone in a restaurant and record what each individual ate. Estimating relative weight by eye, the observers became skillful enough to guess very reliably. They were, to be sure, watching people eat only one of their daily meals, and that in public, where obviously piggish behavior might be embarrassing. But anonymity in the surroundings should have been sufficient protection for anyone who wanted two or three hamburgers instead of one. When the observers' sheets were tallied, Stunkard found that the fat customers had eaten no more than those who were thin.[2]

The Wooleys' and Stunkard's findings are the rule rather than the exception; the Wooleys have cited a score of studies other than their own, all of which show that fat people eat normal quantities of food, or even slightly less. "Any of these studies can be criticized on methodological grounds," they write. "Nonetheless, the congruence of results is so striking that the burden of proof must be said to rest with those who contend there is a difference in the amount that fat and thin people eat."[3]

Less popular than the big-eater theory of obesity have been two others. The lazy-body hypothesis holds that some people eat normally but are fat because they are physically less active than the average. The sluggish-metabolism hypothesis is similar: Some people need less energy than is normal to keep their fundamental biochemical processes going; even though they eat modestly, it is too much, and so the excess must be stored as fat. From time to time, suggestive evidence for one or the other of these notions appears. Currently, the sluggish-metabolism concept is enjoying a revival after thirty years of disrepute, because of laboratory findings suggesting that fat people use less energy than normal for certain important bodily processes.

All three theories share one crucial feature: They assume that getting fat is an accident. If the appetite, physical activity, and metabolic needs of a person all *happen* to be "normal" (whatever that is), then by a stroke of divine good fortune, that person is spared from obesity. But if one or the other of these variables is slightly out of line, the difference accumulates in fat. As an explanation of obesity, any one of these theories leaves much to be desired. Saying of someone, "She's fat because her metabolic rate is low," simply begs the question, "Why doesn't she eat less to compensate?" Worse yet, saying, "She's fat because she eats too much," merely restates the problem.

Setpoint theory holds that fatness is not an accident. Each body "wants" a characteristic quantity of fat and proceeds to balance food intake, physical activity, and metabolic efficiency in order to maintain that amount.

Although it may sound silly to say that a body "wants" a stipulated amount of fat, this really is not a bad way to describe what goes on. Fat storage appears to be managed by a particular portion of the unconscious brain, which can as easily desire fat as the conscious brain can yearn to possess an original Picasso. Yet, in determining the amount of fat the body will maintain —in establishing the setpoint—the brain does not act alone. The cells that store fat apparently release chemical signals telling the brain how much fat they contain and, when necessary, asking for more. The "desire" for fat arises in these cells as well as in the brain; each cell demands to be supplied with a minimum amount of fat.

The cells, however, do not write their own meal ticket; they only provide information that is processed and acted upon by the brain. And the brain synthesizes a lot of data about the state of the body and the environment before "deciding" what the setpoint should be. Sensory impressions—such as the taste and smell of especially rich food—may raise the setpoint; such drugs as amphetamine and nicotine may act in the brain to lower the setting, as we will see in chapter 4. Physical activity also affects the setpoint, perhaps through hormonal signals (yet to be determined) that would also be processed by the brain.

When we speak of the "setpoint mechanism"—the system that determines how fat a body will be—we are clearly talking about a system involving much of the body, not just an obscure cluster of cells at the base of the brain. But when one's weight begins to deviate from the setpoint—as a result of dieting, say, or festive overeating—it is the brain that pulls on the reins. Hunger, of course, is its first resort when food intake is insufficient. Someone who feels famished after two weeks on the latest "miracle" diet is experiencing internal pressure to eat normally and stay at his or her setpoint. Similarly, the bloated feeling that remains after the Christmas-to-New Year's excess is a signal to let fat stores fall back toward normal. Changes in the quantity of adipose tissue are probably the fundamental determinant of hunger; other factors, such as hormones released by the intestine, may affect it in the short run.

Hunger, though, is only one way for the brain to bring an

organism back to its setpoint. And hunger may be ineffective: A person can starve through sheer force of will; an animal or person may be in an environment where there simply is not enough to eat. So the setpoint system, coordinated by the brain, has other tools at its disposal. If it cannot increase the amount of energy, in the form of food, flowing into the body, it will decrease the amount that is expended and, thus, protect whatever fat stores remain.

Energy is expended in two ways. It drives the chemical (or "metabolic") reactions needed to keep the organism in good repair, and it powers the contraction of muscles required for activity. Either of these energy drains may be limited in order to preserve the body's fat. During long periods of semistarvation, people and animals spontaneously become less active. A more subtle form of energy conservation also comes into play: The metabolic rate—the speed at which calories are burned to perform the body's maintenance functions—slows down with underfeeding; overfeeding has the opposite effect. Controls on the outflow of energy must be integrated with the mechanism controlling food intake in order for fatness to be regulated. The setpoint mechanism uses whatever means are at its disposal to make an organism conform to its set requirement for fat.

This fact was vividly demonstrated by a rat that was kept in a Baltimore laboratory at the time when Keys's conscientious objectors were starving in Minneapolis. The animal was subjected to surgery that destroyed a minute cluster of cells in its brain. For years it had been known that this procedure would cause a rat to eat voraciously and grow enormously fat. But the Baltimore rat was not allowed the luxury of overeating. Day by day, after its surgery, the animal received precisely the amount of food that it had voluntarily consumed before its operation. It proceeded to get much fatter than before. The investigators then confirmed this finding with another experiment. They used two virtually identical rats but performed the brain surgery on only one of them. They then measured what the intact animal ate every day, and the next day they fed exactly the same amount to its surgically altered mate. In short order, the experimental animal grew much fatter than its control.[4]

Subsequent research has shown what happened to these animals that got fat without overeating: The brain surgery raised their setpoints. Denied the opportunity to eat the quantities they would have liked, each used alternative methods to increase its body fat. Presumably, after surgery the animals reduced the rate at which they used energy for metabolic needs, and they may also have cut down their spontaneous activity.

For most creatures, most of the time, plenty of food is available, and an increased requirement for energy or fat is met by eating. But this need not be so. If food is restricted an animal may become less active to take on the required fat.

In many ways, pregnancy and lactation mimic the effect of a temporarily raised setpoint by calling for extra energy. In Western societies, women meet this added need by eating more than usual. But in a highland tribe of New Guinea, women eat no more during pregnancy and lactation than they do at other times. They meet their increased energy demands by reducing their levels of activity. During the last three months before and the six months after delivery, they become increasingly sedentary. As one observer has reported, they "walked less, spent longer periods sitting—partly enforced because of the breast feeding—and worked shorter periods in the garden."[5]

Instead of regarding activity, eating, and metabolic rate as three independent functions that may or may not be at a "normal" level, setpoint theory sees them as the means for maintaining a certain quantity of fat. (In other terminology, we could speak of the three functions as playing a "zero-sum game" for which setpoint has written the rules.)

"Setpoint," both as a term and a concept, is borrowed from the science of engineering. In the last ten years, this word has been widely used by students of weight regulation—and it has been sedulously avoided by others (who may, nevertheless, find themselves using a synonym, such as "defended variable"). The term has been criticized by still others, who have argued that the amount of fat an animal carries could easily be an accident—the result of various interrelated processes in a system so complex that it changes very slowly. In this view, a shift in activity, eating, or metabolic rate is simply damped by the response of many other factors that tend to keep the system in equilibrium. To use an analogy, the water level in a lake can be exceedingly stable for years on end, and yet nothing resembling a setpoint controls it.

The arguments against setpoint have been based largely on theoretical models (some tested by computer simulation), purporting to show that it is quite possible to keep weight very stable without even the ghost of a setpoint. These models require some gratuitous assumptions of their own. Meanwhile, a good deal of evidence gathered from animal experimentation confirms the existence of setpoints in species other than our own.[6]

The setpoint mechanism is apparently very good at what it does best: supervising fat storage. On the other hand, it has serious blind spots. It cannot tell the difference between a reducing diet and starvation. If an animal with a high setpoint is forced to lose weight, it reacts with the intensity of the truly deprived. The same appears to be true of human beings. The dieter with a high setpoint who enters into battle begins to experience constant hunger, presumably as part of the body's attempt to restore the status quo.

This experience of perennial hunger is itself evidence that losing weight does not necessarily return a body to "normal" —at least not in its own terms. Many fat people who successfully reduce find that they have to live with constant discomfort. Fats Goldberg is one of them.

Larry "Fats" Goldberg was fat since childhood. As he told his friend, the writer Calvin Trillin, he weighed 320 pounds—double the average for his height—by the time he graduated from college. In his early thirties, Fats successfully lost the "extra" weight and then, in an act of cosmic defiance, he entered the pizza business. Goldberg succeeded in both his callings. The pizza sold well, and thanks to the most rigid diet conceivable, he kept his weight down. Both achievements are exceedingly rare: The rate of diet failure in severely obese people is almost as high as the rate of new restaurants' closing in New York. About half of the dieters regain everything in three years, and the rest succumb within the next seven.[7]

Fats Goldberg has evidently derived some of the psychological strength he needs to stick with his perpetual diet by declaring Kansas City, his home town, a "free zone." On visits there, he eats a meal that lasts all day: eggs, biscuits, milk, sausages, bacon, cinnamon rolls, hot beef sandwiches, Dutch apple pie, half of a second pie and a pint of ice cream, Pepsi, peanut butter and jelly sandwiches, a barbecue, popcorn, Coke, cheeseburgers, a Frosty Malt, a banana split. . . .

Then, upon returning to New York, Goldberg arduously divests himself of the baggage left over from his trip and goes back to normal—except that his state of mind is *never* truly normal. Fully a decade after he lost 160 pounds, Fats was still hungry—unremittingly. Trillin asked him at that time whether life was worth living and recorded his reply: "Well, I figure that in my first twenty-five years I ate enough for four normal lifetimes [certainly an overestimate]. . . . So I get along. But there is a lot of pain involved. A lot of pain. I can't stress that enough."[8]

Binge eating is a typical response to the kind of pain that chronic dieting produces. Just as Keys's volunteers responded to the termination of semistarvation by eating everything they could cram into their stomachs, even the most determined dieters are likely to cave in from time to time.

Determination is the hallmark of dieters who check into the Dietary Rehabilitation Clinic at Duke University's medical center. They are required to disrupt their lives; to move to Durham,

North Carolina, for at least a month; to pay handsomely for the privilege; and to go hungry. When 280 of these patients were asked about binge eating, exactly half reported that they regularly went on a food toot at least once a week. Although this statistic was given the cachet of publication in a scientific journal, it only reinforced the rich lore of tales about explosive gluttony associated with Duke's diet clinics.[9]

Duke's famous "Rice Diet" was devised in the late 1940s by Walter Kempner, a physician who was a refugee from Hitler's Germany. First designed for patients with hypertension, Kempner's regimen consisted of unsalted rice, fruit, and fruit juice. Of course, people who went on the diet lost weight while they were on it, and gradually it was extended to the treatment of uncomplicated obesity. Patients came to Kempner's Durham clinic expecting to lose vast amounts of weight in short order, and many did, but not without setbacks. And not without moments of flamboyant rebellion.

One of the "ricers," as they came to be known by the people of Durham, described her most triumphant moment to writer Burr Snider: how one evening she stole a nineteen-pound turkey from the hospital kitchen, smuggled it into her room, and by three the next morning had consumed the whole bird and disposed of the remains. Because the turkey was freshly cooked when she took it, and she had to hide it under her nightgown, she suffered an unpleasant burn, but she had no regrets. On another occasion, five sizable ricers piled into an old car and blitzed through Durham's fast-food strip with stops at Pizzaville, Colonel Sanders, McDonald's, Dunkin' Donuts, Howard Johnson's, and one or two other places. As Snider quoted the driver, "that car was carrying a lot of accumulated hunger."[10]

Hunger does accumulate; there is really no question of that. Dieters demonstrate it; Keys's volunteers demonstrated it. Any laboratory rat will demonstrate it: Take away its rations until the animal loses twenty or thirty grams, then give it free access to food and it will eat very earnestly until it has restored the missing fat. Satiety also accumulates. Force-feed a rat with rich eggnog through a stomach tube, and if you give it more calories than it needs, it will fatten. When you stop, the rat will eat less than normal until the excess is lost. Sims's overfed volunteers showed the same effect.

What is "accumulating" in a hungry or sated animal is the discrepancy between its actual fat stores and the fat supply its body deems necessary. How this computation is performed is unknown, and until the mechanism is discovered, the existence of a setpoint must be regarded as speculative. There is enough evidence, however, to make an educated guess about how the system functions.

The control of the setpoint does not reside at a particular point in the brain or body. Instead, fat storage is regulated by messages cycling continuously through a system with no iden-tifiable "master switch." Where we begin, then, is arbitrary. We will start with the cells in which fat is stored because, to para-phrase Willie Sutton, that's where the fat is.

The body stores small amounts of energy in the form of sugar —either glucose, a simple molecule, or glycogen, which is a long chain composed of glucose units. If need be, the body can withdraw protein from muscle to use as an energy source. But most of its reserve is in the form of fat packed into cells, which are usually found in clusters like microscopic soap bubbles, each one distended by a droplet of oil. The cell's biochemical machinery, which accumulates or discharges the stored fat on demand, is all squeezed into a thin watery layer at the surface of the oil droplet.

Fat cells seem to abide by certain rules of their own. Each one can accumulate only so much fat; above a certain size (about a millionth of a gram) it simply will not grow, and most fat cells are normally about half that size. If all the available cells are filled to capacity, then new ones must be formed to handle the overload. On the other hand, surplus capacity is never lost; the number of fat cells in the body, so far as anyone knows, never decreases.[11]

This apocalyptic finding was first made in rats a little over ten years ago. When newborn rat pups were nursed in small litters, they took more milk than usual and grew extra fat cells, which then remained with them into adulthood. The overfed rats were stouter than normal, apparently because their extra cells demanded to be supplied with fat. Just as the cells were unwilling to grow above a maximum size, they were unwilling to shrink below a minimum. The experiments also seemed to show that rats easily added extra cells at the beginning of life, but not later.[12]

One of the great dangers to public welfare is scientific research that is hastily applied. The discovery that rat pups could be pushed into lifelong obesity if they received more milk than usual was almost immediately interpreted by the public as a recommendation that human infants should be protected from "overfeeding," whatever that might mean. In practice, pediatricians began to urge the parents of obviously chubby babies to restrict their intake—essentially to put them on diets. The first year of life was thought to be especially critical.

The theory underlying this recommendation went as follows: Fat cells try to keep a constant size. An individual's particular setting—fat or thin—is determined by the number of cells he acquires early in life. After that, all the cells tend to keep a constant size and number—in effect, they determine the setpoint. Overfeeding a baby gives it extra fat cells as lifelong companions.

The popularity of the fat-cell theory was probably due in part to a post-Freudian inclination to blame mothers for their children's disadvantages. Here, instead of the unconscious, fat cells were seen as the target of mothers' misdeeds. This enthusiastic extrapolation from careful research-in-progress was far too simple, as subsequent work has demonstrated.

The number of fat cells a baby has in the first year of life does not foretell its adipose future. Only after its first birthday does a child begin to resemble its appearance as an adult. And by then, as any parent knows, the amount a child eats is firmly decided by the child—whose choices are opposed only at great emotional cost to both parties. The effort in the 1970s to restrain babies from eating what they wanted was a vast, uncontrolled experiment, from which we shall probably learn nothing. The experience of two groups of children born in Sweden in earlier decades suggests that there may be nothing to learn. In humans, early nutritional experience probably does little to set the number of fat cells.

Around 1930, ten baby boys suffered severe food restriction. They had been born with pyloric stenosis, a condition in which the stomach's outlet is constricted. Instead of receiving surgery, the usual treatment, they were placed on a diet of very small meals and treated with drugs to relax the constriction. Eventually they outgrew their condition, but in the process they fell to about half the usual body weight for their age. As adults they were smaller than normal, but when tested they were found to have a perfectly normal number of fat cells.

Ten to fifteen years later, a dozen boys and girls were born to mothers with diabetes that had been poorly controlled in pregnancy. The mothers' high blood sugar meant that the babies developed with an oversupply of calories available to them. They were born big, but by the time they were twenty, like the undernourished boys, they had a normal supply of fat cells.[13]

Perhaps if a child were really force-fed, in the manner of a Strasbourg goose, there would be a noticeable effect. But we doubt whether ethnic mothers, urging their children to "Eat, eat!," can be held accountable. Not, at least, for their behavior. Their genes are another matter.

The tendency to be fat or thin—like the distribution of fat on the body—is influenced by heredity. The question is, To what extent? In at least one respect, genetic control is absolute: Women have more fat than men, and it is distributed in a conspicuously different pattern. This distinction has nothing to do with differences in the way boys and girls are fed; it is hereditary and is mediated by the sex hormones. That is why most women have prominent breasts and most men do not. Less obvious aspects of fat distribution—more or less on the thighs, the torso, and so on—are also, it appears, largely inherited.[14]

It is less clear—and a matter of some controversy—whether genes determine the total amount of fat a person carries as well as its pattern of distribution. Among laboratory animals, heredity does play a major role. At least four distinct mutations in the mouse and one in the rat are known to cause obesity. These single-gene abnormalities produce animals with extraordinary quantities of adipose tissue. The mutant rat was originally called the "fatty" by Lois Zucker, the geneticist who discovered it, and is now universally known as the "Zucker fatty." It grows to double the normal weight by the age of ten weeks, and the entire excess is fat. The animal has a vast number of fat cells, all of them large. The exact reason for this abnormality is not known, but clearly it is not merely a dietary negligence—an inability on the rat's part to notice when it has overeaten. If a Zucker fatty is forced to reduce, or is made to work hard for its food, it takes every available measure to regain any weight it loses. It may be foundering in the midst of adipose plenty, but it acts as if it were *hungry* unless it has all the fat to which it is genetically entitled.[15]

One of the obese mice—code-named *db/db*—early in life turns into a furry tennis ball, with a string tail, pointed nose, and four dainty feet its only outward signs of mouseness. Like the Zucker fatty or the brain-damaged rat, *db/db* is a big eater when given free access to food. But, when several *db/db* mice were pair-fed with normal littermates, the *db/db* animals gained *five times* as much fat as their controls—on precisely the same amount of food. This mutation acts in much the same manner as the brain operation to increase the animal's demand for *fat*, not its appetite per se.[16]

These single-gene defects probably tell us little about the typical genetic difference between fat and thin people living outside laboratories or hospitals—or fat and thin rodents, for that matter. What they do show is that, when a gene is eliminated, some part of the setpoint system is destroyed, with truly drastic consequences for the animal.

Most of the normal variation in a population of animals is caused by a whole group of genes, none of them truly abnormal, which act in concert to push each creature toward some particular place on the spectrum between fat and thin. To demonstrate this fact, two geneticists separated a heterogeneous group of normal mice, some of them slightly chubbier (by mouse standards) than others, into two groups, heavy and light. They then bred these animals for fifteen mouse generations. They mated the heaviest of the heavy with each other, and the lightest of the light. At the end, they had created two races, or strains, one consistently plump and the other lean.[17]

The only rigorous way to show whether the setpoint weight of most people is determined by their genes would be to engage them in a similar breeding experiment. Short of an unwelcome visit from another planet, this investigation is unlikely to take place, and the only alternative is to observe people as they are by using statistical methods to disentangle genetic from environmental or behavioral influences. The simplest way to begin is to ask whether children resemble their parents and siblings. And, of course, they do. From large surveys, it is clear that children are very like their parents, and even more like their siblings in the amount of fat they carry. But this finding only tells us that genes *could* be in control. Families also share an environment and acquire similar habits, which might, instead, account for the similarities.

Stanley Garn, a strong environmentalist, has argued that family resemblances are not evidence of genetic inheritance because husbands and wives, who lack any blood relationship, have similar amounts of fat, much as brothers and sisters or parents and children do. He has also pointed out that a woman's socioeconomic status is strongly correlated with her fatness. Garn seems inclined, on the whole, to remain within the blame-a-mother tradition, and he argues, without direct evidence, that shared experiences and dietary habits are the means by which family members come to resemble one another.

Several features of Garn's own data, however, argue against his interpretation. Husbands and wives *do* tend to have a similar amount of fat, but the resemblance does not increase with the length of marriage. This finding suggests that like attracts like, not that spouses remake themselves into each other's image. Also, inasmuch as mothers traditionally prepare meals and set a household's culinary style, Garn's theory would accord them a disproportionate influence over their children's weight. But children are as likely to resemble their fathers as their mothers —a finding that argues against his environmental hypothesis.[18]

The best evidence on heritability of any human trait usually comes from studies of twins. There are several ways to approach such an investigation—all difficult to execute, and none especially satisfactory on methodological grounds. A few scientists have tried one or another of the methods, such as comparing the difference between pairs of fraternal twins with that between pairs of identical twins. Because the fraternals may have only half their genes in common, whereas the identicals have all the same genes, the relative influence of heredity can be computed with a fairly simple mathematical formula. Unfortunately, this procedure requires some untestable assumptions, and the results must be treated with caution. The few twin studies that have been at least adequately completed tend to agree that fatness is as much as 75 percent heritable. Roughly translated, this means that when two people have different amounts of fat, at least three-quarters of the difference has been caused by their dissimilar genes; the remainder is the result of differences in experience, environment, or habits.[19]

For the sake of argument, assume that this estimate is accurate. It tells us that people who share a relatively similar life-style have different amounts of fat as the result of inherited differences. If two city-dwellers—each with a nine-to-five job, a car, a television set, and a house in a nearby suburb—are dissimilar, it is largely because of their genes.

But other conclusions should *not* be drawn from these estimates. They do not mean that a fat person is genetically fated to remain fat under every conceivable circumstance, as someone with brown eyes is always brown-eyed. Rather, the genes specify a way of reacting to the environment. Change jobs, sell the car, move to a farm—and the same genes might produce a very different effect. The possibility is not just hypothetical. There are now several well-known examples of people who, having held to quite an ordinary weight in one habitat, have become extremely fat upon moving to a new one. The Pima Indians of Arizona, for example, had lived for centuries as subsistence farmers working irrigated land along the Gila River. They prevailed over this unforgiving terrain, but part of their success depended on a hidden compromise. They adapted genetically to the cycle of plenty and scarcity that their land afforded. In the past few generations, however, they have been forced to abandon the old way of life and move into the mainstream economy. The great majority have responded by becoming obese.[20]

The Pimas are an extreme case, but as such they make two important points: The effect of a gene is often defined by its environment, and, working together, genes and environment can become a virtually irresistible force. As Shaw's Johnny Tarleton remarks in *Misalliance,* "No matter how little you eat you put on flesh if you're made that way."

The setpoint system appears to act as the enforcer, the internal mechanism that takes its instructions from DNA and figures out how to adapt them to an organism's living conditions. It is unlikely that the number of fat cells each of us carries dictates, in and of itself, how fat we are to be. Such an arrangement would be profoundly maladaptive for creatures that live in, and cope with, changing environments. To be sure, predictable changes in our need for fat are themselves partially built into the genetic program. For girls, to take one example, the transition from baby fat to childhood leanness is followed, at adolescence, by a return to relative fatness. But if the whole decision as to how much fat will be carried were left to stubborn and unthinking fat cells, serious errors could result. It is quite possible that those people who become exceedingly fat in childhood and enter adult life with a large excess of fat cells, as Fats Goldberg presumably did, are suffering from a hereditary error that gives the cells too much autonomy.

But those people who are ordinarily fat, or pudgy—or who just happen to think they should be thinner—follow the instructions of a control center located somewhere in their brains. It may be faintly discomfiting to think that our conscious minds have not been trusted by Mother Nature to supervise fat storage. We are inclined to assume that intelligence is restricted to those mental processes of which we are aware. Setpoint theory postulates that we come equipped with an unconscious, automatic (but not rigid) device that assesses the body's stores of fat and takes steps to adjust them.

In all probability, the fat cells communicate with the brain by releasing chemical signals into the bloodstream. If each cell released signal molecules in proportion to the amount of fat it contained, blood levels of the molecule would reflect the total amount of fat in the body. Indeed, there is such a material; it is glycerol (or glycerine), a simple substance attached to fat molecules inside the cells that store them. For no apparent reason, every fat cell is constantly detaching glycerol from some of its accumulated fat molecules. This activity appears to result from steady idling of the cell's metabolic machinery (which is all located near its surface). Because the fat cell cannot recycle glycerol internally, all of the material is released to the bloodstream. The amount released is proportionate to the cell's content of fat.

The experiment is obvious. Inject a rat with glycerol, first into its bloodstream and, if that works, try delivering the chemical directly to its brain. Does the animal lose its appetite? The experiment has been performed. The rat injected with glycerol virtually stops eating even though its other behaviors—drinking, puttering about the cage, and so on—remain normal. The following step would be to give the rat glycerol over a long period and see whether it would lose its appetite indefinitely, or stabilize at a lower, "set" weight. Because of technical limitations, the experiment is fiendishly difficult to perform, but results from a week-long trial suggest that a rat receiving glycerol does indeed resume normal eating after a period of weight loss. The injected glycerol, then, is less an appetite suppressant than a false messenger, deceiving the rat into acting as if it had more fat than it does.[21]

Glycerol cannot be the only chemical signal required to regulate the body's fat stores, although it may be the only one released by fat cells. Several other substances, including insulin and hormones with more exotic names, such as cholecystokinin (CCK), bombesin, and beta-endorphin, are capable of influencing appetite. Glucose (blood sugar) also has a marked effect, and for years it was thought to be the sole substance controlling appetite and fat storage. By now it is clear that blood sugar may have a short-term influence, helping to promote the beginning or termination of a meal, but it does not govern the accumulation of fat. How the other substances modulate the setpoint, if indeed they do, remains to be determined.

Periodically, reports appearing in the press to the effect that "the body's own appetite suppressant" may have been discovered raise hopes that the key to obesity has finally been identified. These reports should rather excite suspicion. As the outer surface of the body has a rich supply of visual, auditory, and tactile information about the surrounding world, so the surface facing inward is exposed to a universe of chemicals, and it has sense organs galore with which to perceive and evaluate this internal world. Even as you might stop a man in his tracks by flashing a blinding light at him or setting off a loud explosion, you might dazzle appetite with large doses of this or that hormone. But you would not have discovered the "control" over locomotion, nor would you have discovered very much about normal appetite controls. It is exceedingly unlikely that anything as important as fat storage is governed by a single chemical.

A wealth of internal sensory and chemical information is delivered to the brain, but not to the conscious mind. Instead, sense data are relayed to several regions of the brain's central portion, where they are integrated and evaluated. From there, instructions are sent across to consciousness. The message is never so specific as "eat a candy bar." Rather, it is experienced as a kind of steady pressure—hunger—which requires a behavioral response. Eating a candy bar is only one, obviously, of the myriad possibilities.

The hunger most of us feel at mealtime is probably more a habitual reaction than a serious signal that we're facing a fat shortage. Real hunger is a thoroughly unpleasant sensation, and we learn to prevent it by eating meals of the right size at the right intervals. In fact, most people are very good at anticipating their nutritional needs. The ability to judge the number of calories in a meal is evidently acquired early in life. Newborn babies suckle until their stomachs are full, no matter how many calories are in the fluid. But within a matter of days, they begin to adjust their intake to compensate for changes in the energy content. An adult can be thrown off for a couple of days by unfamiliar food consumed in unfamiliar circumstances—such as liquid dietary food delivered through a tube—but thereafter most people judge very precisely, although unconsciously, how much energy they are consuming.

Hunger and satiety have been described as conditioned

reflexes. As a dog learns to avoid an electric shock by jumping whenever it hears a warning noise, an unconscious part of our brains learns to avoid hunger by inducing us to eat a certain amount at certain times of day. The sensation of appetite, then, is roughly analogous to apprehension—the expectation that pain is on its way. If appetite begins to make errors, within a few days it is coached by hunger—just as the dog is reminded by a real shock when it fails to jump at the warning noise.

To extend this analogy, simple dieting could be compared to the dog's deciding merely to stand there and take it when the shock comes. And behavior modification would be like attempting to believe that the warning noise means something other than "a shock is coming." But if the shocks do come, and they are painful, we might well expect that even a very determined and intelligent dog would take to jumping again.[22]

Rare individuals manage to continue dieting and remain relatively thin, despite permanent hunger. But even dedicated dieters may find, to their dismay, that they cannot lose as much weight as they would like. After an initial loss of ten or twenty pounds, dieters often reach a plateau where they lose weight at a far slower rate, although they remain as hungry as ever.

The body, then, has more than one way to defend its fat stores. Long-term caloric deprivation acts, in ways that are not clear, as a signal to turn down the metabolic rate. Calories are burned more slowly, so that even a paltry diet almost suffices to maintain weight. The metabolic rate, in short, can evidently adjust up or down to correct for deviations from the setpoint. The phenomenon was first identified, not in dieters, but in people who, like Sims's subjects, were experimentally force-fed.

At the turn of the century, in the German city of Kiel, a nutritionist named R. O. Neumann set out to become a compulsive overeater—not, however, in the usual sense. Neumann overfed himself in a carefully planned scientific experiment. Further, he measured and recorded the particulars of his diet with an obsessiveness that must have seemed nearly mad to those around him.

In order to keep accurate records of his daily menu, Neumann limited his meals to certain foods always purchased from the same merchants, who must have considered him an odd, if steady, customer. During one period, he ate only black bread, Saveloy sausage, Romatour cheese, lard, and water. More typically, he ate a balanced diet, including a couple of pints of beer a day. Neumann analyzed and weighed all his food in his laboratory, and he regularly weighed himself.

As the months went by, the dogged nutritionist confirmed what he had suspected: When he increased his intake, he gained a little weight, but then held steady, rather than gaining weight indefinitely. Even when he increased his intake by as much as 800 calories a day over a long period, his weight remained quite stable, and he was far from becoming obese on this regimen. He reasoned that his body must have adapted to overfeeding by somehow wasting the extra calories, and called this phenomenon *Luxuskonsumption*—which translates, roughly, as "extra-burning."

Neumann had showed how difficult it is for even a monomaniac to change his weight by changing his diet. Moreover, he had some understanding of why the task was so difficult. *Luxuskonsumption* represents an increase in the metabolic rate. As he willfully overate, Neumann's body gained some fat but then adapted by burning off his intentional excess, and he became virtually no heavier.

The nutritionist realized that the phenomenon he had discovered could work both ways. On the one hand, he wrote, "It's clear enough that someone who otherwise lives well can take in superfluous nutriment and thereby convert his body to a wasteful metabolism [*Luxuskonsumption*]." On the other hand, he observed, "It appears that the organism can grow accustomed [to eating little] and is able to keep house with a scant but sufficient diet."[23]

Neumann's ideas, in one form or another, have been debated for decades, and the effects of diet on metabolic rate are only now becoming clear. The accumulating evidence shows that excess calories can be burned for the simple purpose of preventing their storage. This type of metabolic heat production—or "thermogenesis," to use the Greek term physiologists favor—is a crucial factor in the body's energy equation. Its importance has been recognized only recently, and Neumann's work has been reconsidered after years of virtual neglect.

Neumann's findings received some early support from animal studies—and from the work of another self-experimenter, Addison Gulick. Gulick, a physiologist at the University of Missouri, described himself as belonging to the "difficulty fattening type." "I had long noted my inclination toward a very copious diet of predominantly starchy nature, in spite of which my weight remained fairly constant, even on a moderate round of activity, at a figure well below the average for my stature," he wrote. "If the hereditary constitution is important in this connection, such family data as I possess seem to indicate that I am derived largely from non-fattening strains."[24]

From March to May of 1916, Gulick, carefully measuring his caloric intake and output, added up the number of calories he required for his estimated basic metabolic needs, daily activities (as measured by a pedometer), and the energy required to digest his food. Gulick found that he ate 21 to 23 percent more calories than he could account for, even though his weight was falling slightly. He concluded that his body must handle calories at a "wasteful rate of oxidation," which accounted for his thinness. Then, from May 1916 to July 1917, the physiologist began overeating—largely by adding carbohydrates to his diet—to see what would happen. He gained some weight, but less than he would have predicted. When the caloric balance sheet was drawn up, Gulick found that his body was now "wasting" 27 to 37 percent of the food energy he consumed, apparently to compensate for the oversupply. Gulick's self-study appeared to confirm Neumann's: Some people, at least, could compensate for overeating through *Luxuskonsumption.*

The findings proved hard to replicate, however. Few investigators, after all, were willing to count every bite they ate or weigh every meal for a year or more, and even fewer nonscientists were likely to cooperate with such an experimental design. Meanwhile, short-term experiments, for which volunteers were found, gave little evidence of the wasteful burning that Neumann had postulated. In 1931, F. H. Wiley and L. H. Newburgh, at the University of Michigan, published a paper entitled, "The Doubtful Nature of 'Luxuskonsumption,' " which purported to show just that. They related the experience of a "very thin young man" whom they induced to eat 5,000 calories a day instead of his customary 3,000. After two weeks of this, the man had gained about ten pounds, roughly what conventional nutritional theory predicted. In this case, there was no mysterious disappearance.[25]

Thereafter, the concept of *Luxuskonsumption* received little attention, until the late 1960s. The prevailing dogma was that the metabolic fires burned with a constant flame; diet had little or no influence on heat production. Except in some rare diseases, metabolic requirements were thought to be constant, so that energy balance was essentially a matter of comparing two variables: energy spent in physical activity and the calories consumed in food. Even though a few experiments did seem to demonstrate *Luxuskonsumption,* at least as many failed to do so. In the last fifteen years, however, new studies have revived the concept that heat production can be variable and is influenced by diet. It now appears that *Luxuskonsumption* begins only after about two weeks of overfeeding, and a cumulative excess of about 20,000 calories is required to trigger it. Once begun, *Luxuskonsumption* is capable of increasing metabolic rate by about 10 percent. Thus, if Wiley and Newburgh had persuaded their "very thin young man" to keep overeating for a few more weeks, they might have concluded that *Luxuskonsumption* was not so "doubtful" after all.[26]

Ethan Sims's observations on overfed prisoners, described in chapter 1, provided some of the first modern confirmation of the phenomenon. Sims had not expected his subjects to undermine standard notions of energy balance. But as the prisoners in his study set about making their Lucullan contribution to knowledge, they simply failed to gain weight as expected. Sims recalls:

As various people began to see our data, they said, "Look, people aren't gaining. What about these old theories of so-called *Luxuskonsumption?*" I remember we used to be really embarrassed to say anything about it. Dieticians have assumed that people simply burn with an even flame; stoke it a little more and they'll just gain weight. But we now know that it's a very dynamic situation.

At this point, enough evidence has accumulated to make *Luxuskonsumption* "almost respectable," Sims says with a characteristically diffident smile.[27]

In laboratory rats, the major site of thermogenesis and therefore, presumably, of *Luxuskonsumption,* has turned out to be a tissue called "brown" fat. Whereas the more abundant "white" fat stores calories, brown fat purposefully and wastefully burns them. When a rat is placed in a cold environment, brown fat helps it survive. Although this tissue may make up only 1 or 2 percent of the adult animal's body weight, it accounts for some 60 percent of the rodent's thermogenic potential. Brown fat is especially active in newborn mammals—including, perhaps, human infants—which must survive the transition from the warm surrounding of the womb to a colder, if not crueler, world.[28]

The metabolic furnace responds to changes in diet, as well as changes in temperature. In 1979, two British physiologists reported that rats fed an especially fattening diet gained far less weight than expected—a classic demonstration of *Luxuskonsumption*—and also increased the size of their stores of brown fat. A hypothesis developed: Brown fat might be responsible for burning off excess calories, and a defect in such tissue could lead to obesity. Studies of genetically obese mice supported the theory. These mice have an impaired capacity for thermogenesis. Kept at four degrees centigrade they soon sicken and die—in spite of their insulating layers of white fat—whereas normal rodents thrive. Brown fat in the obese mice proves to be abnormal.[29]

As we have already seen, however, these mice may tell us relatively little about fat people. Although human beings also have brown fat deposits, their function, if any, is still uncertain. In an editorial, *The Lancet* pointed out that "no-one has yet shown that excess food intake, or cold exposure, or indeed anything, stimulates selective thermogenesis in brown adipose tissue in adult man."[30]

The *Luxuskonsumption* hypothesis, by itself, begs a crucial question. People may burn excess calories when they eat too much —but *how much* is "too much"? How does the body "know" when its owner has been overeating? *Luxuskonsumption* does not seem to be triggered by individual eating bouts, say a single Thanksgiving dinner, but by some cumulative change in the body. The simplest explanation—though it is by no means proven—is that the body only increases thermogenesis when it begins to move significantly above its setpoint for fatness. Deviations in the other direction have the opposite effect: The metabolic rate drops to conserve calories and maintain a stable amount of fat.

The body reacts to stringent dieting as if famine had set in. Within a day or two after semistarvation begins, the metabolic machinery shifts to a cautious regimen designed to conserve the calories it already has on board. The willing spirit is opposed by flesh that is not at all weak; it is perfectly determined to hoard the remaining supply of energy, pending nutritional relief. Because of this innate biological response, dieting becomes progressively less effective and, as we have remarked and generations of dieters have observed, a plateau is reached at which further weight loss seems all but impossible.

This energy conservation plan is reflected in the metabolic rate, which goes down. The cooling off occurs in people of normal weight, such as the conscientious objectors Keys studied, and in fat people on diets, even though they still have an ample energy reserve. Obese people put on extremely restrictive diets—a few hundred calories a day—drop their metabolic rate about 15 percent in a few weeks, regardless of the fact that they are still obese.[31]

Whether this phenomenon is general, and a significant factor in the failure of dieting efforts by normal people, has been a matter of controversy. In 1975 Derek Miller, of London's Queen Elizabeth College, wrote, "It is a common clinical observation that some people cease to lose weight after long periods of dieting. There are two possible explanations; either the subjects are not following the diet or they have become metabolically adapted to it." To see which was the case, he joined forces with Sally Parsonage of Slimming Advisory Services, in London, and set out to find a group of dieters who were particularly hard cases—apparently faithful to their regimen but still stubbornly fat.

The two selected twenty-nine women attending British slimming clubs. All of them claimed to be unable to lose weight on a reducing diet; all appeared to be following their diets; all had been attending a club for more than six months; and all had lost weight when they first began dieting. This last feature was especially important; it served as evidence the women were not suffering from some metabolic anomaly that absolutely prevented them from losing any weight at all.

Miller and Parsonage then revived a venerable English custom—the country weekend—for their experiment. But it became three weeks in an isolated country house, where the women were secluded while they were maintained on a carefully measured 1,500 calories a day. When they arrived, their baggage was searched for contraband food. They were permitted to leave the grounds only when accompanied by a staff member. Contrary to British literary tradition, nobody was murdered. But a lot of people were confronted with some hard evidence.

Of the twenty-nine women, nineteen lost *some* weight by the end of their stay. Evidently, they had previously been eating more than they realized. Nine other women, in contrast, remained at the same weight, and one actually gained a few pounds. These latter ten were distinguished from the others by the fact that they generally had the lowest metabolic rates. The nonlosers were also thinner as a group, and had been dieting longer than the women who did lose some weight. This finding suggests that they were in a more advanced state of "starvation" than the women who could still lose. Miller and Parsonage concluded that it is possible virtually to reach the limit of one's slimming capability; that metabolic adjustments can make any further weight loss nearly impossible short of total fasting. A major flaw of this study was the investigators' failure to evaluate the women for thyroid deficiency. The conclusion must therefore be regarded as suggestive, not definitive.[32]

Still, the study provides ample evidence that dieting can change metabolic processes to slow the rate of weight loss—and to prepare for a "rebound" when normal eating is resumed. Richard Keesey, one of the major exponents of setpoint theory, and his colleagues showed this effect in rats. Rats were reduced to 81 percent of normal weight and then refed for a week while they were compared to normal rats on roughly the same diet. The deprived animals gained almost *twenty times* more during the week of refeeding than the control rats did—and they actually ate somewhat less than the controls during that period. Starvation had prepared them to store calories far more efficiently than usual. [33]

Susan and Wayne Wooley have proposed that recurrent dieting may be a crucial factor in weight gain. The cycle would start when someone who is naturally plump—or simply *thinks* she is too fat—reacts by going on a diet. Thanks to her good intentions and virtuous behavior, she reaches a lower weight, but in the meantime lowers her metabolic rate as well. Satisfied with her achievement, she resumes what her good sense tells her is a normal diet—perhaps with an occasional indulgence. But her lowered metabolic rate does not permit her to keep slender on a "normal diet." Now she gains very easily and begins a long struggle to live "normally" under impossible conditions. "The data for our theory are not yet so strong," Susan Wooley concedes. "But if it is true, it would mean that we are doing things so much the wrong way. . . . We should be taking a very close look at all the aspects of metabolism after dieting."[34]

Repeated dieting may, then, lead to insidious weight gain after the diet is abandoned. In any case, there is no evidence that simple dieting has anything to offer the vast majority of people other than a transitory loss of weight—most of it as fat, but some as protein. The stubbornness of the setpoint defeats all but the most dogged of dieters, and in some cases slowing of the metabolic rate appears to limit even their success. But this seemingly grim conclusion should not be taken as a counsel of despair. Instead, it should lead us to redirect our attention. If attempts to fool or override the setpoint are unavailing, then we should find ways to change it.

4

RESETTING:
AN ALTERNATIVE
TO DIETING

IF the setpoint were rigidly determined by some combination of genes and early experience, we would all arrive at adulthood locked into a particular weight. It might dip for a while from dieting, or rise briefly after the holidays. But otherwise, it would not vary. In fact, however, many people go through a spontaneous change of weight at one time or another—a gain or loss of several pounds that occurs fairly rapidly, and often in conjunction with significant events.

Some of these events are so familiar they are almost a part of folklore. Going away to college often precipitates a gain or loss of ten to fifteen freshman pounds. Many smokers gain weight when they quit. Women are likely to be fatter after a pregnancy than before. An illness or injury often leads to weight gain.

Severe depression may result in weight loss. Changing jobs, getting married or divorced, and moving to a new house can work either way.

The standard explanations are entrenched in tradition: "I ate as a way of coping with my emotional stress," or, "I just never had time to eat a proper meal." Such rationalizations are obviously incompatible with setpoint theory. But if the theory is to be useful, it must lead to a more accurate explanation of the significant, spontaneous fluctuations of weight that do occur in many people.

Some variation in weight is to be expected, simply because no setpoint mechanism could be completely precise. The very term "setpoint," borrowed from engineering, is something of a misnomer. Weight is not held to an exact point, but rather to a *range*. Many people, for example, repeatedly gain and lose the same ten pounds; this pattern could be plausibly explained as a measure of the setpoint's tolerance. But how can larger, long-term changes in weight be explained?

To a large degree, we must rely on analogies from observations of animals. Experiments with them that would not be permissible with human beings clarify the workings of setpoint, and they often illuminate clinical or everyday experience.

Many animals adapt to changing circumstances by altering their setpoints in a precise, programmed way. Sometimes, normal animals spontaneously refuse food—even when it is easy to come by—and lose weight. For example, after a red jungle fowl lays her eggs she settles down for a twenty-day period of incubation. This primitive chicken is exceedingly protective of her eggs, which she rarely leaves for longer than twenty minutes throughout the entire day. She seems to lose interest in food, so her foraging departures from the nest can be brief. She eats at about one-fifth her normal rate and loses over 15 percent of her starting weight, even when she has an ample supply of food in her nest box.

"For anyone who has experienced the sensation of hunger or

who has seen how food-deprived animals can be trained to make great efforts or to perform diverse responses to obtain food," comments Nicholas Mrosovsky, "refusal to eat, or failure to search for food for long periods, needs an explanation." Mrosovsky, a zoologist at the University of Toronto, has found that the hen's appetite is perfectly adjusted to produce a predictable course of weight loss. If he takes away *all* her food for a week and then gives it back, she will eat ravenously until she is as heavy as she would normally have been on that particular day of incubation; she then settles back into eating relatively little.

The jungle fowl is a vivid but by no means isolated example of an animal that goes through an automatic change of setpoint. Ground squirrels preparing to hibernate fatten in the fall and then settle in for a long winter's torpor, during which they lose the fat at a programmed rate. Thanks to countless children's books, we humans are likely to accept this fact with the satisfied thought: "Of course. The little creature knows winter is coming. So it bustles around, eats a lot, stores food in the nest that it has also been provident enough to build, and settles in to reap the just reward of its virtuous labors."

A moment's adult reflection, however, should lead us to wonder whether there is a more plausible explanation than Aesopian foresight for the behavior of this very small-brained animal. Mrosovsky—by interfering with the squirrel's pattern of activity, disrupting its sleep, and periodically cutting off its food supply—has been able to show that the animal goes through a tightly programmed gain and loss of weight. No matter how the scientist interferes, as soon as the squirrel is left to its own devices, it eats what it needs to return to its typical weight for that time of year.[1]

In both these animals the setpoint is temporarily altered. The jungle fowl responds to hormones, the squirrel gets its cue from the arrival of shorter days. Somewhere in the brain of each, these stimuli act to change the setting so that the animal gradually begins to lose weight. The advantage of this arrangement is obvious: Freed from the need to forage, the jungle fowl can concentrate on her eggs, the squirrel can wait out the rigors of winter.

Except perhaps at pregnancy, adult human beings go through no such biologically programmed changes of setpoint. Neither do laboratory rats and mice. But we and our surrogate rodents shift our setpoints in reaction to environmental changes, experimental manipulations, or treatments.

When "appetite suppressant" drugs are given to rats, the animals eat less for a while, and they lose weight. Either amphetamine, which is notorious as the street drug "speed," or fenfluramine, a chemically related but safer substance, produces this effect. After rats have taken these drugs for a time, however, they recover their appetites, as people do, and weight loss tapers off. For years, this phenomenon has been interpreted as evidence of drug tolerance; the drug appears to stop working after several weeks.

This, however, cannot be the case. A rat that has been given amphetamine for a long period of time may have been eating as much as it would without the drug and maintaining a stable weight for weeks. But as soon as the drug is taken away, the animal promptly *gains* weight (incidentally, without eating detectably more than it was while on the drug). If the drug had merely been blunting hunger to begin with—and had lost its effectiveness because of tolerance—there would be no reason for such a rebound.

In fact, "appetite suppressants" are misnamed. They have no direct effect on appetite. Instead, they reach into the brain, metaphorically speaking, and turn down the setpoint, in much the way someone turns down the volume on a radio. Appetite does whatever it can to help the animal adjust to the new setting. The animals never become tolerant; as long as they receive the drugs, they weigh less than they would without them.

At Cornell University, David Levitsky and his colleagues have shown that both amphetamine and fenfluramine lower a rat's setpoint, not its appetite. In their experiments, animals were given one of the drugs and simultaneously starved below the weight they would normally reach while receiving it; they were then allowed to eat as they wished while continuing to receive the drug. Under these conditions, the rats' appetites were hardly suppressed; the animals ate voraciously to make up their "deficit" in body fat. Once they were back up to the weight typical of a rat receiving the drug, they settled down to eating ordinary quantities of food.[2]

People respond to amphetamine and related drugs in much the same way as rats do. They lose weight until they stabilize and appetite returns to normal. When the drugs are stopped, weight rebounds to its old level (or even goes a little higher). As Albert Stunkard has demonstrated, patients regain most of their lost weight within a year after discontinuing the drugs. There is no evidence, by the way, that people taking the drugs feel any less hungry than people who are not taking them.

Thus, it makes no sense to use amphetaminelike drugs as a temporary aid to weight loss. The only way to make these drugs effective is to give them for life—a practice far too dangerous to contemplate, although the fact that amphetamines are addicting means that many people wind up with a lifelong commitment to them.[3]

A very commonly used drug that also, it would seem, lowers the setpoint is nicotine (or, less likely, some other components of cigarette smoke). Cigarette smokers are, on the whole, leaner than nonsmokers, and yet they have been reported to consume as much as 200 more calories a day. It appears that most people who stop smoking gain weight, and the amount is somewhere around twelve pounds, although it varies, no doubt as a function of the individual's reaction and of the amount smoked. Cigarettes have been promoted to women as an appetite suppressant since 1928, when the American Tobacco Company introduced the slogan, "Reach for a Lucky instead of a sweet," and the implication remains in Philip Morris's brand name, "Virginia Slims." Like amphetamines, however, cigarette smoke does not suppress appetite at all. If anything, it increases the amount of food eaten but lowers weight by turning down the setpoint (and thus, probably, increasing the metabolic rate). Like amphetamines, cigarettes are exceedingly dangerous; in exchange for a dozen pounds, more or less, the smoker pays with long-term addiction and a greatly increased risk of dying young.[4]

Amphetamines and cigarettes have been the two means people have used most commonly, if unwittingly, to lower their setpoints. Neither approach leads to very substantial weight loss in most people, and certainly not in those who are extremely, or "morbidly" obese. Lowering the setpoint by fifteen or even twenty pounds has little value to someone whose goal is to lose a hundred, and cigarette smoking should not be contemplated as a form of self-treatment.

Many medical efforts to treat the severely obese have offered very little advantage over dangerous drugs. The least hazardous, but by no means pleasant, approach has been severe dieting (often in the form of the "protein-sparing modified fast" or PSMF, which is discussed in chapter 8). Another, fortunately somewhat rare, method has been jaw wiring: The patient's jaws are fitted with a kind of surgical muzzle that prevents him from ingesting any but the smallest quantities of food and drink. Jaw wiring should theoretically allow the patient to go about his business without the fear of giving in to the binge impulse—though some have evidently found ways to circumvent the contraption.[5]

The most effective method of lowering weight in morbidly obese patients is, when it works well, a form of intestinal surgery known as a "bypass." The operation was conceived as a way of limiting the patient's ability to extract calories from food; the upper segment of the small intestine is attached to the very last portion, and the remainder is simply closed off. With only a very short segment of working intestine left, the patient would be uncomfortable eating a big meal, but if he did, the bulk of it would pass through before it could be absorbed.

In this light the rationale for the procedure is extremely hard to understand. How could a surgeon possibly know precisely the right amount of intestine to leave in place to prevent the patient from eventually starving to death? Although deaths have occurred—too many to justify continued use of the operation in the view of most authorities—they have been the result of various complications, not starvation. When successful, bypass surgery allows patients to stabilize quite comfortably at a relatively "normal" weight. These individuals do not in fact eat enormous quantities of food that then passes right through their abbreviated intestines. Nor do they feel constant hunger, while restraining themselves in order to avoid the discomfort of diarrhea and cramps. Instead they eat appropriately to maintain their lowered body weight.[6]

The most plausible explanation of this effect is that the intestinal-bypass operation effectively lowers the setpoint of at least some people who undergo it. Why the surgery should produce such an effect, however, is not apparent. At present we can only surmise that a normal intestine is involved in the system of signals on which the brain relies to establish its setpoint. This hypothesis is certainly plausible; the intestine produces many hormones that have the potential to affect the brain.[7]

It is theoretically possible to lower the setpoint by operating directly on the brain itself, but this extreme measure has not been sanctioned by the medical profession—despite its apparent willingness to tolerate many other dubious or hazardous measures to produce weight loss. In laboratory rats, however, the surgery is frequently performed. Microscopic brain damage (placed very specifically in a pair of cell clusters located centrally near the brain's lower surface) causes a rat to lose about 20 percent of its body weight. Of course, it eats very little after surgery, and for many years the operation was believed to damage the animal's "hunger center." This notion was proved false by an elegant experiment. A rat was first starved, until it lost *more* than 20 percent of its weight, and was then subjected to the brain surgery. When it awakened from anesthesia, it started eating—unlike a well-fed animal, which would have fasted. Once the starved rat reached its new (low) setpoint, it settled down to a normal intake.[8]

This operation, damaging cells in the lateral hypothalamus (LH) of the brain, does not destroy the setpoint mechanism, it only lowers the setting. Another procedure attacks a nearby region, known as the ventromedial hypothalamus (VMH), and yields a very different result. Its effect is most easily understood through our analogy of the volume control on a radio. Whereas destroying the LH permanently turns down the volume, destroying the VMH has the effect of loosening the knob; it becomes far easier to reset. Instead of being locked firmly in place, the setpoint becomes highly responsive to certain influences, many of them having to do with the nature of the food offered to the animal.

When the VMH animals, as they are known, were first studied, they all "overate" and they all got fat. This observation led to the erroneous conclusion that the damaged region of the brain served, when intact, as a "satiety center" to turn off eating when the rat had "enough." The brain-surgery experiment that we described at the beginning of chapter 3 clearly refutes that misconception by showing that the rat would gain even with normal food intake. Nevertheless, the idea of a "satiety center" has lingered to confuse a great deal of subsequent work.

If a VMH animal is given food that appeals to it, it does indeed eat more than a normal rat would, and it accumulates fat. But sooner or later, it finds a stable weight, and then, as long as the composition of its diet is not changed, it sticks tenaciously to that weight and responds to the usual tests of setpoint by doing what it can to return to that same level. Likewise, if its food is made mildly repellent, the animal loses fat until it stabilizes once again at a lower weight. Because of the way they respond to the quality of their diet, these animals have been called "finicky." The term is misleading. They do not absolutely refuse food that is made somewhat distasteful—say by the addition of quinine. Rather, they reset their setpoint and then eat as much as they need to keep the fat store constant at the new level.[9]

From the behavior of VMH rats, we can draw two inferences about the setpoint of normal animals. First, it is somewhat adjustable; influenced by the quality and nature of the food available, the setpoint can rise or fall. This effect has *nothing* to do with the *amount* of food available—only with such characteristics as flavor, texture, greasiness, sweetness, and smell. Second, the normal rat has a mechanism (the intact VMH) for preventing a runaway response to these sensory stimuli. Destroying the VMH exposes the animal to the full force of its sense impressions, and thus its weight becomes exceedingly responsive to influences that are usually held in check.

The alert reader may think, "Aha! This sounds suspiciously like externality.* The rat is enticed to eat by sensory inducements, so it gets fat. Are rats subject to externality, whereas people are not?"

We argue nothing of the kind. As a series of elegant and critical experiments have demonstrated, tasty food does *not* stimulate the normal rat's appetite (at least not in the long term). Instead, it raises setpoint, and that is a very big difference.

The experiments were conducted by Jeffrey Peck, at the University of Utah. He began with a collection of ordinary, virtually identical laboratory rats, which he divided into groups. The first group was fed a diet of rat chow mixed with vegetable shortening (a rat's version of New York cheesecake); these rats

*Regulating food intake according to external cues; see chapter 2.

grew fatter than normal. The next group received the usual fare for rats, a rat-sized, granolalike bar smelling faintly of straw; these animals held to their customary weight. The third group was fed rat chow adulterated with a small amount of quinine to make it bitter; and these rats became somewhat lighter in weight than the second group. In some experiments, Peck used a fourth and fifth group to receive yet greater concentrations of quinine, and they became thinner still. After a brief period on their various diets, the rats all stabilized at their respective new weights.

Now Peck tried forcing the animals to change their weight to observe whether they would resist. For example, he kept them all in a refrigerated cage for several days. In the cold, the rats all had to eat more than usual to compensate for the heat they were losing. In fact, because the fat, the normal, and the thin rats all lost heat to the environment at the same rate, they all had to increase what they ate by the same amount to avoid losing weight, and all of them did. While in the cold, they adjusted their food intake precisely to maintain their weights.

Peck then tried another approach. Having forced the animals to eat more, he gave them an opportunity to eat less. He fed them a rich solution of eggnog through a stomach tube. He was careful not to let them taste the eggnog (for that would have changed their sensory environment). Eventually, he gave the animals enough to replace one-half to three-quarters of their usual caloric intake. All the animals ate less on this regimen— precisely enough less to maintain a constant weight.

The psychologist also tried more complex routines and found that the animals responded by eating less or more, as appropriate, to maintain their same weight. In effect, Peck was asking his animals: "Which do you care about most, how fat you are, or how much you eat?" And the animals returned a clear answer: "How fat we are."

It seems a matter of common sense that a rich or good-tasting diet would make an animal fatter than normal. But the way this influence works is by no means what common sense would predict. The animal is not, in effect, thinking, "This food is yummy. I want more," then eating more solely to satisfy taste —and incidentally getting fatter. It may indeed think "yummy" with what passes for consciousness in a rat, but the reason it gets fatter is a change occurring elsewhere in its brain.[10]

The animal collects a wealth of information about its food before swallowing (and also, certainly, afterward, but this phase is less well studied). All these sensory data are then sent to the as yet unidentified portion of the brain that determines how fat the animal is to be, namely, the setpoint mechanism. This control system then signals the animal, by making it hungry, to eat enough to gain the necessary weight.

This is a crucial point: Peck's animals clearly behaved as though they were *hungry* when they were deprived. Even the fattest animal, when faced with the hard work of pushing a lever to get food and maintain its fat, would do whatever was required; when temporarily deprived of food, it immediately began the restless foraging activity characteristic of a deprived rat. (In laboratory cages, this amounts to running on an exercise wheel while the experimenter counts the number of turns.)

The chain of causation, then, was not the obvious one—good food immediately and repeatedly stimulating appetite; overeating for aesthetic reasons then leading to fat accumulation. Rather, it went something like this: Good food raised the setpoint, whereupon the animal went from feeling pretty good to believing that it was downright ravenous. It ate enough extra food to supply the fat that it now perceived was missing, and then it returned to eating normally.

Such an arrangement makes eminent biological good sense. Imagine a wild rat rummaging along a river bank. Usually it can make do with the reliable supply of vegetable matter, insects, and what-have-you that it finds there. But then it comes on the remains of a picnic interrupted by rain. If it were to eat only until it was full by its usual standards, the animal would lose a fine opportunity to get a little ahead of the survival game. But if good-tasting food makes it feel *hungry*, the animal will eat more and return soon for the rest.

Peck's finding implies that a river rat that suddenly found itself living near a picnic ground might grow stout indeed—perhaps to its own disadvantage. No biologist appears to have tested the hypothesis in this manner, but a laboratory simulation of the situation has been tried. The laboratory was in Brooklyn, where psychologists Anthony Sclafani and Deleri Springer were trying to induce their rats to become obese. They wanted to avoid brain surgery or repeated insulin injections, which do the job but also derange the animal in other ways, and they were not satisfied with the results of adding Crisco to standard feed, as Peck had done. Then, one inspired afternoon, they went to a nearby supermarket where they purchased a basketful of high-calorie goodies: peanut butter, marshmallows, chocolate chip cookies, bananas, and salami, among other things. Thus was born what is now known in the technical literature as the "supermarket diet" for laboratory rats. The Brooklyn animals responded with the highest spontaneous weight gain hitherto reported for normal laboratory rats, according to the investigators.[11]

The wrong conclusion to draw from Sclafani and Springer's experiment would be that rich food is what is required to make an animal fat. "Rich" is a relative term, as biologists at Duke University discovered when they began to study an unusual kind of rat. The North African sand rat is relatively abundant along the Mediterranean coast of Egypt, where it forages on the plants that not only tolerate but thrive in salt water. The animal eats mainly the fleshy joints of these plants, which contain a sap more concentrated than seawater. Despite the obstacles, a sand rat makes a tolerably good living on a diet that amounts to stacks of heavily salted celery. The Duke scientists, who were interested in the sand rat's physiological ability to handle so much sodium chloride, imported a few to their laboratory, where they fed the animals on standard rat chow. The rats responded by becoming hugely obese—more than twice their usual weight—and they developed diabetes. To keep them alive in the laboratory, the scientists had to feed the animals on fresh vegetables exclusively.[12]

The sand rats are, in their way, laboratory representatives of such people as the Pima Indians, who have moved from a rather austere lifestyle to one that urbanized Americans would consider modest and unremarkable. The laboratory rats exposed to a supermarket diet resemble the majority of Americans, who have had ample diets for generations but now live in an even more lavish culinary environment. Of course, people seem to vary enormously in their responses to food, but so do rats. No elaborate psychological explanations are needed here. The dietary history of one's ancestors is probably the strongest influence.

If the human setpoint responds to food stimuli in a manner somewhat like the rat's, then we can guess that certain features of the food we eat have the potential to make us fatter. High fat content is a major trigger in the rat. Sugar is another, especially when it is presented in solution. The sheer variety of the food presented also encourages a rat to gain weight.

Artificial sweeteners have been accepted into the American diet as a way of keeping the taste without the calories. The experiments we have just described suggest that artificial sweeteners could make people still fatter, by driving up the setpoint. The more convincingly sweet and less artificial they taste (as is claimed for the new sweetener, aspartame), the more effectively they should stimulate users to fatten. Enormous quantities of artificial sweeteners—the safety of which is at least doubtful—are consumed in this country; yet they have never been shown to accomplish what they are supposed to. Studies with rats suggest that the sweeteners have the potential to drive setpoint to a higher setting, and may, therefore, interfere with weight loss.[13]

Although the availability of sweet foods may push some people into becoming fatter, there is no clear evidence that fat people as a group have a "sweet tooth": Indeed, many fat people express distaste for sweet things. Yet we might guess that sweet foods are especially attractive to people below their setpoints, and there is some evidence for this inference.[14]

Besides composition of the diet, there is one other "natural" influence that seems capable of resetting the setpoint: physical activity. It is puzzling that exercise has been so little emphasized as a means of weight control while reducing diets have been a national obsession. For more than forty years there has been suggestive evidence that changes in activity levels strongly influence weight regulation, and studies conducted in the 1950s were exceedingly persuasive.

There may have been three important reasons for the failure of the research community and the general public to recognize the importance of exercise. First, diets appear to be effortless; indeed, the dieter's only activity is to choose one food rather than another, and simply not eating requires no physical effort whatever. Exercise, on the other hand, demands both time and the expenditure of energy, and it may conflict with work and recreation schedules. Second, physical activity is unpleasantly difficult for scientists to quantify. Whereas food calories can be counted, if somewhat inaccurately, and metabolic rate can be measured, monitoring physical activity is far more difficult, and the numbers obtained are quite soft. Third, without a setpoint theory, the effect of physical activity on weight has been difficult to interpret.

In 1939, James A. Greene, an Iowa physician, interrogated more than 150 obese adults about the onset of their condition. He found that fully 68 percent recalled that they had begun to get fat during a period of immobility—usually an injury, illness, or long convalescence. Only 3 percent said they gained initially because they had suddenly begun eating more than usual.[15]

Then, in the late 1950s and early 1960s, Jean Mayer and his colleagues, at Harvard's School of Public Health, began systematically studying the connection between exercise and fatness. In 1954 they had reported a comparison between inactive and active rats. The typical laboratory rat leads an utterly sedentary existence and is plump in comparison with wild rats. When made to run in a treadmill for a few minutes a day, the scientists found, the laboratory rat loses weight and eats just slightly less than usual. At an hour a day of this relatively gentle exercise, it would reach a minimum weight and, as it happens, a minimum food intake. If the animal were forced to run longer —between one and six hours a day—it would begin eating enough to compensate for the additional activity, and would hold to its new, low weight. When forced to run more than six hours, the animal was "run ragged"; it lost its appetite and began losing more weight. (Ultrathin marathon runners may be the human equivalent of these rats.)

Subsequent animal studies have confirmed the general effect that Mayer and his colleagues described: Physical conditioning appears to help regulate the setpoint. With no physical activity, animals spontaneously grow fatter than normal. As they begin to exercise, weight falls, and then, over a fairly wide range of activity levels, it holds constant. Mayer did not use the term setpoint, which was not current when he reported his rat studies, but he clearly demonstrated the phenomenon. He performed several other animal experiments before turning to human studies. One of the more curious, which he reported only in passing, consisted of crossing two genetically abnormal mice. As we have mentioned, several mutations maintained in strains of laboratory mice produce extreme obesity. There are also laboratory mice with a variety of behavioral abnormalities caused by mutant genes. One of these is "waltzer," which forces the affected animal into a lifelong frenzy of pointless motion. Mayer arranged to produce mice that were affected by both the obesity and the waltzing genes. Although they were hefty as mice go, these double mutants, with their ceaseless activity, failed to reach even half the weight of the ordinary obese animals.[16]

One of Mayer's first indications that people might react to exercise as rats and mice do was the finding that high school girls were likely to be fatter in winter than in summer. He and his colleagues surmised that the girls were more active in summer, thus regulating their weight at a lower level. In winter, they were fattened by inactivity. To follow up on this hunch, Mayer next went to a community located on the banks of the Ganges, about twenty miles south of Calcutta.[17]

Collaborating with Purnima Roy and Kamakhya Mitra, he studied more than 200 workers of the Ludlow Jute Co., Ltd., as well as a small group of nearby shopkeepers. These men were assigned to one of thirteen categories by the investigators, who estimated their daily output of energy according to occupation and commuting distance. Each man was weighed and questioned in detail about his food intake. Finally, the estimated levels of activity and caloric intakes were compared with weight.

The relationship exactly corresponded to the rats' pattern. Shopkeepers from the nearby bazaar sat in their stalls all day, ate a lot (around 3,300 calories), and were the fattest men in the study. Clerks commuting to work on foot, and mechanics, who worked largely without power tools, ate about 600 fewer calories a day and were about twenty pounds lighter than their relatively immobile supervisors. The most active workers, the jute cutters, weighed about the same as the clerks and mechanics, but they consumed 1,000 more calories a day.

In sum, above a certain minimum level of activity, the workers ate exactly what they needed to maintain a rather constant, lean weight. The least active men—stallholders, supervisors, and noncommuting clerks—were the heaviest, and their appetites seemed to be released from the normal control. This, at least, was the interpretation Mayer and his colleagues gave their findings. We would speculate that appetite was not "released" but rather that it was serving a higher setpoint. The authors concluded with this observation: "In his hundreds of thousands of years of evolution, man did not have any opportunity for sedentary life except very recently. An inactive life for man is as recent (and as 'abnormal') a development as caging is for an animal. In this light, it is not surprising that some of the usual adjustment mechanisms would prove inadequate."[18]

The West Bengal study is still exceedingly persuasive, although it has been criticized for not taking adequate account of class differences between the various activity groups. Because there has been no attempt to replicate this important piece of research, some questions remain unanswered. One puzzling feature of the Indian study is that the most sedentary, fat men ate significantly more than thin, active ones. In the United States, as we have pointed out, fat people cannot be consistently shown to eat more than thinner ones. Perhaps contemporary Americans are restrained eaters and the Bengalis in the mid-fifties were not. For all we know, the shopkeepers might have been even fatter had they not been spared by *Luxuskonsumption* (see chapter 3).

Some recent observations supporting Mayer's hypothesis have come from studies of serious runners, who consume a lot of calories and remain thin. At Stanford, biochemist Peter Wood has been exploring the physiological effects of sustained, vigorous exercise. Wood began running more than forty years ago. At the age of six, while still living in his native England, he entered a children's race held during the Silver Jubilee of King George V and Queen Mary. Today, thin and gangly, he moves "like an antelope," as a colleague remarked while she watched him lope down the hall to his Palo Alto office. "I mean that as a compliment," she added.

Intrigued by the leanness of long-distance runners, Wood found some sixty of them and compared their intake of food with the diet of randomly selected residents of Tracy, a town in northern California. The runners typically ate 600 more calories every day than their sedentary contemporaries, but the controls weighed 25 percent more than the runners. Like Mayer's jute cutters, Wood's runners illustrate the point that, when a low setpoint is maintained by activity, a person can remain thin on a relatively high caloric intake. (Moreover, by eating and burning more calories, the runners may have a nutritional advantage: a higher intake of vitamins and minerals. As Wood puts it: "I am often asked, 'Should runners eat more vitamins?' And I usually reply, 'They already do.' ")[19]

In a more recent longitudinal study, Wood and his colleagues have found what may be the first strong experimental support for Mayer's Bengal findings. In a general study of the effects of activity, they started forty-eight middle-aged men on an exercise program at Stanford, and compared them, through the course of a year, with a control group who remained sedentary. As might be expected, some of the men took to the idea of jogging more readily than others. By the year's end, some of the "exercise" group were hardly moving at all, while others were logging twenty-five miles a week. Men who ran only a few miles a week—like Mayer's moderately active clerks and mechanics—ate less than the controls. But the men who ran in longer periods increased their caloric intake in direct proportion to their increased activity level.

Wood admits that the study, which required the men to report on their own dietary and exercise habits, leaves room for error. But the data, such as they are, match precisely Mayer's predictions. "Taken at face value," says Wood, "it looks like small amounts of exercise decrease intake, while larger amounts increase it." These middle-aged runners offer further evidence that activity may be more important than the food one eats in regulating fatness. As Wood observes, "Those exercisers who increased their caloric intake the most (and ran the most) were those who lost the most body fat. Or, putting it another way, those who gained the most weight were those who ate the least."[20]

The setpoint theory is, admittedly, somewhat fatalistic. Drugs and surgery, the two treatments that would seem most certainly to lower the setpoint, pose hazards that far outweigh the potential benefits of weight loss. Exercise may provide an alternative way to change the setting. But there is still little hard evidence that activity lowers the setpoint, and, in any case, its effect seems to be limited. Beyond a certain threshold, additional activity may not lead to a significant decrease in body fat. In short, there is relatively little one can do to lower one's setpoint safely.

The notion that fatness is foreordained may seem altogether grim. Health education has emphasized the perils of "overweight" for decades, and fat has come to be clearly linked with fatality in the public mind. The risks, however, appear to have been greatly overstated.

5

FAT MAY NOT BE
HAZARDOUS TO
YOUR HEALTH

INSTEAD of taking comfort from the no-fault implications
of setpoint theory, many readers will find the concept altogether alarming. Those who are fat, plump, or even average may
hasten to the conclusion that Mother Nature has given them a
bad deal. They could hardly be blamed for this alarmist reaction. The notion that body fat is a toxic substance is now firmly
a part of folk wisdom: Many people perversely consider eating
to be a suicidal act. The ritual recommendation to "lose a few
pounds" follows many an otherwise healthy person out of the
doctor's examining room. Nearly every book or article on the
subject of obesity begins with the pious, but unfounded, assertion that "overweight" has become a major threat to public
health.

The very expression *overweight,* which is now used as a well-intentioned euphemism for *fat,* carries an expectation of early death, for it means "over the weight associated with maximum life expectancy." Since the beginning of this century, the life insurance industry has reported that an "ideal" or "desirable" weight exists for men and women of any particular height, and anyone who weighs appreciably more than the ideal is likely to die at a relatively early age.

The industry reached its conclusion through a series of investigations culminating with the massive *Build and Blood Pressure Study,* published by the Society of Actuaries in 1959. For this undertaking the major companies pooled data from 4½ million policies issued between 1935 and 1954. The age, height, weight in street clothes and shoes, and blood pressure of healthy applicants were tabulated, and then the death rates in various categories were compared with those of the whole group. Although the design of the *Build and Blood Pressure Study* left much to be desired (in spite of the huge number of policies involved), its conclusions became, for a time, medical gospel. One of the most important assertions of the report was that the lightest people live longest, and that any increase in body weight is associated with an increase in mortality rate.[1]

The moral of this actuarial fable was condensed into a simple table of "Desirable Weights for Men and Women," published by the Metropolitan Life Insurance Company. The table can often be found on drugstore scales (which also sometimes tell fortunes), and it is reprinted in medical texts and self-help manuals. According to the version still in common use, at least half of all Americans are too fat for their own good. To prevent early death, the *average* young man (at five feet seven inches) should lose about twenty pounds, and the *average* young woman (at five feet three inches) about eighteen pounds.[2]

There is no reason to believe that this is the case. The only direct support for the idea that modest amounts of body fat shorten life comes from these insurance data, which, as we shall see, are so deeply flawed that they should not be regarded as evidence. But even if the industry's findings were accepted at face value, they would not suggest that any great saving of life could be accomplished by a national program of weight loss. In 1979 Frederick H. Epstein, a professor of preventive medicine at the University of Zurich, asked what would happen if all of America's *very* fat people reduced to levels that were only moderately fat, and meanwhile the rest of the population slenderized to within 5 percent of so-called desirable weight. (Needless to say, a nation-wide slimming of this degree would be nothing short of miraculous; it is certainly far beyond anything that currently appears feasible.) From data in the *Build and Blood Pressure Study*, Epstein calculated that there would be only a modest 7 percent reduction in the mortality rate for men between forty and sixty-nine years of age. Other groups would benefit less, so that, for the whole population, the effect would be small indeed.[3]

As everyone knows, however, Americans are not losing weight; they are gaining. In the last fifteen years or so, males of average height have gained four or five pounds and women slightly less. If fat is as deadly as we have been led to believe, somebody out there should have been digging an ever-increasing number of extra-wide graves. But, since 1965, Americans' life expectancy has *increased* by a couple of years. Crude as this measure may be, it does indicate that fatness has not replaced the black plague as an epidemic killer.[4]

However, to answer the critical question, "Does being fat make people die young?," more detailed information is needed, and, for several reasons, assembling the required evidence is exceedingly difficult. First, inasmuch as there is no economically practical way to look at every American, a sample of the whole population must be studied. But if that sample is not typical of the whole, it may tell us little that is worth knowing. As we shall see, this was one serious defect of the insurance data. Second, the sample must be selected at the start of the study and then followed long enough to see what happens. There is no reliable way to reason backward from a sample of people who are already, conveniently, dead. Third, the fat and thin people in a sample must be utterly comparable, except for their weight. If the fatter people are older, sicker, or otherwise at a higher risk of dying at the start, the results will be distorted (almost certainly the case in the insurance studies). Fourth, a disease process could first make its victim fatter and then kill him. Unless statistical care is taken to sort out the correct relationship, "overweight" might be interpreted as the cause of a death when it was actually only an augury of it. This is a particularly treacherous problem for analysis and a rich source of controversy.

Before about 1970, there was nothing to gainsay the insurance industry's conclusions; the only sources of information on weight and mortality were records on policyholders. Since then, evidence accumulating from careful studies carried out all over the world has demolished the credibility of "ideal" weight tables, but this fact is only slowly being acknowledged. In part, no doubt, intellectual inertia is a reason, but a praiseworthy conservatism has also played a role: It seems safer to warn people against nonexistent hazards than to risk overlooking real ones. Perhaps aesthetic bullying has also contributed; it is far easier to say, "Fat is bad for you," than to say, "I don't like the way you look."

The evidence that moderate fatness is not particularly harmful comes from investigations begun in the 1950s, although it has only been published in the last ten years or so. These studies have a common format. The sample studied is a randomly selected group of subjects taken from the whole population living in one community, or from all the personnel working for a single, large employer. Samples of this type are thought to be the least likely to differ from the population at large (whereas people buying life insurance are known to be atypical). At the beginning of the study, the subjects are carefully examined, and then at intervals over a period of five to twenty years they are reexamined. Along the way, their illnesses and deaths are monitored. At the study's conclusion, statistical methods (which have become more powerful in recent decades) are used to distinguish between fatness as a cause of death and fatness that is only associated with early death, perhaps because it is a by-product of the fatal process.

One of the most thorough and distinguished investigations of this type was the Framingham study. In 1950, about half of all the people between the ages of thirty and fifty-nine years then living in Framingham, Massachusetts, agreed to participate in a series of questionnaires and examinations that would continue for twenty-four years, or until death. Every two years, those subjects surviving from the original 5,209 men and women were questioned, examined, and diagnosed. All deaths were recorded and their causes established. Although this sample was much smaller than the millions of policyholders counted by the insurance companies, it was far more representative of the American people, and the methods used to investigate it were the best available at the time.

The Framingham study was designed primarily to explore the causes of heart disease and stroke. When it was begun, cardiovascular disease, after a stunning forty-year increase, had reached virtually epidemic proportions in the United States. The founders of the study hoped to learn ways of identifying people who were at high risk of cardiovascular death. From their data, they hoped also to extract clues to effective prevention. Well aware of the insurance industry's conclusions about weight, the investigators evidently were inclined to believe that fatness was risky, but they were prepared to test the hypothesis.

After the study had progressed for fifteen years, it appeared that the heavier subjects did not have a high risk of developing cardiovascular disease. Another nine years of data collection led the Framingham investigators to revise this conclusion, but

111

only partially. The heaviest subjects now did seem to develop more cardiovascular disease than the lighter subjects. However, the results could be interpreted as showing only that fat people are especially likely to have symptoms of heart disease—such as angina pectoris—that are present but "silent" in thin people. In any case, the investigators did not explore the possibility that excessive weight was a by-product of other factors that were the real cause of disease, and the analysis still had not answered the basic question: Are fat people more likely than the average to die young?[5]

In 1979, three of the Framingham investigators decided to see whether they could confirm the (by now venerable) *Build and Blood Pressure Study*. To do so, they had to rearrange their own data to correspond with the actuaries' presentation. When they had finished, they discovered a flat contradiction between the Framingham experience and that of the policyholders. Life expectancy was the *worst* for the thinnest men of Framingham, whereas it had been the best for the equivalent group in the *Build and Blood Pressure Study*. Above this lowest level, weight simply had little effect on the men's mortality rate. Similarly, the very lightest and the very heaviest women of Framingham had a mortality rate higher than average, but between the extremes, weight had a negligible correlation with mortality.[6]

Other projects, somewhat less ambitious than the Framingham study but carefully designed and analyzed, have come to the same conclusion: "Desirable" weight is a statistical fiction. In Alameda County, California, 6,928 men and women of various ages were observed for five and a half years. In Chicago, 1,233 employees of the Chicago Peoples Gas Company, men aged forty to fifty-nine at the beginning, were followed for fourteen years. In Stavely, a village in Derbyshire, England, 387 men between fifty-five and sixty-four were studied for a decade. More than 1,100 men, twenty-five to ninety years old, living near Baltimore, have been intensively studied every other year since 1958. In each of these groups, premature death has come to the very thinnest and the very fattest groups, but in between, over a very wide range, weight has made little difference to life expectancy. Unlike the insurance results, findings from carefully designed, prospective research have not revealed any clear-cut "ideal" or "desirable" weight at which mortality falls to a minimum. To the extent that some data do hint at a "best" weight, it is *at or above* the average for men and women in general.[7]

In some ways, this result is surprising, although the consistency with which it appears in well-executed studies suggests it is real. Even though there is every reason to mistrust the insurance companies' overall findings about build and mortality, a great deal of medical evidence indicates that obesity is a feature of some common and potentially fatal diseases, notably diabetes and high blood pressure. This effect should show up as a trend toward higher mortality among heavier people. The fact that it does not may mean there are disadvantages to underweight that offset the recognized drawbacks of fatness. At present, no clear explanation has offered itself.

Another possibility, of course, is that the health consequences of "overweight" have been overstated, and this is also certainly true. The accumulated ills charged to overweight include heart attacks, strokes, certain forms of cancer, kidney and liver diseases, arthritis and degeneration of joints, diabetes, high blood pressure, gallstones, pneumonia, complications of pregnancy and childbirth, hernias, skin disease, postural abnormalities, flat feet, and a peculiar disorder of the heel pad, which is injured by excessive thumping. This indictment is sometimes recited indiscriminately—especially by weight-loss entrepreneurs—as a scare tactic. But the list is padded, even more so than the people to whom it is addressed. In some cases, such as kidney disease and postural abnormalities, virtually no association with overweight can be shown; inadequate research conducted long ago produced findings that were simply false.

Many of the other afflictions can indeed affect people who are severely obese—those whose bodies are composed of one-half to two-thirds adipose tissue. But these are a minority of the population, with distinctive health problems. From a medical standpoint their obesity is not merely an extreme version of the common spare tire.

And some of the so-called complications of obesity in this list may actually be causes. Arthritis is a case in point. It has somehow seemed obvious that joints should be damaged if they have to bear a lot of weight. So, once a fairly weak statistical association between overweight and arthritis was demonstrated, joint disease was promptly included among the disorders caused by overweight. When the Public Health Service undertook a large survey to clarify the relationship, its investigators indeed found that fat women were more likely to have arthritis than thin women. But the women had the disease in their *hands* as much as their feet. Unless fat women are inclined to walk on their hands a good deal—which seems unlikely—their extra weight hardly explains the findings. The likely reason—ignored by the authors of the report—is that the women developed arthritis first, then found it difficult to remain active and gained weight as they became more sedentary. Support for this interpretation comes from other studies, which have found no evidence that fat people have more arthritis than usual in their hips—the major weight-bearing joints of the body—but they do seem to experience more pain when the disease is present. It is probable, then, that some people with arthritis begin to suffer a vicious cycle: Joint pain limits their activity, so they gain weight and consequently experience more pain.[8]

In the heterogeneous list of diseases possibly related to fatness, however, one group cannot be dismissed. Repeatedly, stubbornly, "overweight" has been incriminated as a cause of heart disease either directly or as mediated by diabetes and high blood pressure.

The old speculation that excess poundage makes the heart work too hard makes no sense at all; other forms of exercise are thought to strengthen the heart and improve circulation. It is possible that the mere presence of adipose tissue on the body alters metabolism of fats in the blood and encourages deposition of fat in the blood vessels, but such a phenomenon has not been demonstrated. More plausibly, fatness might contribute to heart disease only when it is associated with high blood pressure or diabetes, both of which conditions are known to damage circulation, and both of which are exacerbated by large amounts of body fat. But before we delve too far into the possible connections between overweight and heart disease, we should look at the evidence to see whether they are as closely linked as they are conventionally assumed to be.

Again, we can use major statistical trends to reassure ourselves that fatness cannot be a very important cause of cardiovascular death. From World War I to mid-century, the rate of death from heart attacks and strokes increased dramatically in the United States, but since the early 1950s, the age-adjusted rate has declined almost as fast as it rose. The decline accelerated after the mid-1960s, but in this same period, as we have already pointed out, Americans of both sexes and all ages became, on average, fatter. If the weight gain was favoring heart disease, the influence was clearly a weak one and was offset by some other change that was much more important. (We might speculate that both trends, at least partly, reflected the national change in smoking habits. From 1954 to the present, the proportion of Americans smoking cigarettes has declined. At least some of both the weight gain and the improvement in cardiovascular health can be attributed to the reduced proportion of smokers.)[9]

Detailed epidemiological studies, too, show no impressive connection between obesity and cardiovascular disease. One of the most ambitious investigations was organized by Ancel Keys, who conducted the Minnesota starvation experiment. With his flair for large-scale research, Keys spearheaded a ten-year study of 12,763 men living in Japan, Yugoslavia, Finland,

Italy, the Netherlands, Greece, and the United States. When the data from the Seven-Country Study, as it is known, were analyzed, Keys could report: "In none of the areas of this study was overweight or obesity a major risk factor for death or the incidence of coronary heart disease." In reviewing his own work and that of other recent investigators, Keys wrote:

The idea has been greatly oversold that the risk of dying prematurely or of having a heart attack is directly related to the relative body weight [an index of fatness]. For middle-aged men, the best prospect for avoiding death in ten or fifteen years is to be about average, or a bit over, in relative weight. The risk rises somewhat with departure in either direction from the happy middle ground, but risk increases substantially only at the extremes of under- and overweight.[10]

On the other hand, it may well be that fatness shortens life or makes it more uncomfortable once heart disease is present. Among 18,403 British civil servants who were first examined between 1967 and 1969, the overweight men did not seem to acquire heart disease earlier than the others; once they had it, however, they were more likely to suffer complications and death than were the lighter men. Also, in this group physical exercise seemed to protect against heart disease, but after evidence of cardiac trouble appeared, physical activity became somewhat risky. These were preliminary findings, but they are compatible with other results, and they suggest that extra fat may indeed put a burden on the heart that is already diseased, much as does inappropriately heavy exercise.[11]

Keys and the investigators he quotes distinguish between fatness in itself, which hardly appears to be a risk factor for cardiovascular disease, and associated disorders, such as high blood pressure and adult-onset diabetes, which are known to be important risk factors. Both high blood pressure and diabetes, if inadequately treated, increase the likelihood that cardiovascular disease will develop. Both conditions appear to be associated with obesity, and both are easier to treat if the fat patient loses weight. But the connection between fatness and the two intervening diseases is not clear. Thin adults can develop both diabetes and hypertension, and many fat people develop neither.

There are only two plain facts about overweight and high blood pressure (or hypertension). The blood pressure of fat people is likely to be higher than normal, and losing weight lowers it. Once that has been said, the picture becomes complicated. The statistical association between overweight and high blood pressure is very strong. If you have a roomful of fat people and a roomful of thin ones, your chances of finding someone with high blood pressure are about a hundred times higher in the fat group. Even so, most of the fat people will have perfectly normal blood pressure, so it cannot be said that fatness in itself *causes* hypertension. Now, shuffle the crowds in your two rooms. Put all the hypertensives into one room and all the people with normal blood pressure into another. With this arrangement, your chance is a thousand times higher of finding a fat person in the room with the hypertensives, but the overall difference in weight between the two rooms will be very small. The average hypertensive man in his late thirties has 23 percent body fat, the man with normal blood pressure has 21 percent—a very small difference.[12]

Despite the confusing statistical relationships, it is clear that individuals who are both hypertensive and fat can lower their blood pressure by losing weight. This fact alone argues that there must be some connection between fatness and blood pressure, but nobody claims to know for sure what it is. Fortunately for fat people who have difficulty reducing, physical conditioning also lowers blood pressure, whether or not weight is lost. The long-range benefit of weight loss to hypertensives has not been established, although most authorities assume there is one.[13]

More is known about how the common form of diabetes (which begins in adult life and does not require insulin for treatment) is related to fatness. For practical purposes, any form of diabetes can be defined as a relative lack of the hormone insulin. Whenever digestion takes place, insulin is produced by an organ located behind the stomach, the pancreas, that secretes the hormone into the bloodstream. The hormone passes throughout the body to all its cells. At the surface of many of these cells it encounters special "receptors," which it activates, much like a grocery boy pushing a doorbell. It thereby signals the cells that food is on its way and should be taken inside for use or storage. When this process fails to occur as it should, the load of sugar in the bloodstream builds up to abnormally high levels and begins to cause trouble.

There are two ways in which insulin deficiency can come about. First, the pancreas may fail to produce enough hormone. This is the situation of so-called juvenile (or Type I) diabetics. Both heredity and viral infection seem to play a role in triggering this type of diabetes. Fatness is not an important cause.

In the other main type of diabetes, the pancreas may produce *more* insulin than normal, but the hormone is less effective because certain cells become relatively indifferent to it. This situation is now known as Type II diabetes and usually appears in middle age or later. This form of the disease is eight or nine times more prevalent than Type I, and the people affected are eight times more likely to be fat than thin.

In either type of diabetes, sugar (as glucose) remains in the bloodstream at abnormally high levels instead of being removed for storage within cells. For reasons that are not completely clear, the excess of circulating glucose damages the smallest blood vessels (capillaries and arterioles), and sooner or later this damage leads to impaired circulation of the blood. Insufficient blood supply, in turn, injures a variety of organs, notably the heart and kidneys.

The crucial question about adult-onset diabetes is, "Why do cells become insensitive to insulin?" and not, as with juvenile diabetes, "Why isn't there enough of the hormone?" There probably is more than one reason for the relative insensitivity. A hereditary defect that shows up late in life appears to be the major factor; heredity is even more important in Type II than in Type I diabetes. Accumulation of body fat appears to be another influence. The more adipose tissue a body carries, the less it is capable of lowering blood sugar in response to insulin. Fat cells themselves, as they increase in size, take in less sugar at any given level of insulin. Moreover, as the total amount of body fat builds up, it somehow influences muscle and liver cells to become similarly less sensitive to the hormone. It is this latter, indirect effect that is most important, because the liver is the major organ responsible for removing sugar from the blood. To a point, the pancreas can compensate for the liver's diminished sensitivity to insulin by releasing more of the hormone than it usually does.

Although the excess of insulin helps to keep blood sugar under control, indirectly it makes matters worse. The reason is that the hormone has a second function, which is not impaired: Insulin promotes the accumulation of fat. Thus a vicious cycle is temporarily established. Extra insulin, secreted in an attempt to lower blood sugar, adds fat to the body. The fat interferes with the sugar-storing action of the hormone, so blood sugar rises. In response, yet more insulin is secreted.

Eventually the system may stabilize. In this case, the individual becomes fat and has more circulating insulin than normal, but levels of blood sugar are adequately regulated. Alternatively, the system may break down: Insulin production then falls short of the amount needed to lower blood sugar, and the individual becomes diabetic.

Evidently, being fat does not, in itself, cause the diabetes. Some other factor, or group of factors, tips the balance and precipitates the disease. Indeed, recently reported evidence suggests that being fat does not, in and of itself, increase the risk of developing diabetes, unless the tendency is already present. However, because lowering stores of fat automatically increases the body's sensitivity to insulin, weight reduction is a crucial part of any treatment for diabetes. Efforts to find a safe, effective, and lasting means of weight control would be warranted purely for its benefit to diabetics (and hypertensives). Dieting —with all its drawbacks and discouragements—appears to be a necessary part of the treatment for many adult-onset diabetics. But, once again, exercise may prove to be at least as useful as dieting, if not more so. As we have already indicated and will discuss at greater length in chapter 9, physical conditioning appears to act directly on setpoint. But even if moderate activity does not immediately lead to weight loss, it appears to increase insulin sensitivity and thus help counteract the effect of excess fat.[14]

Diabetics, hypertensives, and people who suffer from extreme obesity can all benefit from weight reduction. Relatively modest measures, perhaps emphasizing physical activity, can help the first two groups. Patients with extreme obesity may need more drastic forms of therapy, but as yet the evidence is not very persuasive that the cure is better than the disease.

"Morbid" obesity—in which half or more of the body's weight is adipose tissue—affects about 600,000 people in the United States. Obesity of this degree is clearly associated with illness and early death, and younger people appear to be more at risk than older ones; indeed, morbidly obese men between the ages of twenty-five and thirty-four have a mortality rate twelve times higher than average. As you might expect, no one has ever proved that the obesity is in itself responsible for the poor health of people affected. But most authorities take it for granted that the excessive fatness, whatever its origin, causes fatal disease—principally in the form of heart attacks and strokes. Nor has anyone managed to demonstrate that the life expectancy of morbidly obese people is improved by weight loss. Undeterred by this lack of certainty, however, many physicians in the past few years have been willing to experiment with drastic methods to produce weight loss in such patients. Much of the initiative has come from patients themselves, who suffer inordinately from the social stigma of their obesity and are insistent that their doctors "try anything."

Two main approaches have been taken. One is semistarvation. Patients permitted only 10 percent or less of their usual daily intake do lose weight but, given the chance, many of them also give up. Those who diligently stick to the diet may actually damage their health. Clinical observations of near-fasting regimens show that they may upset the heart's rhythm, and the popular liquid-protein diet was linked to about sixty sudden deaths. Part of the problem may be a lack of trace minerals; even when vitamin and mineral supplements are taken, they may be incomplete. It's also likely that stringent dieting breaks down vital protein (even on the so-called protein-sparing modified fast), and cardiac tissue can be damaged when protein is withdrawn from the heart muscle. In other words, even a very fat person may react to semistarvation by literally eating his heart out.[15]

As was described in chapter 3, intestinal-bypass surgery has also been used in an attempt to override a patient's eating behavior (although in fact, if inadvertently, it may serve to lower setpoint). This procedure occasionally works, but it has led to so many and such horrendous complications—infection, severe vitamin deficiency, outright malnutrition, and liver failure, among others—that an editorial in the *Journal of the American Medical Association* recently concluded, without mincing words, that the medical profession is "compelled to reject [intestinal-bypass surgery] as metabolically and physiologically unsafe." Currently, experimentation continues with a less drastic form of surgery in which the stomach is partly stitched up to make it feel full when it contains only small amounts of food. This procedure has no physiological rationale (inasmuch as the perception of a "full stomach" is not what makes one cease to feel hungry); it is technically difficult; and patients are prone to serious complications immediately after surgery. In the long run, stomach surgery is not likely to work, because patients learn how to "eat around" their limited capacity. But, since it is less dangerous than intestinal surgery, attempts to improve the procedure continue.[16]

Although medical efforts to control morbid obesity have intensified in recent years, on the whole the medical fear of fatness is very gradually giving way to a more moderate outlook. Partly, this change is a response to evidence from better sources than insurance policies, but it has also received some impetus, unexpectedly, from recent insurance data. In 1979, twenty years after the first *Build and Blood Pressure Study*, the Society of Actuaries published results of a repeat performance, intended to keep insurance companies up to date on the changing patterns of mortality among their policyholders.

The new *Build and Blood Pressure Study* reported one unsurprising fact: Americans had been gaining weight. And it reported another that should have been regarded as altogether astonishing. As before, the actuaries found that for every height one particular weight promised the lowest mortality. For every increment above this weight, they found a steadily increasing risk of death. But the "desirable" weight as of 1979 was as much as ten to fifteen pounds heavier than in 1959![17]

The actuaries' announcement met with mixed reviews in the general press. Some writers took the cheerful attitude that we could all breathe a little easier and diet just a little less strenuously. Others huffed that a formerly abysmal situation had now become merely disgraceful: Whereas half of all Americans had been above the old standard, now it was a third—hardly cause for rejoicing.

Both of these reactions missed the real point of the actuaries' new "finding." It simply beggars credulity to argue that (1) fat is still lethal, but (2) within a generation we have all been given an extra, free ten-pound allowance before the effect begins to operate. Some kind of divine intervention would have been required to bring about this change in human biology; nothing short of a miracle could have altered our nature so profoundly. Alternatively, of course, the research methods that produced the *Build and Blood Pressure Study* could have been faulty. But even if we were to assume that God had better things to do in the last few decades than to raise America's "desirable" weight, we would be left with a problem. If the actuarial data were simply a mistake, the life insurance industry could well be out of business, for its profits depend on actuarial precision.

This very point has been made in the past when skeptics have questioned the insurance companies' evidence. Indeed, the modern belief that body fat is a mortal threat to its owner is mainly due to the fact that, for many decades, the insurance companies had the sole evidence, and if it was wrong they would presumably have had to close their doors. To understand our national fat phobia, then, we need to learn a little about one chapter in the history of America's life insurance industry.

At the turn of the century, few people thought moderate amounts of fat were anything but an advantage. Tuberculosis, not heart disease or cancer, was one of the most common ways to die and one of the most feared diseases. Because tuberculosis was a wasting process, it came to be associated with a lean physique. People assumed, naturally enough, that the plump were less likely to harbor tuberculosis and communicate it than were thin people, and that they were less susceptible to the illness. They were probably right. Death rates from infectious disease had begun to decline earlier in the century (well before a germ theory was proposed or antibiotics even imagined), and, in retrospect, improved nutrition probably was an important reason for the change. An adequate and varied diet helped to preserve health, and a modest reserve of fat would have improved resistance when infection struck.[18]

Out-and-out corpulence, of course, was considered unhealthy in the nineteenth century, much as it has been throughout history. In 1810, William Wadd published in England a medical treatise on the subject, *Cursory Remarks on Corpulence,* which advocated a vegetarian diet to treat extreme obesity. Two generations later, in 1863, William Banting, a very fat Englishman of sixty-five—and probably an adult-onset diabetic—successfully lost weight. In his enthusiasm, Banting published a famous pamphlet, *Letter on Corpulence.* In it he vividly characterized the drawbacks of obesity, which he called the most distressing "of all the parasites that affect humanity," and he put forth the first low-carbohydrate diet. The book struck a responsive chord and had gone through many printings by 1900. Among its other accomplishments, it gave the English a term for dieting: "banting."[19]

Still, few people believed that moderate fatness was a medical disadvantage. Banting himself published a table of healthy weights for adult men (which was remarkably similar to the 1959 insurance standards) but went on to describe it "only as an average—some in health weighing more by many pounds than others. It must not be looked upon as infallible, but only as a sort of general reasonable guide to Nature's great and mighty work."[20]

Banting's table had been devised for a British insurance company by a physician who gauged health mainly by the volume of air a man could move in one breath. (Interestingly enough, this quantity may indeed prove to be the best way to predict longevity, according to William B. Kannel and Helen Hubert, of Boston University Medical School, who made a preliminary report of their finding in 1981.) Premiums issued by the company were evidently based in part on this table, although neither the British nor the American insurance business had yet developed an industry-wide policy on weight.[21]

By the close of the nineteenth century, however, life insurance companies were beginning a systematic search for ways to predict which of their policyholders would die young. In America, this effort was part of a radical change in the way the life insurance industry conducted its business. Before 1840, virtually no life insurance was sold in the United States. Then, until 1900, the business went through a phase of rapid and unruly growth. High-living insurance executives (some of them, incidentally, quite fat), had used their policyholders' premiums for speculative investment. Scandals and setbacks ensued; there were investigations; and by 1907 widespread regulatory legislation was put into effect.[22]

Once life insurance companies were prevented from gambling in the stock market, their further financial growth was limited by the kind of sound, conservative investment that yields steady, but not spectacular, returns. In order to expand, the companies were then obliged to sell as many policies as possible. To sell policies, they needed to keep their premiums inexpensive. And to keep the whole enterprise from suffering a nasty shock in ten or twenty years, they had to be sure that the newly insured would not die prematurely. The ability to predict how long policyholders would live, and to screen out risky applicants, thus became even more important than it had been before. The companies began to look for inexpensive, simple ways to screen applicants, as well as to seek reliable omens of their early demise. Medical directors became increasingly important figures in most companies as this effort picked up steam.

A pioneer in the enterprise was Oscar H. Rogers, a physician with the New York Life Insurance Company. A patrician figure, much revered by his colleagues, Rogers was largely responsible for two innovations in the business. He instituted the practice of *systematically* looking for risk factors that would predict a higher mortality rate in applicants, and he developed a method for rating "substandard" applicants to whom insurance would be sold at an appropriately higher premium.[23]

In 1901 he reported that the mortality rate of fat policyholders was higher than average. Rogers's assertion, based on a small sample of his company's records, was widely accepted, and it undoubtedly led insurance companies to begin discriminating against fat applicants. Subsequent collaborative studies would confirm the finding that "overweights" were substandard risks.[24]

The industry's conclusion was extremely persuasive. It was based on many policies, and the sheer force of numbers seemed to authenticate it. Moreover, if it were grossly misleading, the firms depending on the actuaries' figures could be expected to suffer financial loss (though a lesser loss than they would suffer if they had *under* estimated the mortality of fat people). The very success of the American insurance industry seemed to argue for the accuracy of the tables.

They may have been accurate enough, for insurance purposes. Yet the tables had, and still have, severe limitations as a guide to the biological meaning of fatness. To begin with, the issue was clouded by a growing prejudice that fatness was a Bad Thing. Rogers had originally found that *underweight* applicants also suffered higher mortality, but this association was generally underplayed. Likewise, the insurance studies have sometimes suggested that especially tall people, for some unknown reason, are statistically more likely to die young. But "over-height," as a concept, lacks the moral cachet of "overweight," and the connection has never been pursued.

A more basic defect, one that still bedevils insurance studies, was that people buying life insurance, particularly at the turn of the century, were very unlike the American population as a whole: They were mostly white men of northern European descent, they had relatively high incomes, and they lived in Eastern cities. They were, as a group, leaner than the general public. Even if the early studies had proved that any degree of overweight was bad for these men, they would not have guaranteed that the same was true, say, of a recent immigrant from the Ukraine or a rural black woman.[25]

Also, the mere fact that the people being studied had all bought life insurance surely distorted the results. At the turn of the century, American men did not automatically buy coverage as a matter of prudent financial management; they often had some other reason. And there were, as yet, no fixed standards for selecting men to be insured; much was left to the discretion of examiners. These factors could have so seriously distorted the sample of men buying insurance that their pattern of mortality was not even representative of Eastern, upper-income, white, urban males.

A case in point comes from the experience of insured women in the nineteenth century. A dozen life insurance studies conducted between 1843 and 1886 all agreed: Insured women died younger. Yet some thirty-four mortality tables published between 1746 and 1899 showed that women in general lived at least as long as men. The reason for the discrepancy was not known, although a discussion of the problem in 1900 turned up some imaginative suggestions: By wearing corsets during medical examinations, women could prevent the doctor from detecting grave illness; or women's intuition might give them a special ability to predict their own demise and thereby beat the odds when taking out insurance. A far more likely explanation came from the observation that a higher-than-average proportion of insured women were married. Husbands may have arranged to insure their spouses in the knowledge that they were sickly or self-destructive. One could imagine Rhett Butler taking out a policy on Scarlett.[26]

Bias in insurance statistics is a troublesome problem because it is self-perpetuating. Once people in a category—be it women or overweights—are defined as high risk ("substandard"), they are charged an extra premium for their insurance. After that, the very fact that they are willing to pay an extra premium suggests that these applicants have some special reason to fear for their health.

Despite their flaws, the life insurance studies probably revealed some sort of fact. Whatever the reason, fat people buying policies did die at a somewhat faster rate than their thinner contemporaries. This information was worthless to anyone concerned about public health, but it was not recognized as such until the 1970s, because no other data were available to contradict the insurance records. For actuarial purposes it was enough, and the companies had little incentive to probe for cause-and-effect relationships.

What led insurance companies to look at weight in the first place was its easy measurability. Decades of experience had taught them that elaborate attempts to assess the moral character, habits, and lifestyle of applicants were often more trouble than they were worth. The companies needed simple, measurable traits and verifiable facts: age, height, weight, occupation, marital status, income. In its search for clear-cut, quantifiable attributes, the insurance industry also began very early to measure blood pressure and perform urinalyses, and it invested in improving the necessary technology.[27]

The point about all this effort is that it was not truly a search for the *causes* of early death; the insurance studies were never designed to give such information. In reality, they were looking for markers: easily spotted traits that, for one reason or another, would identify people in high-risk categories. They might well have recorded the mortality rate of people with tattoos, for example—if only there had been enough tattooed applicants to make it worthwhile. Had they done so, the companies would probably have found that tattooed men die young, not because wearing a tattoo is bad for one's health but because people with tattoos live more dangerously than those without them.

This kind of guilt by association may partly—even largely—account for the bad record of "insured overweights." If overweight was a moderately reliable marker for some other trait that was lethal, the overweights would indeed have died young. We can only speculate as to what those traits might have been. It is possible, for example, that fat applicants smoked more cigarettes. Although cigarettes are widely believed to lower weight, and in some people evidently they do, a recent survey of British men reveals that, among the upper classes, smokers tend to be fatter. If the same association held for American men fifty years ago, "overweight" would have served as a code word for "heavy smoker" in the insurance records. (But until very recently, insurance companies have evinced no interest in smoking habits—even though cigarette use reliably predicts early death—because measuring cigarette consumption is difficult.)[28]

Likewise, overweight could have been a sign of alcohol abuse. Heavy drinkers, especially beer drinkers, are likely to get fat before their alcoholism progresses to the stage at which they lose weight, and one of the early insurance studies found that overweights tended to die of cirrhosis of the liver. But contemporary research has found no association of fatness with severe liver disease (except in extreme degrees of obesity).[29]

These questions about the nature of the insurance data are not quibbles; they are crucial to deciding whether some or all fat people die young *because* they are fat. Rogers and the other medical directors at the turn of the century did not concern themselves with uncovering fundamental biological truths. They apparently saw their contribution as helping the life insurance industry to do business more rationally; they were not public health crusaders and did not mount a campaign to slenderize the American people. That task was assumed by a man who entered the insurance business just as Rogers, the pioneer, was about to retire.

By 1910 it might have seemed progress enough that insurance companies could be relied upon not to squander the premiums they collected. But having acquired commercial respectability, some went on to style themselves almost as public charities. One of these was Metropolitan Life of New York, a relatively small business at that time, which distinguished itself by writing a large proportion of its policies for working people—so-called industrial policies. In 1909 the leaders of Metropolitan had resolved to spend some of the company's money trying to prolong the lives of those they insured. They opened a Welfare

Bureau, which conducted educational programs and demonstration projects in public hygiene. The bureau even provided free home nursing service to its policyholders.

Soon after, Metropolitan's Welfare Bureau established a statistics department and hired a bright young zoologist named Louis I. Dublin to work in it. Dublin's job was distinct from the actuaries' labor of setting premiums and regulating the firm's fiscal activity. Instead, he was supposed to produce new information, for example, to monitor the cost-benefit ratio of the home nursing program and to develop new methods for identifying substandard risks. Dublin proved more than equal to the task. Not only would he contribute to Metropolitan's growth, he would be tireless in promoting public-health measures—and would become the person who, almost by himself, persuaded the world that any degree of overweight is potentially deadly.

Dublin was an exemplar of the good citizen in America's Progressive period. He had been brought to the United States from his birthplace in Lithuania in 1884, when he was two years old. He grew up on the Lower East Side of Manhattan, where his father worked as a tailor. He distinguished himself in public school and at the City College, where he majored in mathematics. From there, in 1901, he went to Columbia for graduate study in biology—seemingly an odd choice for a boy who had grown up in the human tumble around Henry Street and had no acquaintance with wildlife. But in college he had become fascinated by Darwinism, and he hoped to take part in the excitement of the new science.

He came to the right place at the right time. The laws of genetics that Mendel had divined in 1865 were just at that moment being rediscovered, and it was at Columbia that much of the fundamental work would be done. Dublin immediately began work with one of the pioneers, Edmund B. Wilson. Meanwhile, he studied statistics with the great anthropologist Franz Boas and took courses in human biology at the medical school. Summers were spent at the laboratories in Woods Hole, Massachusetts, and Cold Spring Harbor, New York, which were just becoming the work-and-play resorts of America's biological elite.

In retrospect, Dublin's career was full of promise for a bright academic future, but in 1904, with a new Ph.D. in zoology, he had trouble finding a job. No doubt anti-Semitism, which permeated the universities, played its role. Dublin supported himself by teaching algebra and geometry to freshmen at City College, while he kept his hand in biology by conducting independent research in Wilson's laboratory.

It was there that Dublin came close to, and lost, what would have been the discovery of his life. He was examining the large chromosomes of an improbable organism, the squash bug. Nobody knew what chromosomes were at that point, but the scientific smart money said they were important. Dublin noticed that all the bug's chromosomes could be grouped into pairs of equal size except for two, which were mismatched. He asked Wilson for advice on how to pursue this curious finding. The professor borrowed the set of specimens and kept them for several months, while he quietly started to study the phenomenon on his own. Wilson concluded, correctly, that the unpaired chromosomes were responsible for determining an animal's sex. With an offhand, footnoted, nod to Louis Dublin, he published this discovery. Wilson's investigation paved the way for another Columbia professor, T. H. Morgan, to prove that chromosomes carry all genetic information.[30]

The experience of having his research problem swiped by his professor—and, no doubt, his recognition that academic opportunities for an immigrant Jew would be limited—led Dublin to reassess his future. After his marriage in 1908, Dublin sought a position in the life insurance business, which, he believed, would put his mathematical and biological background to good use. On his first job, at Mutual of New York, Dublin compiled a new table of standard heights and weights for men and women, a table that was widely used by the industry for years afterward. Then, in 1909 (the same year the word "gene" was coined), Dublin was offered a job at Metropolitan by the new head of the Welfare Bureau, a man whom he had known from "volunteer social work" a few years before. The young man who might have become one of the great names of twentieth-century biology eagerly accepted the opportunity.

At Metropolitan, Dublin served for over forty years, not only as a statistician but as the house intellectual and publicist. He arranged to purchase prototypes of I.B.M. punched-card computers and started to churn out data. He worked indefatigably, producing upwards of 600 papers, popular articles, speeches, and other publications in his tenure there, and eventually became what has been called a "visible scientist"—the sort of authority to whom the press would turn for pronouncements on scientific matters. His publications ranged over the years from the drily technical ("An Experiment in the Compilation of Mortality Statistics") to the practical ("The Health of Musicians: A Statistician Looks at Their Ways of Life and Death") to the sweeping ("Is American Vigor Declining?"). Dublin was passionately committed to public health and health education. He was a prominent member and, sooner or later, president or a director of half a dozen organizations dedicated to public health. With extraordinary energy he pursued his intellectual, civic, and business interests almost to his death at the triumphant age of eighty-six.

One of his last and most influential undertakings was an effort to persuade Americans that obesity was killing them. Single-mindedly, and very nearly single-handedly, Dublin managed to persuade a whole generation that "overweight is one of the prime factors in shortening life." In his typical, prolific style, he wrote articles for both professional journals and popular magazines, articles sounding the alarm: With the conquest of infectious diseases, people were now dying of chronic, degenerative illness of which overweight was the most significant cause. Dublin coined the phrase "America's No. 1 Health Problem" for obesity and used it in the title of a 1952 article in *Today's Health*, then a widely read magazine. He attempted to enlist the antagonists in the war between the sexes for his campaign against fatness. An article in *McCall's* asked, "Do Husbands Like Plump Wives?," to which the answer, of course, was no. And, in the *Reader's Digest,* he ordered the American housewife: "Stop Killing Your Husband" by overfeeding him on fattening foods.[31]

Dublin had, at that point, a considerable reputation. Coming from him, the message seemed plausible enough, and he backed up his point with statistics that seemed impressive indeed— though in fact they were at least as deeply flawed as Rogers's had been.

By mid-century, several insurance investigations had repeated the finding that overweight predicted early death. As before, however, the people studied had been atypical of the general population. As time went on, and the insurance industry's antipathy to overweight applicants increased, fat men were more likely to be discouraged from buying life insurance (unlike men of normal weight, who were actively recruited). At the beginning of his career, Dublin had recognized the analogous flaw in the industry's approach to women. Then, he had been quick to cut through nonsense about corsets and premonitions. He had pointed out that insurance companies would wait for women, or their potential beneficiaries, to apply for life insurance, whereas they were vigorously marketing their policies to healthy men. This difference automatically meant that the insured women were more likely to be poor risks than the men. But, at the end of his career, Dublin failed to perceive a comparable disparity between his normal and overweight populations.[32]

To make his case, Dublin also drew on his own analysis of the meticulous records kept by Union Central Life Insurance Company. His finding, published in 1930, was that fat policyholders were dying of "organic heart disease and angina pectoris, arterial diseases, diabetes, nephritis and cerebral hemorrhage," and, to a lesser degree, "cancer, influenza, paralysis, appendicitis, cirrhosis of the liver, and typhoid fever"—the works. This list contains some of the familiar, hardy perennial diagnoses, but also some others that are altogether puzzling, in particular the category of "nephritis," which implies that the policyholder died of kidney disease (although the term was used somewhat loosely before the 1950s). Whatever it was, this disease was the largest single cause of excessive mortality among Union Central's overweights—fully 20 percent of the extra deaths. Yet today *no one* claims that there is a direct association between obesity and kidney disease. We could speculate endlessly as to what "nephritis" may have signified, but the hard fact is that Dublin's list, which was extensively cited well into the 1950s, was utterly uninterpretable from the day it was published. Reciting it, however, has been a favorite rhetorical device of writers on the perils of obesity; the grisly diagnostic terms created satisfying overtones for the basic note of doom.[33]

Dublin was himself somewhat cognizant of the flaws in the evidence he presented (as were some of his more discriminating contemporaries). Individuals from a select group were weighed and measured once, fully clothed, and then were never heard from again until their heirs put in a claim. Cause of death, when it was ascertained, came from death certificates—a notoriously unreliable source of diagnostic information.

Dublin's ace in the hole was a study he had completed in the late 1940s; it purported to prove that fat people who lose weight live longer than those who do not. He correctly realized that this finding, if valid, would be the best possible proof that fat is a health hazard (even as the improved life expectancy of people who quit smoking belongs with the best evidence for the hazards of cigarettes).

To collect his evidence, Dublin went through Metropolitan's records and found the applications of some 2,300 people who received a first policy when they were overweight but later, after reducing, were granted a second policy, at a standard premium. (Like other insurance studies, this one was carried out on policies, not people. Nothing is known about what happened between the two examination dates, or between the second examination and the end of the study.) He compared the slimmers with the whole contemporary group of overweights insured by Metropolitan and found that they indeed had a nearly normal death rate (or, in one group of women, better than normal). Dublin and his associates placed great emphasis on this statistic, which they cited at least half a dozen times in papers published during the 1950s.[34]

Nowhere, however, was the study published in full. Fragmentary accounts of the methods and the results were given in various journals. So, today it is impossible to fully reconstruct the investigation, and there are questions that even a full report would doubtless have failed to answer. For example, as we have indicated, it is exceedingly rare for people to lose significant amounts of weight and remain at their lower weight. The 2,300 people in Dublin's group would have been atypical indeed had they managed it. But Dublin himself knew only two weights for each applicant. Moreover, the findings themselves do nothing to inspire confidence: The apparent benefit of losing weight was greatest for old men and negligible for young men. Yet, if fatness were a cause of chronic degenerative disease, as Dublin so freely claimed, we would expect the reverse.

In sum, this study was so badly designed and inadequately presented that it cannot be taken as evidence of anything. Yet it was highly influential in its time—the results appeared in the "best" medical journals—and it helped to persuade a generation of physicians that reducing diets are, almost in and of themselves, therapeutic. Dublin's study (repeated with all its inadequacies in the *Build and Blood Pressure Study* of 1959) remains to this day the *only* published evidence we have found that weight loss improves life expectancy.

Louis Dublin's greatest influence today stems not from his research on overweight but from the table of "Desirable Weights," which he devised and published in the *Statistical Bulletin* of the Metropolitan Life Insurance Company. Although the table was, in significant ways, Dublin's *invention,* it has come to be treated as though it recorded biological truth as faithfully as Moses' tablets proclaim the Ten Commandments. Most medical research for the last twenty years has relied on the "Metropolitan Life" table as a way to judge whether or not subjects are fat. The numbers in its columns have been used as a goal for countless dieters. They have been accepted as the absolute standard of human normality, at least with regard to height and weight.

The form of the table is simple enough, and it fits tidily on a single page. It is split into two parts, labeled "Men" and "Women." The left column lists heights. To the right are three columns labeled "Small Frame," "Medium Frame," and "Large Frame." For each sex, height, and frame size, the table gives a range of "weights (in indoor clothing)." Thus, as of 1959, a woman who was five feet six inches tall with a medium frame should have weighed between 120 and 135 pounds throughout her adult life. A six-foot man with a small frame was allowed 148 to 158 pounds.[35]

The table was based on the same type of data that Rogers had first collected: the height, weight, age, and survival of applicants holding insurance policies. Dublin based his first table, published in the early 1940s and presumptuously labeled "Ideal Weights," mainly on this kind of information collected within his own company. But in 1959, after his retirement, he revised the table with data from the massive *Build and Blood Pressure* investigation conducted by the Society of Actuaries. Although it compiled statistics on several million people insured by twenty-six large companies in North America, the Actuaries' study corrected none of the inherent defects in the earlier investigations. All it did was to study a more recent population and expand the sample size.

Using the actuaries' biased data, Dublin constructed his table with the aid of two completely gratuitous assumptions. He *decided* that there was no reason to get fatter after the age of twenty-five—although nearly everybody does—and so he based his "ideal" on statistics for twenty-five-year olds. Thus, his table makes no provision for weight gain with age. This feature of the table has a perverse consequence: According to the insurance records, overweight is most dangerous at younger ages; at later ages the risk is considerably diminished. Thus, older people are most likely to be above the desirable weight but least likely to be affected by their fatness, even if the Actuaries' data are accepted at face value. The table, in effect, puts the greatest pressure on a group with the least "need" to reduce.

Dublin next *decided* that a group of people of the same height could be sorted into those with large, medium, or small musculoskeletal systems. Accordingly, he took the Actuaries' range of desirable weights for each height and split it, more or less evenly, into three categories of "frame" size. Plausible as this maneuver might be, it has no basis whatever in evidence. There is no accurate way to measure or estimate "frame" size. "Frames" are even harder to evaluate than fatness, and there is no objective criterion for distinguishing between a large and a medium, or a medium and a small frame.

Louis Dublin was intelligent and sophisticated. His tendentious use of sloppy statistics to mount a campaign against overweight seems out of character with the man and his career; it calls for an explanation, that may, perhaps, be found in his thwarted ambition to become a biologist.

Dublin was approaching retirement when he began his anti-obesity evangelism. In proclaiming the hazards of overweight, he found a swan song and, perhaps, a justification for his career in the insurance industry. On the face of it, no justification was needed; for forty years Dublin worked vigorously and with some effect to bring about improvements in human health. But his contribution, and that of his industry, was small. To be sure, from the time Dublin joined Metropolitan to his retirement, life expectancy in America increased by more than twenty years— a fact with which Dublin was much preoccupied. But the improvement came about thanks largely to improving nutrition, lowered mortality from infectious diseases, and tighter control of occupational hazards—all changes with which the insurance industry had little to do.

Overweight was another matter. Insurance executives had "discovered" the health hazard, and Dublin evidently believed that he had conducted the critical experiment, as it were, in his study of policyholders who lost weight and lived longer. A biologist *manqué,* Dublin the statistician could conceive of his work on overweight as an example of a biological fact revealed by insurance records. And he could argue that this knowledge would make one of the last great contributions to prolonging life. In the event, Dublin was wrong.

At the same time that the insurance companies were making their case against overweight, laboratory scientists were beginning to put rats (or mice) on restricted rations. They found that keeping the animals below their normal weight caused the whole process of development and aging to slow down. If the restriction was drastic and begun at an early age, the animal's growth was stunted and it matured slowly, but it lived twice as long as a littermate fed the standard diet. Less extreme deprivation also had an effect; a slightly skinny rat would live a little longer than its control.[36]

Predictably enough, these results have been interpreted as evidence bolstering Dublin's unsupported assertion that people should lose weight to live longer. The gerontologist Alex Comfort, who made his name and his fortune as author of *The Joy of Sex,* took up the cause in the early 1970s. In the guise of recommending more human research on the possibility, Comfort speculated that dietary restriction beginning at an early age could prolong the human life span by 20 to 40 percent. More recently, Roy Walford, an immunologist at the University of California at Los Angeles, has explored semistarvation as a way of life. Walford, who conducts experiments on the immunity of underfed mice, himself fasts two days of every week. He has expressed a hope that the maximum human lifespan can be extended well past the present limit of about one hundred years.[37]

The reasoning behind the inference that semistarvation may benefit human beings appears tenuous indeed. In the first place, caged laboratory rodents have a life cycle that is radically different from the human life cycle. These animals live in a metabolic fast lane; they are designed to survive only three or four years at a maximum, not three or four score, like a human being. The laboratory animals also live under conditions that are very different from those of their free-living cousins. Protected from infection, prevented from exercising, they have a highly aberrant lifestyle. There is no particular reason to believe that rats rummaging along subway tracks and picking their way through garbage dumps would benefit in the least from underfeeding. Moreover, because the laboratory rats have lived in cages for generations, they have diverged genetically from the wild strains; they are not even necessarily representative of their own species.

There is no indication whatever that the human *lifespan*—the maximum useful life that anyone can hope to achieve—is improved by deprivation. Reports that hardy peoples living in rugged mountains, the Caucasus and the Andes, live twice the normal lifetime have proved to be erroneous—a result of the confused record keeping that often goes along with primitive living conditions and a spare diet.[38]

Meanwhile, if anything, improved nutrition and a gradual, slight increase in fatness have led to an increase in human life *expectancy*—the chance in any given population of making it from birth to a ripe old age.

The only major medicosocial experiment that has attempted

to improve the health of normal people by limiting fat accumulation took place in the 1950s and 1960s. It was an uncontrolled and unscientific effort to induce women to restrict their weight gain during pregnancy. For a while, the obstetricians' standard practice was to limit their patients, if possible, to a gain of fifteen or at most twenty pounds.

The rationale for this recommendation was, in retrospect, somewhat bizarre. A relatively uncommon, but serious, complication of pregnancy is toxemia—which causes high blood pressure and fluid accumulation (edema). It can, if untreated, lead to convulsions, coma, and kidney or heart failure. One sign of toxemia is an abnormal weight gain, mainly from accumulated fluid. Because women with toxemia gained weight, the false conclusion was drawn that weight gain predisposed to toxemia. On the basis of this error, until the early 1970s, expectant mothers were urged to curtail their food intake—often quite severely—during pregnancy. This policy not only had no rational or empirical basis, it was counterproductive. The fat gained during pregnancy is demanded by the body as an energy store for the late phases of pregnancy, the time of birth, and lactation. Deprived by dieting, the pregnant body takes measures to limit the size of the fetus. Far from being at an advantage, the smaller baby is more likely to face complications around the time of delivery, and to suffer illness at the beginning of its life.[39]

Women struggled to cooperate with this regimen, not only because they genuinely believed it was better for them and their babies, but also because they dreaded looking fat and matronly. Since the vast majority of American women do not breast feed their babies—or do so only briefly—they are left at the end of their pregnancies with fat that normally would be consumed during the months of lactation. Without nursing, the fat is hard to get rid of. The only alternative is to limit weight gain during pregnancy—which makes the cosmetic task easier but adds a burden of risk.

It was both ironic and predictable that women would be the object of this misguided attempt at medical slenderizing. The woman's body has become the unfortunate Galatea of two Pygmalions. Contemporary fashion demands that she whittle her contours to an almost boyish litheness, whereas millennia of evolution have worked to mold her with an ample reserve of fat.

6

ORIGINAL THIN:
THE EVOLUTION
OF SETPOINT

WOMEN are fatter than men. Men are fatter than monkeys. Some people are much fatter than others.

These observations are commonplace—but what do they mean? Why are humans generally fat in comparison with their closest relatives, the apes and monkeys? Why is a young woman's body proportionately twice as fat as a man's? And why is the human race so exceedingly variable—with individuals ranging from the bony to the amply proportioned to the downright corpulent?

By now we hope our readers will resist thinking to themselves, "Of course the human species is fat. We have more food than other animals." Sheer quantity of available food does not explain why an individual gets fat, much less a whole species.

The fundamental reason that we humans are, as animals go, a chubby lot is that our way of life has made the ability to fatten crucial to survival. From about ten thousand years ago until the middle of the eighteenth century, most of the earth's people lived in constant jeopardy of famine—sometimes several famines in a single lifetime. Before about two hundred and fifty years ago, these food crises were built into the agricultural economy, which was far more prone to periodic, severe breakdowns than the hunter-gatherer lifestyle that humans had pursued for the three or four million years before the garden was invented. Being fat (or, more accurately, having a relatively high setpoint) was one means by which our recent ancestors managed to survive the consequences of their own ingenuity.

The nature of human reproduction has made it even more important for women than men to have high setpoints: Each human infant is nutritionally dependent on its mother for a matter of years, and until recently a woman to a large extent had to nourish her baby from her own body. To manage, mothers had to protect themselves and their infants by carrying a reserve of fat, and this insurance policy has been so important to human survival that it is now automatically required by the woman's reproductive system. Women cannot get pregnant unless they have enough fat to make the risk a reasonable one. A "reasonable risk," of course, is defined not in modern terms but according to the ancient experience of our species.

Despite the hazards of agriculture and the leisurely pace of human reproduction, our ancestors did manage to reproduce, and, some seven or eight millennia ago, to form relatively dense, sedentary populations with a network of trade relations. As these networks grew sufficiently extensive to include several thousand people, the intercommunicating population began a less profitable form of exchange: Epidemic diseases would periodically sweep through a region, often in the wake of a famine. The unlucky died; the fortunate were merely disabled. These epidemics must certainly have killed those individuals who lacked an adequate energy reserve, thereby favoring survival of the fatter ones.

The fat we see on human bodies today is not merely a sign of present luxury; it is evidence of past hardship. Paradoxically, the greatest hardship, from a nutritional point of view, came after the introduction of agriculture. Before about ten thousand years ago, people fed themselves in much the same way as other animals, by foraging. They took what they could find, and we can guess that they did not get particularly fat, even when they came upon a nutritional bonanza.

It is not a fact of nature that animals react to an abundance of food by getting fat (unless, like sand rats brought into a laboratory, they experience an abrupt and radical change of environment and diet). Instead, they have babies. And, from an evolutionary standpoint, this seems to be the only response that makes sense. Given a choice between getting fat or reproducing, the animal that puts its energy into reproduction is the one that leaves descendants. Fatness calls for an explanation because, at first glance, it seems to be a poor evolutionary strategy for animals with plenty of food. Indeed, the more food available to an animal species—provided the supply is reliable—the leaner it should be.[1]

Because fat does not leave fossils, we can only speculate about the evolutionary events that made people not only the smartest primates but also the fattest—and created the odd difference in body fat between our two sexes. We are also hampered by the fact that scientists have given little attention to the subject. The eighteenth-century anatomist John Hunter set the tone when he declared that adipose tissue is "not animal substance" because "the animal is the same with as without it," and variants of his attitude have persisted to the present. Part of the reason, no doubt, is aesthetic; many biologists seem inclined (for no good reason) to view fatness as a shameful, degenerate aspect of human existence. And part of the reason is theoretical. The concept of a setpoint for body fat has only recently been developed, and without this notion, thinking sensibly about the evolution and ecology of corpulence can be difficult indeed.[2]

Natural selection acts to preserve animals with certain traits that are beneficial in a particular environment. Height, color, shape of wing or leg, chemical characteristics of blood or tissue —such features can be measured or described in a fairly straightforward way, and they are the ones most likely to be studied by evolutionary biologists. Fatness is not such a trait. The most significant aspect of body fat is that its amount is subject to change; fat is an energy reserve to be drawn upon in times of need. A successful animal may easily be fat at one time and thin at another. Consequently, natural selection does not systematically choose between fat and thin animals. However, an environment could—and almost certainly does—favor a particular kind of control system to manage the setpoint. It is this control system, rather than any particular amount of body fat, that is subject to natural selection.

This may seem like hair-splitting, but it is not. Take an obvious example. Many animals that hibernate or migrate, as we have already pointed out, gain fat for the purpose. Consider the ruby-throated hummingbird. This creature, weighing less than a nickel, makes a 600-mile flight across the Gulf of Mexico twice a year. To do so, it doubles its weight with fat—enough to supply it with the twenty-three calories needed to power its entire flight. (A man could travel about a thousand feet on that same supply of energy.) Once the bird has reached the farther shore, it returns to a world of abundant flowers and nectar. Lugging an extra gram or so of fat would impose an energy burden on the hummingbird as it hovers in flight at flower after flower, gathering sugar water or swooping to snap up an insect. And here the fat is unnecessary: Food is more conveniently stored in the environment. So, the hummingbird streamlines; it fails to regain the fat it lost while migrating, until it has to prepare for the return journey. Nature has not selected the hummingbird to be fat or thin; rather, it has selected a setpoint mechanism that makes appropriate choices for the hummingbird's migratory cycle.[3]

The human setpoint has no such obvious seasonal changes, but, as we have observed, it appears to be reset by changes in the body's level of physical activity. A person who is fat while sedentary becomes leaner with regular exercise. This phenomenon appears to be no accident; it is a coordinated response, and we shall presently consider whether there has been an evolutionary advantage in this arrangement.

To take another example: Men live perfectly comfortably with less body fat than women, and in many, if not most, species, the female is no fatter than the male, except when she prepares for pregnancy. Moreover, a human female can, with a good deal of effort, reduce the amount of fat she carries to that typical of a lean, young man. She can survive perfectly well, if uncomfortably, without the fat, but her menstrual cycles are likely to be interrupted; she becomes infertile. Why have the human sexes evolved with different setpoints, and why is the female's setpoint tied to her reproductive cycle?

Questions of this nature are now being asked, but the role of body fat—let alone setpoint—in human evolution is still a much neglected subject. For example, a recent, very long and generally excellent book on primate and human diet in evolution devotes exactly one paragraph to the subject of fat storage.[4]

We can assert with some confidence that the capacity to become fat has been a critically important asset to human survival. A relatively high level of fat storage has probably contributed to the evolution of our long life span and ability to care for offspring over a prolonged period. A flexible setpoint, which responds to both activity levels and types of food in the diet, has given us the ability to colonize an endless variety of habitats and to exploit the food resources they have to offer. The ability to get fat has also, no doubt, been the means by which our ancestors managed to survive their dependence on agriculture

—often an exceedingly precarious way of life. And it has provided a form of resistance to infectious diseases, which became an increasing peril as human populations reached ever higher densities.

There is little direct information about the first human beings, and there is some dispute as to who they were. But certain agreed-upon facts seem to be emerging. Like virtually all animals for all time, the first people lived by gathering their food from what the land afforded. (Ants had evolved a system of domesticating aphids long before the beginnings of human husbandry, but as exceptions go this one is minor.) The new, upright, and relatively hairless apes almost certainly consumed a variety of foodstuffs—fruits, nuts, young leaves and shoots, insects, and perhaps small mammals and lizards. They lived at the edge of the great east African forest, say three to four million years ago, in a region of copses and woodland stretches patchily intermingled with grassland. To begin with, they probably lived mainly in trees but traveled as need be across open areas to find fresh stocks of food in nearby wooded areas.[5]

We can conjecture about the setpoints of these creatures. First, because they lived by scavenging and gathering, and because their world did not undergo marked seasonal changes, they were probably quite lean. Fat on any animal is a sign that its food intake fluctuates in time. Hibernation, migration, rutting, or brooding are all regular, seasonal events during which an animal eats less than usual, either because food is unavailable or because the animal has something more pressing to do. Animals that live in seasonal environments, especially those that depend on fruits and vegetable matter, are likely to get fat; bears, badgers, and raccoons are familiar examples. But creatures that live in equable climates, with a year-round supply of food, such as most of the monkeys and apes, are lean. Their habitat is a fairly reliable storehouse, and the cost of carrying fat, especially for a tree dweller, is significant. In this situation, the insurance provided by a reserve supply of fat is not worth the cost of the premium—the energy needed to carry it.[6]

Second, our ancestors were large omnivores, constantly on the *qui vive* for rich sources of calories and nutrients. Accordingly, their setpoints probably responded to the type of food they encountered. In particular, sweet or fatty foods (as with modern rats) would have raised their setpoints and thus allowed them to take advantage of high-yield foodstuffs when they were available. These suppositions about our remote ancestors require more comment.

Animals do not live in a state of constant hunger. Nor do the few hunting and gathering peoples that have persisted into modern times. Most often, foraging animals or people live in a world that offers them an ample supply of food in return for a reasonable effort to gather or catch it. This is an utterly remarkable fact: Most living forms have evolved in such a way that they do not push their potential resources to the limit of Malthusian misery. Quite often, animals even have calories enough for conspicuous consumption, in Veblen's sense. Male birds of paradise, for example, turn excess energy into fancy plumage, and elks produce massive antlers. Among many animals, elaborate ritual behavior also uses up a lot of surplus calories. None of this could go on in the animal kingdom if food supplies were so limited that an animal could not, if it "chose" to, get fat. The idea that limited food supplies prevent wild animals, or non-agricultural people, from getting fat makes no sense at all. When we look at thin animals or people, we may be tempted to assume they are hungry. Observation, however, indicates that they are not. Although there are some interesting exceptions—such as lemmings, voles, and other small mammals living mainly in temperate or cold climates—as a rule, animal populations cease growing before they reach the point of exhausting the surrounding resources.[7]

Why animal populations so seldom increase to this point is an interesting and difficult question. There appear to be several reasons. Fertility and reproduction are often very sensitive (as they are in people) to minor food shortages; an adult animal may survive easily enough from season to season but fail to reproduce when calories are somewhat limited. Predators and disease also prevent most animal populations from becoming exceedingly dense; indeed, they may be the major factors preventing denizens of a natural ecosystem from overharvesting the food it provides. The young, the ill, and the old are the first to go, and their lives may seem unenviable. But for normal adult animals, as for normal adults among hunting and gathering peoples, life is not "nasty, brutish, and short," as Hobbes described it.[8]

The !Kung San, or Bushmen, who live in the Kalahari desert of Botswana illustrate the point. (The "!" represents one of the four click sounds in their language.) The !Kung spend several days a week gathering food, but by no calculation are they forced to work what we would consider long hours for adequate nutrition. They rely on the mongongo nut, which grows abundantly in their range, as the staple of their diet; they also consume a wide variety of vegetable and animal foods. Even in severe drought, they appear to be quite capable of satisfying their nutritional needs without putting an undue strain on their resources. The !Kung population is sparse, and births are spaced at rather wide intervals. Infant mortality is high, but not because of brute starvation. The !Kung make virtually no effort to store food at their camp sites, evidently because they can rely on finding more as soon as they want it. Living as they do, within the limits set for them by their environment, the !Kung rarely experience famine and show little inclination to grow fat, although their weight fluctuates somewhat with the seasons. Their overall slenderness is not a sign of deprivation, then, but of stability in their food supply.[9]

If the experience of peoples like the !Kung and of animals living in warm climates are any indication, humans started out as a lean (but not especially *hungry*) species. Even then, they probably had some marked dietary preferences. At present, the most reasonable assumption is that the human lineage has always been fundamentally omnivorous—willing to eat a little of this and a little of that—rather than specialized as exclusively leaf eating, or meat eating, or nut-and-seed eating. In some ways, "omnivorous" is a poor description of the human feeding strategy. So-called omnivores don't eat just *anything* that comes their way. Rather, they seek out a variety of foodstuffs that are high in calories or other nutrients but relatively hard to find or catch. By contrast, grazers and leaf-eaters, to take two types of "monovore," are adapted to a routine diet of rather low quality but high availability. When they eat a lot of the same thing—perhaps supplemented by an occasional treat—they get the calories and other nutrients they need.

A major difference between monovores and omnivores is in the "pleasure" they get from eating. Monovores seem to be indifferent to taste, texture, or variety in their diets. Their culinary choices are limited to eating either some or a lot of the same fare. In contrast, omnivores are highly sensitive to the taste of food, and they seem to seek variety. As we saw in chapter 4, this reaction to food is not purely a matter of "taste." Rats—like people, classic omnivores—show taste preferences: Given the choice between plain or sweetened water, they'll drink the sweet; between plain or greasy food, they'll choose the greasy; and given a variety of items, they'll sample some of each. This aspect of their behavior clearly reflects an aesthetic predisposition: The animals have been endowed by natural selection with a hankering for precisely those foods that yield the most calories. But their response has a second component as well: The rat's setpoint rises in the presence of varied, sweet, greasy foods. This is a wonderful adaptation, as long as such items are not abundant. The induction of a higher setpoint means that the animal feels greater hunger in the presence of high-yield foods and is thus motivated to seek them by more than sensory pleasure. The temporarily raised setpoint thus allows the animal to store the calories it has harvested, pending a return to more ordinary conditions. In a seasonal environment —and even the tropics have slight but appreciable seasonal changes—this pattern of response is likely to pay off by encouraging the omnivore to grow fatter when good food is abundant and allowing it to live at a reduced weight when the larder is less rewarding.[10]

There is every reason to believe that the dietary history of the human race has equipped it with responses very similar to the rat's. For three million years, human beings have sought high-energy food in a world that offered precious little of it. They succeeded, thanks to a strong preference for sweet and fatty foods—and the intelligence to find, or later produce, such a diet. It is unlikely that, in the normal course of events, our remote ancestors suffered often from brute deficiency of calories, but doubtless they frequently failed to find the concentrated sources of energy they preferred. Wild fruits and berries would have been somewhat sparsely distributed and available only in season; they were also far less sweet than their domesticated descendants. Pure sugar was available only in the form of honey. Significant amounts of dietary fat were even harder to come by. Game animals usually contain very little fat, and wild vegetables even less. Indeed, many hunting and gathering peoples eat insect larvae for their high fat content. Among the hunter-gatherers surviving into modern times, fat, not protein, is the most prized component of the diet, and it is eagerly consumed from sources that Europeans or Americans find distasteful.[11]

A strong preference for high-calorie foods was beneficial in another way. These foods are also likely to contain nutrients— vitamins, minerals, essential fatty acids—that otherwise are in short supply. Thus, in a setting that offered people little opportunity to overdo it, a strong built-in preference for sweet, fatty foods would have been highly beneficial and would have carried little threat of obesity. Three million years ago, Mother

Nature had no way of knowing that one day cheesecake would be invented.

It can be presumed, then, that our remote ancestors were originally slender but endowed with a physiological inclination to get fatter whenever they found high-yield foods. The composition of their diet before the invention of agriculture was so varied, and the occasion for excess so uncommon, that this characteristic of the setpoint rarely or never led to outright obesity.

As long as humans were gatherers and hunters—that is, until very recently in evolutionary time—they had to move around frequently to find the kinds of food they favored. The extent of the movement required by any habitat was as much a feature of the human diet as the calories it provided. The fact that setpoint is lower when people exercise than when they are inactive probably reflects this basic condition before agriculture: The quantity of food a person ate was closely correlated with the extent to which that person had to move around. It seems somewhat mysterious, if this is so, that setpoint rises during periods of inactivity. Purely as speculation, we suggest that people ordinarily became inactive only during periods of severe shortage or when they were disabled. A higher setpoint (and consequently a more efficient metabolism) might well have been a protective response during such periods of enforced inactivity. If we think (inaccurately, but perhaps usefully) of natural selection as a designer of bodies, the reasoning would go as follows: Any creature that is moving is also eating, except in such special circumstances as rutting. When it is moving, then, it doesn't *need* a lot of fat. But if it is sedentary for a while, its food supplies are almost surely running out. If its setpoint is raised at such times, it will metabolize what fat it has more sparingly, and it will have more energy with which to find what additional food it can.

The dietary habits of the first people would scarcely have distinguished them from other animals with similar tastes, but new kinds of behavior soon differentiated humans from all other primates. At some point very early in our species' existence, the two sexes began to divide the labor of getting food. Women specialized in gathering plant matter, insects, and possibly small animals. Men became hunters or fishers. Now, it is not unusual for the two sexes of other primate species to search for somewhat different types of food, but they are not known to make a regular practice of sharing their provender with each other. The human sexes not only came to seek quite different kinds of food, but even more remarkably, they made a regular practice of returning to a home base where they processed and presumably *shared* their respective harvests.[12]

The division of labor in obtaining food and the custom of sharing it are virtually universal features of modern hunting-and-gathering peoples, and are presumably exceedingly ancient practices as well. We can guess they have had an important influence on the way the two sexes store fat.

In a curious way, men and women moved into somewhat different ecological niches. Men came to act more like carnivores, whereas women stayed with the older patterns of the omnivores. Presumably the two sexes always *ate* much the same sort of thing because they shared their food. But they went about getting what they contributed to the common meal in different ways, and it is entirely reasonable to assume that the difference in foraging styles led to some differences in the amount of fat they routinely stored.

Successful carnivores are lean animals because they must chase their prey, and at high speeds every added ounce of flesh appreciably increases the cost of running. Large size in itself may benefit a hunting species by protecting it from its own potential predators and by enabling it to bring down larger game. But the major component of its large body should be working muscle, not fat. Thus, typical carnivores, such as wolves, foxes, and cats, are very lean—unlike the omnivorous bears, badgers, and raccoons that live in the same climate.

When they seek to store food energy beyond what they can ingest during a big meal, carnivores do not store fat on their own bodies. Rather, they conceal dead prey in a cache, although they run the risk that it will putrefy or be stolen.[13]

To succeed at hunting, early men must have been good sprinters because, although most of a hunt is likely to be conducted at a fast walk, the closing phase often requires bursts of speed. And, to be good sprinters, they had to be lean. Women, on the other hand, were engaged in steady walking, stooping, reaching, and carrying. They would not have been penalized by a modest amount of fat. In this regard, their ecological role would have tolerated a fatter body than that of the males, even if it did not encourage fatness.

However, another distinctively female role, child care, almost certainly pushed women to acquire fat. The human child is dependent on its mother for a very long period in comparison with the young of most animals. This prolonged helplessness of the infant has presumably been part and parcel of the growth of human intelligence. It has allowed our species to develop a brain that works more by learning than instinct, and in that sense it can be seen as an advantage. But it has also been a somewhat risky business: The longer a mother takes care of her child, the more she has to lose if it dies—in not only a personal but an evolutionary sense. A woman has comparatively few opportunities to produce progeny; each infant she bears and begins to raise entails a large investment of her reproductive lifetime. In a hunting and gathering society she can expect to spend three or four years carrying her baby, foraging all the while and in most instances nursing it as well. It has been estimated that a !Kung mother carries her infant some 5,000 miles in the first four years of its life—an extraordinary expenditure of energy.[14]

Babies are easily endangered by malnutrition. Their own reserves of fat are limited, and deprivation makes them highly susceptible to infection. Thus, even a mild food shortage that might make little difference to an adult is a significant threat to the infant. Any mother who faces the prospect of carrying and nursing her child for years on end does well to accumulate fat reserves that she would not need for her own protection but that her baby might well require if there were even a slight reduction in the availability of food during her three- or four-year period of nursing.

The importance of fat as an insurance policy for reproduction was evidently sufficient to induce the evolutionary process to build it into the physiology of all women. Rose Frisch, of the Center for Population Studies at Harvard, and her colleagues have argued persuasively that menstruation cannot begin in girls until they acquire a certain, critical amount of adipose tissue. The magic number appears to be about 20 percent of body weight. As a girl approaches puberty, her body grows fatter (unlike the preadolescent boy's, which tends to become leaner). This process of adding fat almost certainly reflects a change in setpoint. The exact mechanism by which puberty is turned on is not known, but it is thought that some kind of internal clock times the necessary bodily changes. Much as a seasonal animal, such as a ground squirrel, responds to lengthening nights by getting fatter, the human female's setpoint responds to some internal signal by rising in preparation for her reproductive career. The added fat itself may serve as the trigger for menstruation to begin. There is some evidence that adipose cells can make female hormones, and Frisch and others have speculated that these estrogens, as they are called, help to initiate puberty.

Severe weight loss—of the sort seen in famines, concentration-camp victims, patients with anorexia nervosa, and exceedingly active athletes—always delays puberty or, if menstruation has already begun, interrupts the cycle. Only when fat is regained does fertility return. Indeed, postadolescent women need even more fat, 22 percent of their body weight, to recover fertility than they did to begin menstruation. The typical adult woman in the United States carries a comfortable margin; 26 to 28 percent of her body weight is adipose tissue.

Frisch proposed in 1978 that the growth of human populations might have been limited, at least in part, by the availability of food, and that this factor has been important in the course of relatively recent history. If calories were in short supply, she has argued, girls would acquire fat at a later age than usual and thus would delay the arrival of their firstborn children. Subsequent births would come at widely spaced intervals because both nursing and a limited food supply would keep a woman near or below the critical level of fat needed for ovulation to begin again. If Frisch is correct, she has demonstrated a way in which populations might be naturally regulated to prevent them from overwhelming their food resources. Female fertility would be diminished at a fat reserve of 20 percent, well above the point at which overt starvation sets in. From the woman's point of view, this is the best evolutionary "strategy": She protects herself from the risk of a wasted pregnancy or a sickly infant fated to die despite her care. She waits out a lean time and thus improves her chances for a healthy pregnancy to produce a viable infant when times are better. An incidental, but important, result is that the population as a whole benefits by not growing so fast as to swamp its resources.[15]

It is obvious that women would have benefited individually from delaying reproduction until they were fat enough to maximize their chances of success. But the leanness of males is a little harder to explain. If food was shared, and if women supplied most of the calories, as !Kung women do today, it seems unlikely that a poor hunter would simply have starved to death. If nothing else, he could have joined or at least imitated the women and survived by gathering his food. So it is unlikely indeed that absolute survival of the human species, or even of the male half, ever depended on the hunting prowess of men, at least not in the equatorial climates where humankind originated.

But mere survival is not the only requirement for evolution; reproduction must also take place. If a poor hunter were kept from breeding, or if good hunters had preferential access to women, then the successful hunter's physique would have been passed on to his male descendants, even though, within any single generation, the nonhunters lived full and comfortable lives. Even if natural selection were fully tolerant of male gatherers, women (or their families) might have preferred hunters and reserved the right of reproduction to them. The choice of sexual partner could easily have been based on some proven record of hunting skill; it could also have been influenced by a physical appearance connoting a talent for the hunt—leanness and obvious muscularity, for example. To some degree, the reverse consideration could have affected women: If those with a certain promising amount of fat were able to make favorable alliances, they would have been the ones most likely to leave many thriving offspring.

In a sense, then, fat or its absence in human beings can be regarded as a form of display, like a peacock's tail or a lion's mane. Because we humans mostly lack hair, one of our most conspicuous features is the fat we carry under our skin—rather than fur or feathers, which other animals use for display. For several million years our ancestors all lived in a climate that permitted them to wear little clothing. The contours of fat deposited under the skin were likely to have been an altogether conspicuous physical feature of these people.

In modern humans one of the most obvious aspects of adolescence is a rearrangement of subcutaneous fat that emphasizes differences between the sexes—a phenomenon that has virtually no precedent among the other primates. Human babies are born with a fairly even layer of fat under the skin. As they get older, this baby fat, as it is aptly named, remains evenly distributed but diminishes in thickness. Young children may be quite lean in appearance, but much of the smoothness and *childishness* of their skin is due to the fat they retain. At adolescence, both sexes undergo a striking change. Boys begin to lose the fat that has covered the muscles of their arms and legs, as well as any that has remained around the waist and flanks. Thus, the contours of their muscles become visible. Typically, what fat remains on the adolescent boy's body is located high on his trunk and along the outer contours of his shoulders, where it emphasizes the musculature. Thus, the relatively small amounts of subcutaneous fat remaining on a lean adolescent boy help him to "cheat" in a visual sense—to look more muscular than he really is—much as a ruff of feathers or fur helps the male of another species to look bigger and more ferocious than he otherwise would.[16]

The changes in the male's body, though obvious, are subtle in comparison with the changes in the distribution of fat on an adolescent girl. Not only does the proportion of fat on her body increase, but it is stored in specific conspicuous locations— notably the breasts, several fat pads at the hips, on the thighs, and even at the ankle, where males generally carry no fat. This patterning of fat, which we take for granted, cannot be explained as a biological necessity. Although the fat confers a reproductive advantage on human females, there is no particular *physiological* reason for its being distributed as it is. Even breasts, which are made prominent by fat and not by the milk-producing glands, could function perfectly well if the fat were located elsewhere. Here again, the pattern of fat distribution appears to be a form of reproductive advertising—a way of saying, "I am healthy and well-nourished and able to nurse children," even as the male's prominent muscles convey a promise of hunting prowess.

There is no need to imagine that people thought explicitly in such terms—or even that they had a theory of paternity—to argue that they systematically based sexual choices on such physical attributes. To the extent that many healthy children resulted from the choices they did make, the traits would have been preserved. Even when they conferred no other survival advantage, sexual displays would have become a kind of self-perpetuating criterion of desirability, reinforced by the taste they had created.

After the prime reproductive years, fat returns to the male body, and in the female it tends to be redistributed, making the two sexes appear more similar. That is, in both sexes, fat becomes concentrated on the stomach and at the flanks. Fattening after middle age is an almost universal feature of human development, and it is usually regarded as evidence of the gradual degeneration that leads to senescence and death. It may be, in part. But in males it may also more simply reflect a gradual reduction in physical activity, as we shall suggest in chapter 9.

The rearrangement of fat on the female body is harder to account for. One provocative idea has been advanced by Caroline Pond of the University of Pennsylvania, who has suggested that fat on the middle-aged woman still serves the purpose of display, but the message has changed. Instead of advertising her reproductive potential, the older woman may be announcing with her thickened trunk that she is someone to be reckoned with. By looking more "formidable," as Pond puts it, she is warning others who might threaten her children that she is ready and able to protect them. Females of certain animal species, including such diverse examples as the Barbary partridge and the reindeer, appear to do precisely this—to mimic masculine features as an aid to protecting their young.[17]

The traits described so far were most probably acquired in the millions of years during which humans and their immediate forebears lived predominantly in eastern Africa and southwestern Asia. The differences between the sexes, the responsiveness to diet and exercise—these characteristics would have evolved during the leisurely dawn of human existence. Then, about forty thousand years ago, the direct ancestors of all living people began an explosive outward migration. Earlier emigrations from the same region had carried human beings of a somewhat different type into Europe, southern Africa, Indonesia, and China, among other places, but these pioneers appear not to have survived. They were either displaced or absorbed by the men and women who left the eastern Mediterranean in a wave that recolonized Europe and Asia and then, perhaps twenty thousand years ago, entered the Americas.

At the beginning of these great migrations people were probably quite homogeneous; they shared a common pool of physical and biochemical traits, some of which can be inferred from living populations. But their new habitats placed varied demands on them, with the result that they began to diverge from the ancestral type. Although some genes may have been acquired by interbreeding with the indigenous populations remaining from the preceding migrations, many of the distinctive "racial" traits we now see have emerged as adaptations to the vastly dissimilar environments that people have entered.[18]

The legacy of our species' great centrifugal movement is the wide variation of skin colors, facial features, hair color and texture, and stature—as well as myriad invisible traits that biochemists detect. The mechanism controlling the setpoint for body fat has also been affected by this great diaspora.

There are two principal ways in which the long human migrations have created the typical divergence of human groups. First, when a small band of colonizers broke away from its ancestral home and moved a good distance away—for example, across a mountain range or over a long sea route—it was unlikely to have carried a full representation of the genes in its parent stock. Sheer luck of the draw would have given the emigrants a distribution of genes differing from that in the whole population from which they departed. Second, as the wanderers moved into their new homes and became established, they adapted to the new environment. Part of that adaptation was undoubtedly genetic, although cultural innovations were also a major means of accommodating to each new home. In a thousand generations or so, fugitives from the eastern

Mediterranean, partly by accident and partly under pressure of circumstances, became the types that we now know—people adapted to life in habitats as diverse as the Australian desert and the sub-Arctic tundra.

It was not until the past seven hundred years or so that a new wave of voyages, crusades, conquests, and colonizations revealed to humanity how diverse it had become. In the process, a major reshuffling of the genetic cards began, and it is still under way. In the face of all the dazzling variety of human types, the belief that one of them is the single, perfect ideal has persisted with incredible tenacity. Even though it is now out of fashion in most circles to say that one particular skin color is the "proper" one and all others are inferior, few people hesitate to identify bodies as "too fat" or, less commonly, "too thin."

Human dispersion into a variety of environments has led to some variation both in the amount of fat that is customarily carried and in the way it is distributed on the body, but exactly what forces have been responsible is far from clear. One of the most venerable and popular, although least plausible, hypotheses is that fat serves human beings in place of fur as an adaptation to cold. According to this climate-control hypothesis, people who live near the poles are better equipped to survive low temperatures if they are short, with short arms and legs, and nicely insulated with a layer of fat. By contrast, those living near the equator handle the torrid climate by becoming elongated and exceedingly lean.[19]

This theory is shaky indeed, and it requires some very selective attention to the evidence. It is true, as nineteenth-century biologists observed, that when a single animal species is widely distributed over the earth's surface it tends to be stocky in cold climates and somewhat more gangly in warm ones. By some accounts, the same is true of *Homo sapiens*; anthropologists have prepared lists of the body measurements of various peoples and found that they conform to the general rule. Favorite examples are the Nilotics of the Sudan, who are tall and breathtakingly slender, and the Eskimos, who are relatively short and stocky in build—and, in the picture books, look quite chubby. (Of course, the Nilotics are all but naked in their pictures, whereas Eskimos are always bundled into heavy furs.)

The generalizations about animal form probably do apply in an approximate way to human body build, but not to fatness. Although the Nilotics are exceedingly slender, other African peoples in similarly hot environments are not. Some, in particular the women, may become quite fat. And Eskimos, though stocky, are not especially plump; they carry no more subcutaneous fat than do Caucasians living in Toronto.[20]

Clothing, a cultural adaptation, has undoubtedly been far more important for insulating people against the cold than fat ever has, if only because adipose tissue is primarily stored energy and therefore unreliable as insulation. If the weather became cold and food scarce at the same time—a likely coincidence—fat would have to be withdrawn and metabolized for food energy. As it happens, the subcutaneous layer of fat is the first to be removed. We suspect that climate has had only a minor influence on setpoint, except as it has affected the constancy of the food supply.[21]

The process of migration itself may have led, in some instances, to changes in a people's average setpoint. The Polynesians, it has been suggested, are one such group. These island people fatten easily, either with age or in response to a change of dietary composition and activity patterns. According to one tentative hypothesis, the ancestral Polynesians, who made canoe voyages across thousands of miles of uncharted waters to settle pristine archipelagoes, may have suffered fairly severe food shortages until they finally established themselves in their new territory. Perhaps the survivors were either those who began with a reserve of fat or were able to shift their metabolism to an efficient mode. In effect, they would have passed through the eye of an evolutionary needle. Certainly the Polynesians, with their inclination to get fat, are markedly different from their presumptive ancestors, the peoples of eastern Micronesia or Melanesia, who are consistently quite lean. The idea that evolution could act so rapidly—presumably within a generation—at first seems implausible, but recent observations of a population of Darwin's finches on Daphne Major, an island in the Galápagos, suggests that significant evolutionary change can result from a single, brief episode of severe deprivation.[22]

By the time European explorers encountered the Polynesians, late in the eighteenth century, the islanders' colonizing voyages were long past. Descendants of the canoe-borne explorers had settled into a variety of stable societies and were hardly malnourished. More than one early account of the Maoris of New Zealand, for example, expresses disgust over the items in their diet, which consisted of a fern root as the staple and occasionally the flesh of dogs or enemies killed in war, as the writers reported it. But the native New Zealanders were, admittedly, the picture of health. William Anderson, a surgeon's mate on Captain Cook's second voyage to the Pacific (1771–1773) noted, "The natives do not exceed the common stature of Europeans . . . few that I have seen are corpulent." But even then a few Maoris were fat, and the modern Maoris have proved highly susceptible to the fattening influence of modern diets. There is no indication that the gathering economy of the islanders was unstable at the time of contact with Europeans; it may thus be that the experience of deprivation was confined to the voyages or the earliest period of settlement.[23]

As the great era of migration was coming to its close some twelve to fifteen thousand years ago, another revolutionary change in human existence was beginning: the invention and spread of agriculture. The shift from gathering to gardening or farming had staggering consequences for human history, of course, but it is of interest here as the most important cause of the human species' ability to get fat. Not because it produced abundance, however; quite the reverse. The invention of agriculture ushered in an epoch of recurrent famine and chronically compromised nutrition.

As we observed earlier in this chapter, the hunting and gathering lifestyle requires relatively little effort, often yields a highly varied diet, and at least in tropical climates is reliable the year around. Farming may require twice the effort that gathering does to yield the same caloric return; since the typical farming economy produces only a few crops, nutritional variety can be severely limited; crops are vulnerable to drought, frost, disease, pests, and mismanagement of the soil. Further, agriculture lends itself to taxation, exploitation, and tyranny.[24]

Indeed, farming looks like such a poor alternative to gathering that it is now rather difficult to see how the practice came into being in the first place. Why would the first farmers, if they were sane, labor to cultivate a garden while their gathering neighbors were still able to make a comfortable living? One plausible theory is that gardening began in a zone intermediate between shore communities of fisherfolk and an interior region inhabited by gatherers and hunters. Caught between the two economies, the people living at the margin of both found that they could keep their foothold by raising some of their own food. This activity most probably began simply enough as the act of harvesting food from the tangle of growth covering rubbish heaps.[25]

Once farming began, however, it persisted. In good years, which might come in sequence for a generation, gardening or farming could produce many calories from a relatively small plot of ground. Thus, populations could become quite dense, and once they reached a certain number of inhabitants per square mile, it would have been impossible for individuals to return to the gathering way of life.

Agriculture was capable of sustaining very rapid population growth—and it did, over and over again. But inevitably a crisis would arise, followed by famine for a matter of months or, at worst, years. Population crashed at such times, only to resume growth as harvests improved. Thus, the number of people on earth increased very slowly after the agricultural revolution. The regular boom-and-bust cycle persisted in western Europe until 1740; thereafter, improvements in trade networks and innovations in technology (known as the "new husbandry") created a steady food supply. But until that came about, nearly every generation experienced at least one, and often several, bad years. Thus, virtually all agricultural peoples have been subjected to repeated selection favoring those with the capacity to grow fat, and probably this circumstance more than any other has made us a fat species in comparison with other primates.[26]

Starvation has not been a uniform experience, of course. In some regions and among some classes of people, prolonged hunger has been rare. We would expect such people to be among the world's leaner groups. In any case, the converse relationship also appears to hold: The tendency to extreme obesity in some groups seems to reflect a history of even greater hardship than was the norm for agricultural peoples. The Pima Indians of southern Arizona are one of the best known and most thoroughly studied examples. The Pimas and their forebears have lived on the banks of the Gila River for about two thousand years. Relying on a sophisticated irrigation system, they have managed throughout much of their history to produce an adequate diet of corn and beans from this arid and unforgiving land. But periods of drought taxed their resources and stamina to the limit.[27]

In recent decades the Pima have abandoned their traditional ways—in part because water has been diverted upstream to meet the demands of white farmers. On receiving a stable supply of calories in the form of relatively rich foods, the Pima have become fat, even while eating a modest diet by usual American standards. Half have also become diabetic by the age of thirty-five. The Pimas present a classic example of what geneticist James V. Neel, of the University of Michigan, has termed a "thrifty" metabolism "rendered detrimental by progress." Having lived for so many generations at the edge of starvation—and forced to work hard in the best of times for an adequate but austere diet—they evolved a metabolic means of using calories efficiently. If starved, a Pima would long outlive the average American, but the era of famines is, at least temporarily, behind us, and the thrifty metabolism has become calorie-wise but pound-foolish, as it were.[28]

The rise of agriculture, despite its drawbacks, made possible high population densities, which led to cities, and thus to civilization. But in tandem with increasing density and a larger network of trading populations came a new scourge: epidemic disease. Hunters and gatherers typically suffer infestation with parasites and other chronic illnesses, which continuously drain their energy supply but may still be endured without great debility. Yet, because their contact with other people is relatively infrequent, bands of hunter-gatherers are protected from exposure to epidemics. To flourish, an epidemic disease usually requires a large pool of regularly communicating people, among whom the disease organism can always find new, susceptible individuals to infect. Otherwise, the disease would simply die out for lack of a host.

Within a few thousand years after farming began, agricultural societies became dense enough, and trade routes extensive enough to maintain recurrent waves of disease. Certainly cities, the densest aggregations of people, were so thick with disease that until very recently their populations were not self-sustaining. Urban populations depended for their existence on an influx of healthy new citizens from the countryside.[29]

In many ways, an epidemic can be regarded as a form of famine, and recurrent plagues have probably been as important a pressure favoring fatness as have food shortages. Fighting a disease requires extra energy at a time when the ability to obtain, eat, or digest food is impaired. The net effect is a severe drain on energy reserves. As recently as this century, thin people have suffered disproportionately from infectious disease. On the other side of the coin, improvements in the availability and quality of food in the last century began to reduce the severity of infection long before specific treatments were discovered.

It is little wonder, then, that slender bodies were more disparaged than admired in times past. In particular, the image of a thin woman was often associated with deprivation and disease. Even Lord Byron, who was himself one of the first crash dieters, preferred women of full figure. According to his buxom friend, Lady Blessington, "Talking of thin women, he said, that if they were young and pretty, they reminded him of dried butterflies; but if neither, of spiders, whose nets should never catch him were he a fly, as they had nothing tempting." The year was 1823 when Byron dismissed such women with the imagery of death and desiccation.[30] Just a hundred years later, no fashionable woman would think it possible to be either "too rich or too thin."

7

THE CENTURY OF
SVELTE

IN 1979, Bloomingdale's—a department store that, in its way, defines the taste of America's upper-middle class—advertised its summer line of women's clothing: "Bean lean, slender as the night, narrow as an arrow, pencil thin, get the point?" The fashions, and the bodies they enclosed, were illustrated with sketches, perhaps because not even a model could achieve the designers' ectoplasmic ideal. Certainly the average American woman, even the average upscale American woman, could only look at the drawings and eat her heart out—she had better not eat anything else.[1]

Her husband, meantime, might have browsed through the pages of *Playboy*—because it was the only magazine in the barber shop, or because he liked to read the interviews—and contemplated photographs of women who set a rather different physical standard. Although the centerfold is hardly a typical woman, it does show a woman with a three-dimensional body, and an ample supply of subcutaneous fat, judiciously distributed—so much so that she would have a bleak future modeling for *Vogue*. As one *Penthouse* model said, "I've stood around while some skinny bit who thought she was It strutted her stuff in front of the camera. It's nice to find myself the focus of attention for a change."[2]

Contemporary women have the unhappy opportunity to compare themselves with two distinct and incompatible "ideals" as portrayed in the two types of periodical devoted to the female body: women's fashion and men's skin magazines. Given these divergent tastes, a woman might be thought happiest if she had two bodies—one of them dressed, public, and stylish; the other unclothed, semiprivate, and unconditionally sexy. The fashionably clothed body is thin-to-bony; its contours offer minimal competition to the fall and drape of the fabrics that cover it. High-fashion garments only imply the presence of breasts and intimate a tiny, rounded bottom that forms a single unbroken curve from the base of the spine to the top of a minimal thigh. By contrast, nothing is implicit about the breasts of a "bunny" body; in any competition with whatever covers them, they win the viewer's attention. Likewise, hips and thighs, though supernaturally smooth and firm, *fill* the pants or skirt they wear. The contrasting body types converge in only two significant aspects: Both are narrow-waisted with board-flat abdomens, and both are distinctly long-legged.

The *Vogue* body is a product of the twentieth century. The *Playboy* body, on the other hand, is a modern, streamlined version of an older ideal. Actually, it isn't all that old: The basic design—prominent breasts and hips with a relatively low, narrow waist—emerged just a little over 300 years ago. Earlier still, sex appeal had had a different outline; a woman's chief erotic attribute was her full, swelling abdomen, above which her breasts were pleasing, but not necessarily prominent, satellites.

The human frame limits the range of forms we can imagine

as beautiful. But it allows considerable latitude, and a great deal of change has occurred just within the last 600 years. In each succeeding era, an ideal has evolved that suits the temper and needs of its time. One medium for defining the image of perfection is the visual arts, provided they employ certain "realistic" conventions—as did Western painting and sculpture from the late Middle Ages until around 1900. Human figures in this artistic tradition are ostensibly imitations of real bodies, but they are also held forth as images of perfection. Thus, art, by imitating life, in fact sets a standard for the living. The striking variety of ideals in the artistic tradition of the West is proof enough that there is no natural standard of physical beauty—a point that Kenneth Clark makes in his now classic study, *The Nude*. [3]

Another way to define the ideal is through clothing, as Anne Hollander has so persuasively argued in her book *Seeing Through Clothes*. In many ways, the Western nude has been conceived as the body that best fits the clothing of her time; her nude body is a reminder of what she would look like if she were dressed. [4] (The *Vogue-Playboy* dichotomy appears to be a partial exception to this rule.)

But why do body styles change? And why is preternatural thinness so prized in our time, after centuries in which art glorified female forms that are simply fat by current standards?

Men's bodies have been idealized and distorted in various ways by art and fashion, but far less so than women's, and body fat has played a small role in the masculine image. Most of what we know about the ideals of the past has been filtered to us through the vision of male artists. What men admire in the bodies of other men has been a muscularity that ranges from slight and lithe to brutish—but that almost always conveys a potential for movement and action, whether erotic or competitive. [5] Women's bodies have been a screen onto which different values have been projected by men: receptive sexiness and the promise of fecundity, in the main. For hundreds of years, these attributes were manifested in the fleshiness of the woman's figure.

Clothing has also expressed these ideals, and played out their ramifications. In fact clothes have to a large degree established the values that artists have portrayed. Yet we should not easily assume that clothing styles have been determined entirely by masculine tastes and desires. If we could "read" clothing as we read written or pictorial material, we might find a dialogue between men and women, a discourse on the roles of sex and the sexes. However, until the beginning of this century, the dominant interest being served was the man's. A fashionable woman's clothing, for example, served to indicate that she was or could be of value to her man, and it advertised his status.

Not long after 1900, women's fashions rather suddenly began to express a new ideology: that a woman's body could serve her own purposes, independent of any man's requirement. Women have claimed a right to move as actively as men, without restraining garments, and to pursue their own sexual destiny, freed from the inevitability of pregnancy. The central expression of the new, liberated woman was her thin body, which came to symbolize athleticism, nonreproductive sexuality, and a kind of androgynous independence. Almost immediately, however, this symbol of liberation itself became oppressive. As it was co-opted by fashion, the "bean-lean" body became, arbitrarily, a mark of status, sexual competitiveness, and self-mastery. By now, it is at least as oppressive to the majority of women, who are not naturally skinny, as were the extremes of Renaissance or Victorian high style.

In all, Western taste has idealized three types of woman since about 1400. The first was tummy-centered and often quite fat; we call her the *reproductive* figure. Somewhere around 1650— certainly by 1700—taste changed pretty much throughout Europe. The new ideal was all bosom and bottom; her narrow waist only emphasized these ample endowments. Although slender women of this outline, which we call the *maternal*, were sometimes portrayed on canvas, the overwhelming majority were at least plump by any standard. Then, rather rapidly between 1910 and 1920, the full-blown figure lost its place in the sensual aesthetic mainly of Anglo-American culture. The new woman was lean, with no remnant of the promising, reproductive tummy and with minimal breasts and buttocks. This slender, at times almost tubular, form has become emblematic of the sexual *free agent,* the third idealized type. Also in this era, the taste of men and women has diverged, with men's preference clinging somewhat to the unstylish maternal figure.

In this succession of types, we believe Western sexual symbolism has superimposed changing values on biological reality. For millennia, fatness not only represented fertility, it also contributed in fact to a woman's reproductive success. Since about 1910, limitation of fertility has become increasingly important to men and women, and so has sexual expression. The cultural conflicts engendered by these two trends have been expressed in a cultural obsession with weight control—even as birth control has made it technically easy for a woman to have sex but not babies.

In European art, open preoccupation with the female figure reappeared late in the fourteenth century after a hiatus of nearly a thousand years. From roughly the fourth to the fourteenth centuries, the weight of official Christian doctrine disparaged the flesh and discouraged artistic representations of sexually appealing women. Celibacy was held up as the holy, highest goal; marriage was an acceptable, but less worthy, alternative. Sex certainly did not disappear in that epoch, and we can assume that people had criteria of physical attractiveness in mind when they contemplated making love. But we also suspect that physical appearance was a far less erotic issue than it now is. To begin with, people probably saw few images of any kind, let alone the kind of purportedly realistic representations that create erotic standards. Church art was stylized to convey a spiritual message; when it depicted naked bodies, they were in torment more often than not.

In real life, the range of erotic opportunities must have been exceedingly limited. Because the largest towns rarely exceeded a population of 20,000, most people lived in less dense aggregations. Considerations of age and rank further restricted social interaction, so most people's sexual partners must have been limited to a small subset of their neighbors. Marriages in this society were concluded for the sake of property and prestige, not only among those of high status who set the standards of taste and fantasy, but also quite probably among the serfs. Near total lack of privacy must have severely limited opportunities for sexual play, and in any case people probably wore a good deal of clothing during sex. In these circumstances, we can speculate, sexual intercourse lacked much of the aesthetic mystique it has since acquired in Western culture, although the erotic imagination did produce some great works of art.[6]

Even so, out of the late Middle Ages there emerges from the Gothic north a distinctive ideal of feminine beauty. First portrayed as a nude Eve, she is a woman whose abdomen is prominent and gracefully swelling, though she is not otherwise fat. Her breasts are high and small, her flanks comparatively slender. Clothing styles of the thirteenth century (and well into the seventeenth) did everything they could to emphasize the woman's stomach, sometimes covering it with masses of gathered fabric; sometimes revealing it with long, tight bodices that flattened the bosom to lengthen the abdominal expanse; sometimes supplying a kind of false front, the stomacher, as a promise of the sensual reality beneath it. The sexual appeal of this prominent tummy was manifestly its association with pregnancy.

Their emphasis on fertility makes these paintings look strange to modern eyes. In discussing one of the very first nude images of this type—a fifteenth-century painting of Eve by Hugo van der Goes—Kenneth Clark confesses his disinclination to see the figure as glamorous: "The docile mother of our race, homekeeping, childbearing, flatfooted with much serving, has seldom been depicted with so little attempt to modify the humble usefulness of her body." But he then allows that "these unathletic proportions, which are so far from our own idea of grace and desirable beauty," in fact were compellingly erotic in their own time. Writing more recently, Anne Hollander denies that the large, rounded stomachs of the Gothic Eves could have symbolized pregnancy; in her view, the abdomen "connoted elegance rather than fruitfulness." She claims it was a reminder, in the shape of a nude body, that the real woman idealized as Eve would customarily appear "in sumptuous clothing," with her skirts richly gathered at the waist.[7]

Both of these eminent art historians seem to betray a modern bias that fecundity lacks elegance. Yet, throughout the Middle Ages, the ability to bear children was the single most important capacity of a high-born woman. Important marriages were contracted virtually sight unseen, and often before the parties were old enough to have refined erotic tastes. The criterion of marital success was production of an heir. Miscarriage and infant mortality were phenomenally frequent, such that repeated pregnancy was the only promise of a secure posterity. On balance, pregnancy would seem to have been more desired than feared, difficult as this may be for sexually active moderns to imagine. Premarital pregnancy was not seen as a disgrace; bastardy, although potentially embarrassing, was not always a serious disability; and the prevailing morality effectively permitted discreet infanticide when it was inconvenient to keep a child.

The elegant nudes of the fifteenth and sixteenth centuries—and their clothed counterparts—*look* pregnant, even when they are portrayed in circumstances that make real pregnancy inappropriate. For example, Eve before the Fall could hardly be depicted as pregnant. And yet in the early images (the *Hours* of the Duc de Berry, van Eyck's and van der Goes's panels), Eve not only has a prominent abdomen swelling up from below, her navel is prominent, like a pregnant woman's, and it is displaced away from the upper body as if by the growth of a fetus. Moreover, a dark line sometimes appears to run from the navel toward the pubic area of these figures—a feature resembling the typical "linea nigra" of pregnancy. The painters have treated Eve's stomach as a symbol, it would seem, of the promise of fertility. No doubt the cut of clothing had a similar purpose, for stylish dresses were indistinguishable from maternity garments. Because of these conventions, when an artist wanted to portray a pregnant woman, he could not rely on a large stomach, as Hollander points out. Certain clues, such as an "otherwise unwarranted disarrangement of clothing" or a hand placed on the belly, were used.[8]

The desirable female who emerged from the medieval cocoon continued to have a prominent stomach for hundreds of years. As Hollander puts it: "In the erotic imagination of Europe, it was apparently impossible until the late seventeenth century for a woman to have too big a belly. This has decidedly not been true since then; breasts and buttocks have become (and remained) far more acutely erotic than bellies." All the beautiful women of Renaissance painting are fat by modern standards. The bellies cease to look as explicitly pregnant—perhaps under the influence of the late Classical models' being rediscovered— but they continue to be *big*. Not only are stomachs prominent, they are supported by enormous buttocks and thighs. Their breasts, in proportion, are often quite modest.[9]

When this simple fact is pointed out today, the listener is likely to lean back, nod, and say, "Ah yes, Rubens." But Peter Paul Rubens (1577–1640) did not paint fatter women than those his contemporaries painted; he merely made their fleshiness more difficult to ignore. Looking at the paintings of other artists, modern viewers can follow a train of thought that automatically slenderizes their women: "This is a beautiful painting, therefore this woman is beautiful, therefore she must be thinner than she looks." Rubens makes this impossible; he painted female figures with a strikingly puckered, dimpled and rosy skin that serves to call our attention to their bulk. Hollander explains that Rubens's attitude toward skin reflected his attitude toward fabrics and clothing: "Nameless anatomical bubbles and unidentifiable waves agitated the formerly quiescent adipose tissue under the mobile hides of nymphs and goddesses as they simultaneously agitated the satin sleeves and skirts of the newly fashionable free-flowing clothes."[10]

In the decades around 1600, the female belly achieved the ultimate in grandeur, no matter who the painter was. The general rejoicing in opulence epitomized by these fleshy women was undoubtedly part of an exaggerated symbolism, expressing delight in the return to earthly pleasures after long centuries during which they were condemned by ideology, albeit probably enjoyed by anyone who had the opportunity, even in the darkest times. However, fat women also offered certain practical advantages to the men who married them. They were likely to be healthy and to resist infection. And, as before, they promised fertility.

Well into the seventeenth century, women still had very little chance of raising large numbers of children. Except among the great aristocrats, women married in their mid-twenties—at least in England—and they entered menopause around their fortieth year. Either the wife or her husband was likely to die young, thus reducing even further the likelihood of leaving offspring. Any degree of malnutrition or illness simply tightened the limitations while causing more wasted pregnancies. An ample supply of body fat was certainly the best visible insurance against reproductive calamity, and it hardly seems surprising that sexually desirable women were dressed to look fat and artists painted them as fat.[11]

The rich association of erotic pleasure, fatness, and pregnancy is alien to a generation that has grown up dreading the missed period. But in the past the prospect of making babies was far from an erotic turn-off. Consider the crowds of pudgy baby boys that populate paintings from 1400 to around 1800. Of course there are innumerable representations of the Christ child, the baby St. John, and various cherubs in religious art, but a dominant element in explicitly pagan, erotic painting is the little cupid or Eros, gamboling somewhere in the background or slyly playing the part of the man he will become—toying with the armor of a sleeping Mars or fondling Venus's body with undisguisedly sexual gestures.

As these artistic conventions were being developed, explored, and taken to their limits, the European outlook on sex and procreation began a radical change. First came a gradual shift in the ideology of marriage, and then an increasing warmth toward children. In altering the status and role of women, these developments transformed the nature of feminine beauty.

The ideal marriage of the high Middle Ages had been an alliance between two clans. Under this arrangement, a woman was the representative of her own extended family. Backed up by her relatives, and retaining rights to her own property, the high-born woman could have considerable private clout, although she lacked any legal standing. Then, beginning as early as 1100, very gradually, this situation had begun to change, largely as a result of the waning influence of noble families— clans—in European politics.[12]

By the year 1500, marriage was becoming less an alliance of two clans than a union of two individuals—essentially a nuclear family in which the woman became a part of her husband's personal property. The process of change, and the conflicts it created, sprawled over centuries, with no sharp break between the end of one system and the beginning of another.[13] (Thus, in the decades around 1600, Shakespeare could write about both patterns of marriage with great feeling. In *Romeo and Juliet* he presents the tragedy of two youngsters who are driven by misguided erotic passion to flout the old order of allegiance to kin and clan. In *The Taming of the Shrew* he presents a comedy of the new order: A woman of mature judgment submits to her husband's absolute authority because she sees that the only alternative is chaos.)

The rise of the nuclear family—and a host of associated changes in mores—put new pressure on women. They not only had to be fertile, they did well to be pleasing in body and personality besides. Whereas in earlier times the married woman's body was primarily an *instrument* to produce heirs, thereafter it became more a *commodity* of value in itself, existing to give her master pleasure as well as to provide him with children. (We are referring here to the upper classes, who expressed their fantasies and commissioned the art that served fantasy.) Men could, of course, turn elsewhere for gratification, but that was all the more reason for an otherwise powerless wife to protect her interests by maintaining her appeal.

In this same period, the late 1500s, Protestant theology began to stress the mutual comfort that husband and wife should give each other in marriage, whereas earlier the primary justification for marriage had been reproduction (and still is, in the formal Catholic view). Partly for this reason, and largely, no doubt, because living in a nuclear family is more pleasant when the partners are on reasonably good terms, after about 1600 affection and sexual gratification were seen as an ever more important part of the good marriage. These changes in the nature of the marriage relationship may themselves have contributed to the growth of erotic art, in which woman is represented as sexually appealing, as a luxurious object—and, occasionally, as an individual much beloved by the painter.

As the bond of affection between man and woman came to be emphasized, attitudes toward pregnancy and children also shifted. By 1600, in England and parts of Europe, excessive fertility in marriage was undesirable. Solutions of herbs and oils to be taken orally, to be used as douches, or to be prepared as genital baths were widely recommended as antiaphrodisiacs, contraceptives, or abortifacients. Whereas in the Middle Ages, illegitimacy, abortion, and infanticide had been lamented as the legacy of ungovernable and illicit lust, the plight of excessively fertile women was sympathetically characterized in a French medical work translated in 1574: "For they haue scant a monethes rest in a whole yeere, but that they are continually ouercome wyth sorow and feare. . . ." Beginning around 1650, there is clear evidence that upper-class families were limiting the number of children they produced—presumably not by using "radish root, agarick, and saram boiled in barley water to be taken when cool," but rather through coitus interruptus, abstention, or noncoital sex.[14]

Fertility was beginning to be perceived as a burden, perhaps for several reasons. It is possible, owing to improvements in the food supply and a reduction in disease, that women were having more frequent pregnancies than before. But if this was so, the effect was almost certainly small. Infant mortality may have been declining also, but neglect of children—some of it perhaps intentional—was still so common that the scant statistical evidence from the 1600s shows little improvement. Even in 1622, as the historian Philippe Ariès relates, a woman observing the birth of her neighbor's sixth child could offer the comforting thought: "Before they are old enough to bother you, you will have lost half of them, or perhaps all of them." The preceding centuries of exceedingly high infant mortality had ingrained this "idea of necessary wastage," as Ariès terms it, which in turn, no doubt, allowed parents to engage in a certain amount of *unnecessary* wastage. A profound consequence of these high rates of infant and juvenile mortality was the emotional isolation and chill that prevailed within families. Parents and children seem not to have formed the kind of intimate, affectionate, and very special relationships that have become the norm in the past 250 years or so. Childhood memories were quite unlikely to include images of a warm, nurturing, protective mother.[15]

By 1700, the casual attitude toward babies—which had allowed parents to abandon them, if only to a wet-nurse, or neglect them if they were unwanted, and which had also protected parents from repeated mourning—was giving way to tenderness. Children were "discovered" and parent-child affections markedly intensified. This change most probably began in the middle and upper-middle classes, rather than among the highest aristocracy or the poor. As a result of this warming emotional climate, a generation of articulate men was born, some of them artists, who had fond, not merely formal, memories of their mothers—and these memories could be worked into their erotic imagination.

This extraordinary alteration in family relationships and in the emotional experience of people growing up in the seventeenth century appears to have resulted in a radical revision of the ideal woman's body. The difference is visible in the portrayal of two women painted within a few years of each other in the 1650s. Rembrandt's "Bathsheba" is in many ways the culmination of the tummy-centered tradition: Her abdomen and hips are full and fleshy, as if she has already carried several pregnancies; her breasts are high, widely separated, and modest in proportion to her ample body. Velázquez's "Rokeby Venus" is envisioned according to an altogether different ideal—the one that was coming into style. The goddess, facing away from the viewer, reclines on a simple bed and regards her own face in a mirror, which is held by a fetching boy whose features are individualized and very real, despite an improbable wing sprouting from his shoulder blade. The little Eros looks at his mother with manifest affection. What he sees is a woman with a narrow waist and broad, tapered hips. We can guess that her breasts, which are hidden from our view but not from his, are full and sensual.[16]

Henceforth, the female belly as the emblem of pure fertility was to be systematically minimized, both in art and in clothing styles. Instead, the breasts and lap, attributes of nurturing, became the dominant parts of the woman's body. The *fertile* figure gave way to the *maternal*. A conspicuous bosom and buttocks, emphasized by a slender-to-tiny waist, became the erotic ideal that has lasted into this century—and is still preserved in the pages of *Playboy, Penthouse,* and *Hustler.* Obviously, this change in taste did not represent out-and-out abhorrence of fertility. Until early in this century, sterility was an erotic disadvantage for a woman of high status—even when a pregnancy was not desired—and sex without the possibility of procreation was thought to be altogether perverted. One artistic indication of this view is the fact that babies—boys—remained a fixture in erotic painting until the early nineteenth century.

In any case, fertile or maternal, a woman still needed plenty of fat to be considered beautiful, as well as to fulfill her reproductive function. Although fashions changed (with increasing frequency) from 1700 on, and waists were often pinched in, the essential fatness of the woman's body was preserved and often emphasized. In this regard, it is important to remember that recurrent famines, many severe, ravaged Europe in cycles until around 1740. Cultivating a slender body was simply not advisable for anyone whose food supply might be reduced for a year or so, least of all for a woman, who had to meet the nutritional demands of pregnancy and lactation.[17]

The maternal ideal emerged at a time when sexual attractiveness was becoming more important, and more problematic, than ever before. Young people, at least those of the propertied classes, were beginning to choose their own mates rather than submit to the choice of their parents. Sexual attraction was, naturally enough, a component of the decision, though not necessarily the main one. At the same time, however, there were new pressures to avoid unwanted pregnancy—and, thus, to control sexual desires. At their most doctrinaire, the Puritans attempted to impose strict, mechanical rules to control the conflicts that these social changes created. By the end of the seventeenth century, they had failed, and the great era of sexual experimentation began in earnest. Sex became an object of attention, a pursuit, a matter of technique and taste, of prescription, proscription, regulation, and supervision in a way that it had not been before. From being a natural force, which people had to contend with or contain lest it get them into trouble, sex became something to be manipulated and explored for its own sake—sometimes hedonistically, sometimes morally, sometimes medically, sometimes artistically.[18]

Representations of women in painting change dramatically in this period. The maternal outline becomes predominant, and nude women are more explicitly painted for purely erotic reasons. Classical allusions, often the pretext of telling a story in which the female character happens to be wearing no clothing, tend to disappear. The woman's charms are displayed, more or less unabashedly, for their own sake. In this way "art" begins to converge with pornography, which emerged as a commercial enterprise late in the seventeenth century and reached a grand scale in England by the end of the eighteenth.[19]

Because the economic status of women had continued to deteriorate into the eighteenth century, the marriage market acquired extraordinary importance for well-born women, and *fashion*—as a way of molding and clothing a body to compete in the market—also gained in importance. The main object of style throughout much of the eighteenth century was to create an impression of enormous bosoms and bottoms. To enhance the effect, a tiny waist and poker-straight back were deemed essential. Young women were forced into tight, rigid corsets, which would compress them into the proper outline.

For the first time in recent history, women began to go on reducing diets. Before the eighteenth century it is doubtful whether Europeans, who lived with the constant threat of famine, found the notion of voluntary hunger at all appealing. But by then, the English upper class had a relatively secure food supply, and dieting was something they could contemplate without sheer terror. Because the upper and lower body could be—and were—padded to make up for whatever was missing, girls dieted to make their waists ever smaller. Nutritional deprivation, sometimes aided by purges and enemas, had another cosmetic benefit, pallor. Pale skin was an indispensable feature of the beautiful woman, and anemia from inadequate diets was one acceptable way to produce milk-white skin. A girl who survived all this would wear a wirework bodice to make her breasts look large and a cork bustle to make her buttocks look huge—contraptions that remained in vogue until the 1790s. In 1801, reminiscing on this style, an Englishman wrote: "Formerly, when the women wore strong stiff stays and cork rumps, you might as well sit with your arm round an oaken tree with the bark on, as around a lady's waist."

As an adjunct to her mammary and gluteal display, the eighteenth-century woman required a rod-straight spine. For a time, young girls were braced for hours a day with various devices that were meant to assure the growth of a perfect back. One woman recalled

. . . a frightful kind of neck-swing in which we were suspended every morning, whilst one of the teachers was lacing our stays, all which contrivances were intended and imagined to improve the figure and the air. Nothing was thought so awkward and vulgar as anything approaching to a stoop.

One overenthusiastic mother, concerned about her daughter's marital future, managed to kill her at the age of twenty. The autopsy revealed that

. . . her ribs had grown into her liver, and that her other entrails were much hurt by being crushed together with her stays, which her mother had ordered to be twitched so straight that it often brought tears into her eyes whilst the maid was dressing her.

Lawrence Stone, who cites these examples, tartly comments that the brace-, frame-, and corset-makers of the eighteenth century were "the affluent equivalents of the orthodontists of late twentieth-century America, who also cater for a real need as well as a desire for perfection in a certain area thought to be important for success in life."[20]

As the century progressed, the image of woman in upper-class England underwent a remarkable transformation. Pallor, delicacy, and languor—these were the hallmarks of a woman of high fashion. Women had always before been conceived of as vigorous, lusty creatures whose impulsive nature and sexual appetite were bound to get them into trouble unless they were contained. Men, who made it their business to contain women's sexuality, had regularly used external restraints: spies, chaperones, chastity belts, imprisonment in houses or convents, threats of physical violence. Curiously enough, when the great century of liberty arrived, the tactic began to change. Human nature, as it applied to women, had to be reconstructed: Women were to deny their physical nature and to pass themselves off as frail wisps of exquisite sensibility and passive sensuality. At the height of the Age of Enlightenment, the asexual woman was invented.[21]

It would be a mistake to interpret this creature as solely a product of the masculine imagination. By presenting herself as frail, vulnerable, and limited in her capacity for passion, the eighteenth-century woman may have protected herself from some of the dangers of sex, for sex was becoming a very scary business. Women were probably becoming more fertile after about 1700, as nutrition throughout Europe improved and the great famines, a regular feature of life for centuries, began to abate. Venereal disease was reaching epidemic proportions in this period. The economic status of women in all classes was deteriorating—thus they were all the more vulnerable to the promises and threats of men, and the burden of an illegitimate child was potentially greater than before. Increasingly, young women left home to work and were thus deprived of their parents' protection. Effective means of birth control had not come into use. Although condoms could be purchased, it was thought unseemly to employ them for contraception; men were most likely to use them "for the prevention of disease only" during intercourse with whores.[22]

Meanwhile, men were exploring the possibilities of sexuality with a fervor and versatility that had not been known since the Roman Empire. Not only did erotic art thrive in the salons and printed pornography in the bookstalls, but "personal" advertisements appeared in some newspapers, and sexual hardware of various sorts came onto the market.

Prostitution and illegitimacy were inevitable in a society that gave men so much license and women so little protection. Men were certainly aware of this situation. A literature of sexual cruelty blossomed in the eighteenth century. Samuel Richardson's *Clarissa Harlowe* (1748) and the Marquis de Sade's *Justine* (1791) are only two of the best-known novels that fantasize about the plight of virtuous women in a world of sexually liberated men. In both works, young women of unspotted, conventional virtue suffer torture and eventual death at the hands of unscrupulous seducers or rapists.

Both men and women reacted to the unstable sexual situation of the late eighteenth century, as well as to the changing views of women's natural abilities and rights. Explicit feminism was making its appearance, whether in Abigail Adams's patient and private admonition to her husband to "remember the ladies" or in Mary Wollstonecraft's more vigorous defense of women's rights, published the year after *Justine.* Men's ambivalence and anxiety in response to the change found literary expression in, among other ways, a "fatal man," as Mario Praz has called him—a mixture of swashbuckler and melancholy philosopher, of fallen angel and upstart Prometheus. The character takes several forms in the Romantic imagination, but he has two constant features: He is a rat with women and something is eating him. The fatal man always has wild, searching eyes, he is usually pale —and he is thin. The appearance of patients suffering from tuberculosis may well have provided the model, as Susan Sontag suggests in *Illness as Metaphor.* It could also have been derived, as a kind of guilty internalizing, from the image of ethereal, fashionable women that had emerged in the eighteenth century.[23]

The slender figure of the Romantic hero was also, indirectly, a reference to classical ideals. Early in the nineteenth century a new wave of interest in ancient Greece, and particularly its representation of the human body, washed over Europe. In England, the Elgin marbles, which went on display in 1807, inspired several generations of artists and writers.

Before the fourth century B.C., the Greeks had portrayed perfectly formed, athletic youths whose physiques anticipated those of today's well-rounded college athletes. Physical and spiritual perfection were fused in this ideal, which entailed a harsh edge of intolerance for the less-than-perfect. The point is emphasized in a satirical vase painting: Two muscular boys go through their workout at the athletic field while two others, one tall and skinny, the other short and chubby, idle their time in a pointless argument. Greeks of the Classic era did not portray older or imperfect bodies as belonging to happy people. (On the other hand, their contemporaries, the Etruscans, produced realistic funeral sculptures of fat men who, in the glow of maturity, regard the world with complacent smiles. In its infatuation with classical models, the nineteenth century bypassed Etruscan realism for the Greek ideal.)

The "ideal" in later, Hellenic art split into two dissimilar types: the Hercules and the Apollo, each of which enjoyed its vogue during the nineteenth century. The Hercules was a massive strongman—an emblem of physical or political power. The Apollo was somewhat boyish, slighter in build, and was often portrayed with a hint of softening, subcutaneous fat; he embodied eroticism, inwardness, or spirituality.[24]

The slighter figure predominated among the "fatal" men of Romantic poetry. For example, in 1814, Byron described his "Corsair," Conrad, as "Robust but not Herculean—to the sight/ No giant frame sets forth his common height." These tormented heroes were not ninety-pound weaklings, but their creators often were. The French writer Théophile Gautier commented on this curious literary vogue of the early nineteenth century: "When I was young, I could not have accepted as a lyrical poet anyone weighing more than ninety-nine pounds." Among the English, Keats and Shelley couldn't help being thin; they had tuberculosis. But Lord Byron was naturally chubby; he became thin—and thus an "acceptable" poet—only through a dogged program of dieting.[25]

Byron's parents were fat, his mother especially so, and, to compound his difficulty, he was born with a club foot. John Hunter, the same anatomist and surgeon who thought fat was not "animal matter," was called to consult on the deformity, but he could offer no hope of a cure. The foot limited Byron's physical activity, although he did swim (famously), and he grew fat; by age nineteen, at five feet eight and a half inches tall, he weighed 202 pounds.

At this juncture, Byron began the first of the stringent diets that he would follow for the rest of his life. For this first venture he limited himself to a "quarter of a pound of butcher's meat a day"; later it would be biscuits and soda water, or "a thin slice of bread, with tea at breakfast—a light, vegetable dinner, with a bottle or two of Seltzer water, tinged with vin de Grave, and in the evening, a cup of green tea, without milk or sugar." Byron never found his regimen easy, and took to chewing tobacco, then smoking cigars, as a way of suppressing the hunger he felt. He seems to have justified his need to be thin in part on the grounds that walking hurt his foot more when he was fat. However, by the end of his life, when he is described as unnaturally or skeletally thin, that can hardly have been the reason. He was cultivating his figure and his image by then.[26]

The Romantic figure was slender, as opposed to meaty. Descriptions emphasize that he was not musclebound, and being fat was simply out of the question. By contrast, 200 years earlier Hamlet, who might be taken as something of a forebear to the Romantic type, is casually described by his mother as "fat and scant of breath" (though thanks to the Romantic influence today, the part is virtually never cast with a chubby actor). And, in real life before about 1800, adult men seem to have been content to display some fat. Henry VIII was evidently pleased with portraits that emphasized his bulk, and 250 years later, George III seemed equally unabashed by his portly figure. Indeed, in the last decades of the eighteenth century, potbellies seem to have enjoyed a certain social and sartorial cachet. Men's waistcoats emphasized the swell of a prosperous abdomen, and outercoats flared back over the buttocks in a way that magnified them.[27]

But in Regency England, views changed. The Regency opened the era of self-made men, in several senses of the term. A man's physical appearance became one of the means by which he placed himself in society, and his appearance began to matter as much as bloodlines—perhaps more. The prince regent himself (eventually George IV) became perhaps the first ruler in modern history to suffer open taunts on account of his girth. Byron, several years into his own diet, couldn't resist the opportunity to describe the regent as he danced the waltz, at that time a novelty and a craze in England:

> Round all the confines of the [woman's] yielded waist,
> The strangest hand may wander undisplaced;
> The lady's in return may grasp as much
> As princely paunches offer to her touch.
> Pleased round the chalky floor how well they trip,
> One hand reposing on the royal hip;
> The other to the shoulder no less royal
> Ascending with affection truly loyal![28]

Byron did not claim authorship of the poem, largely because of this passage. It was published anonymously, in 1812.

Another Regency celebrity (it was the age when celebrities were invented) was George Bryan "Beau" Brummell, who virtually created the very influential concept of dandyism. Brummell made himself famous by making himself a gentleman—out of whole cloth, so to speak. Unlike Byron, he had no aristocratic antecedents whatever, and he purposely obscured his background. Brummell's sole qualification for the status of gentleman was the way he lived—primarily, in fact, the way he dressed. Cutting a perfect figure—and nastily cutting anyone who fell below his standards—Brummell established himself as a legend without ever *doing* anything. At about the time when Byron published "The Waltz," the prince regent, who had been friendly with Brummell, withdrew from the association, in preparation for ascending the throne. "The most famous of all Brummell anecdotes," as the late Ellen Moers related it, "has it that the Prince came down the street one day in company with Lord A———, and met Brummell and Lord B——— strolling in the opposite direction. The Prince stopped to chat with Lord B ———, ignoring Brummell; the Beau, who had taught a whole generation how to cut, turned to Lord A——— and inquired loudly, 'Who's your fat friend?' " Whether it happened or not, this immortal instance of lèse-majesté illustrates the way in which personal attributes were coming to overshadow even the highest rank.[29]

The Romantics and the Dandies had their heyday in the early decades of the nineteenth century. Then, both passed out of fashion, perhaps largely because they were subversive characters. And the thin, ethereal body type they made famous ceased to be a male ideal. As the century progressed, the robust, muscular, active, and manly figure—close to the Greeks' Herculean type—became the dominant Victorian ideal. It seems clear that fear of the sexuality turned loose during the preceding century, and disapproval of the self-centeredness that went with it, were major reasons for the change of taste. The terrifying impulses that had preoccupied the Romantics, on the one hand, and the ambiguous—even effeminate—sexual character of the Dandy, on the other, were both roundly rejected. Self-mastery and masculinity were pursued with an obsessive anxiety for most of the rest of the century by mainstream Victorian males.

The visible evidence that a man was not a slave to his sexual impulses was taken to be a big, muscular body. William Acton made the point perfectly explicit in his very popular book *The Functions and Disorders of the Reproductive Organs,* first published in 1857. Acton was a physician, a health educator, and something of a liberal reformer, who managed to give almost perfect expression to the official Victorian ideology about sex. In discussing the problem of masturbation, he confidently asserted, "It is not the strong athletic boy, fond of healthy exercise, who thus early shows marks of sexual desires, but your puny exotic, whose intellectual education has been fostered at the expense of his physical development." Repeatedly, Acton describes the physique of the masturbating boy: "The muscles are small, soft, and flabby; the body is generally emaciated, the adipose tissue being but feebly stored up; the complexion is . . . as a rule, pale." Again: "The pale complexion, the emaciated form, the slouching gait, the clammy palm, the glassy or leaden eye, and the averted gaze indicate the lunatic victim to this vice." With a brighter eye and somewhat firmer muscles, this could have been the Romantic man of a few decades earlier.[30]

With nothing resembling evidence, Dr. Acton was able to sell edition after edition of this nonsense to the credulous and worried public. Indeed, he was something of a Dr. Herman Tarnower of his day, and we are tempted to suggest that the diet books of our own time are very similar in character to the antimasturbation literature of the last century. The Victorians worried that excessive sexual activity—whether masturbation or intercourse—threatened physical and mental health. Having abandoned self-control, the sex addict would never regain his equilibrium; and sexual excess itself was thought to be physically weakening. Because it was still believed that more than a quart of blood was needed to manufacture each ounce of semen, the whole argument seemed to make some kind of sense, and it served to scare a lot of people. The diet doctors have managed to create a whole literature of advice that has little more justification than the Victorian attitudes toward sex—it certainly makes no better use of evidence—and it embodies much the same philosophy: If you eat too much, you'll be ugly, you won't be healthy, nobody will love you, and you'll be showing the world that you are a slave to self-indulgent passions.[31]

Muscularity was not only a way of achieving and demonstrating self-mastery, it was also a rejection of the androgyny that lurked in the figure of both Dandy and Romantic. It served further to identify another sort of self-made man—one more in keeping with late Victorian tastes—a man who did not depend on heredity, artifice of clothing, or "refinement" to prove his worth.[32]

Taste in men's bodies has continued to pass from one extreme to the other since the turn of the century. The male ideal has never been fat, although an epidemic of corpulence afflicted men in public life during the Gilded Age. Even then, however, fatness appears to have been regarded as a somewhat unfortunate by-product of high living. Certainly, William Howard Taft, who was the United States' fattest president, was dismayed by his bulk and struggled to reduce it.[33] The importance of the vicissitudes of the masculine form in the nineteenth century lies mainly in their influence on perceptions of women's bodies. The slender Romantic man, as we shall show, became incorporated into the feminine ideal, whereas the Herculean type as the male ideal seemed to be emphasized largely as a way of underscoring the weakness of women.

After the brief, libertine period around 1800, when women's clothing was soft and clinging (and very revealing of the bosom, a style partly justified by the vogue for breast feeding), fashion returned to corsets and padding. The object of dress design reverted to the earlier goal: to create the impression of ample flesh above and below. Nudes of the period clearly reveal what

191

men imagined was underneath all the voluminous yard goods women wore. Slenderness was not prized, even though belief in the official mythology of women as weak, diseased creatures had by now reached epidemic proportions.

Women, their sexuality, and their reproductive potential were the focus of something approaching mass hysteria in Anglo-American culture by the middle of Victoria's reign. The fecund queen could afford children and produced nine. But for most other women of the period, fertility was worrisome indeed. Victorian prudery may have been a form of self-defense—a way for middle-class women to avoid the issue altogether. The official mythology was that "the majority of women (happily for them) are not very much troubled by sexual feeling of any kind," as the ever-confident and successful Acton proclaimed. But they were much troubled, according to virtually every prominent physician of the era, by their reproductive organs. The uterus was seen as the center of female infirmity—a reason why women should not be educated, why they should not exercise, why they should not be trusted to manage their own, or anybody else's, affairs. At the same time, the lascivious imagination of men produced pornography in which a timid woman only awaited the right man to awaken her dormant, but potentially enthusiastic, sexuality. In painting, the fleshly delights of that promise were meticulously depicted.[34]

Taken together, the proper Victorians and the "other" Victorians, as Steven Marcus has called them, constructed a mainstream view of sex that kept the genders distinct and assigned to "traditional" roles that were, in part, an innovation of the period. Middle-class women gained some control over their own reproduction evidently by retreating from sex. The important, indeed the central, feature of this ideology was that the sexuality of women remained absolutely tied to their reproductive potential. The notion of sexual intercourse without the potential of pregnancy was, even at this late date and in Protestant countries, profoundly subversive of the relationship between the sexes. The plump Victorian body, which seems both voluptuous and maternal to us, was precisely that—because voluptuousness was not yet dissociated from fertility.[35]

A birth-control movement did nevertheless come into existence in England as early as 1820. Its adherents included some of the more courageous and spirited reformers of that generation and those that followed. The basis of their argument was not, however, that contraceptives would free women to have sex without the fear of pregnancy. Only one of the early reformers, Francis Place, published his view that contraceptives would permit young people to marry and have sex when they could enjoy it most. He was furiously criticized by other advocates of birth control; in fact, the historian William L. Langer thinks Place set the movement back by publicizing his views and outraging the public. Throughout the century, birth control had to be justified as a way to limit the number of the poor and thus to spare society the burden of supporting them, not to free sexuality from restraint. Even Victorian pornography did not shy away from the mention of pregnancy. If anything, the prospect was used to add spice to otherwise routine and stereotyped descriptions of sexual activity.[36]

The Victorians' conflict-laden attempt to draw up a manifesto for correct sexuality engaged them for more than half a century. Meanwhile, the Romantic exploration of sex, which was psychological and individualistic, continued. It became an alternative, or "countercultural," development that persisted through the 1800s.

While the Victorians cultivated their image of a virtuous, fertile, inwardly fragile and outwardly plump little lady, the counterculture produced a woman who was sexually free, childless, more dangerous than vulnerable, and *thin.* This creature, known as the *femme fatale,* or "fatal woman," dominated painting, sculpture, fiction, theater, and opera. As Salome, Judith, Circe, the Medusa, the Sphinx, Gioconda, or Cleopatra, as nameless images, or as literary characters like Hedda Gabler and Miss Julie, the *femme fatale* was everywhere in European consciousness as the century ended. After World War I she lost her grasp on Europe's imagination, but she left her figure firmly ensconced in high fashion.[37]

The *femme fatale* was, very precisely, a female incarnation of the fatal man of the Romantics. She acquired his physical attributes—pallor, intense eyes, and a thin body. She eventually added a trait of her own—masses of flowing hair, usually dark. And she surrounded herself with the gloomy accoutrements that the fatal man had found indispensable: skulls, daggers, mysterious books in dead languages, snakes, and bats. The bloodsucking creatures were especially important associates of the *femme fatale,* who was often characterized as a vampire. The fatal man—Byron's Manfred, for example—lived with the unhappy knowledge that his unbridled passion had irreparably harmed the woman he loved. The *femme fatale* threatened to return the compliment; she would take her men, suck them dry, and discard them. Reduced to the simplest terms, the *femme fatale* was the embodiment of masculine performance anxiety. With her sexuality released from all constraints, she demanded more than any man could produce.

Just as the image of the passionless, pure Victorian lady was a fiction through which men and women could negotiate domestic relations in the nineteenth century, the *femme fatale* was a construct women used to cope with public life—at first more common on the Continent than in England or America. A prototype, if not the founding mother, of the role was Princess Cristina di Belgiojoso (1808–1871). The wealthy scion of an ancient Lombardy family, she married a poorer, but glamorous and altogether frivolous man, Prince Emilio di Belgiojoso, when she was seventeen. The prince, to marry Cristina and her money, gave up a relationship with the Countess Teresa Guiccioli, who had been Byron's mistress until his departure for Greece two years earlier. Princess Cristina later acquired another souvenir of Byron—his famous custom-made traveling carriage—which she used for her own frequent travels.[38]

The princess also appears to have taken from Byron many elements of her public style, which she exploited to wonderful effect in her early years, for she passed herself off as a kind of female Manfred. It was no disadvantage that she looked the part: "Pale, skinny, bony, with blazing eyes, she would strike the pose of an apparition or phantom," according to Marie d'Agoult, the mistress of Franz Liszt, who left her briefly for an affair with Cristina. The princess often set off her striking features with black or white dresses that were themselves odd— never precisely fashionable. For a time, she was seen in public wearing the "squalid, ash-coloured robe of the Grey Sisters, with—supreme coquetry—a garland of white flowers on her head."

In 1831, installed in Paris and cut off from access to her fortune because of political unrest in Italy, the princess established herself in a modest fifth-floor garret in Clichy. Instead of her name on the door, she put up a card that said only "La Princesse Malheureuse." Inside, on an easel, was a portrait that "made her seem paler and thinner than when I last saw her," according to a visitor, who went on to observe:

Further away a gaping skull reposed on an open book, which on approaching I noticed was printed in Hebrew—yes, Hebrew! Further away still were a guitar with broken strings, tubes of paint and a palette. A sharp-bladed stiletto lay in a prominent position on a table. . . .[39]

The princess' finest hour as a *femme fatale* came in 1849, when the Austrian secret police searched her villa at Locate for subversive papers and found, instead, a coffin with the corpse of a young man who had served her as a research assistant and who had been her lover—and possibly the only man other than her husband that she ever really loved, although Napoleon III, Lafayette, Liszt, Heinrich Heine, and Alfred de Musset (on the rebound from George Sand) had all fallen in love with her. The scandal of the lover's body, which the princess and a friend had themselves embalmed after his death from tuberculosis, was circulated and enjoyed throughout Europe.

What the literary gossips and fashionable scandal-mongers failed to recognize was that Princess Belgiojoso was a gifted, serious, and utterly determined woman. Her posing served not only to draw attention to herself but to disarm the men who might otherwise have dismissed her as a ridiculous and pretentious "bluestocking"—a derisive term applied to women seeking to enter the intellectual and political life of their time. While posing as a mysterious, sensual but cold-hearted, and faintly dangerous person, she managed to turn out a substantial body of political journalism, which was published anonymously and read by a public who thought the author was a man; a large book on the origins of Catholic dogma; a study of the philosopher Vico; and a history of her native Lombardy. Along the way, she sketched for publication most of the deputies to the French National Assembly. She was an impassioned patriot, intent on freeing Italy from foreign rule and uniting it under a republican government, and she used her notoriety as a way to gain access to influence and find allies within the French government. When the revolution of 1848 erupted, she was in Naples. There she chartered a ship to take men and arms to Genoa. After they were under way, the 200 men aboard asked her to become their commander; thus she acquired her own army, which she led into a revolution—another echo of Byron's life in hers. She later organized a nursing corps—four years before Florence Nightingale went to the Crimea. Back on her estates after all this, she experimented with social welfare programs to benefit her own tenants. Near the end of her life, in 1866, she wrote her first candidly feminist essay.[40]

The revolutionary Cristina Belgiojoso was the inspiration for Henry James's rather dull version, the Princess Christina Casamassima. Of the real woman, James wrote:

[She had] a strange, pale, penetrating beauty, without bloom, health, substance, that was yet the mask of an astounding masculine energy. . . . [She reminds] us that the great political or social agitator is most often a bird of curious plumage, *all* of whose feathers, even the queerest, play their part in his flight. We must take him in either sex as the wild wood produces him; he is not to be plucked as for preparation for the table.

Most of Cristina's literary legatees were far more conspicuously engaged in the war between the sexes than in wars of national liberation, as she had been. The male imagination of the late nineteenth century was inclined to deride the aspirations of women who sought to break out of traditional roles in society; nevertheless it took the sexual liberation of women, antagonistically, in dead earnest.[41]

The male anxiety expressed in literary and artistic images is partly that men themselves will be destroyed either by a women's unrestrained passion (as with Salome) or by her indifference to his devotion (as with Carmen). Partly it is that the woman will become an "unnatural" mother, or fail to become a mother in accord with the decree of nature. This theme crops up in turn-of-the-century images of fatal women. Alphonse Mucha designs a poster of Sarah Bernhardt as Medea murdering her children; Edvard Munch makes a lithograph of a slender, half-somnolent, half-inviting "Madonna," and gratuitously sketched in one corner is the image of an aborted fetus, which seems to be floating in preservative. The Italian symbolist painter Giovanni Segantini obsessively paints, and paints again, images of "wicked mothers" being tortured by their unborn babies (one of the nasty little creatures, for example, implacably bites the nipple of a swooning female caught in the barren branches of a tree). The women in all these images are, of course, very thin.[42]

Even if a liberated woman were to have children and not, mantislike, destroy their father, the man could torture himself with uncertainty as to whether he was, in fact, the father. One of Strindberg's characters is driven mad by a wife who makes him doubt his paternity in order to gain control over their child. (Strindberg, whatever his views of women might seem to be, was irresistibly attracted to unconventional and liberated women; he married three of them and fell in love with another who was, as you might expect, "very slender with the lines of a thirteenth-century Madonna and a smile that drove men to distraction.")[43]

The ubiquitous *femme fatale* of late nineteenth-century art and literature was, of course, the preoccupation of male artists. Women—with rare exceptions—found other subjects. The best known exception was Sarah Bernhardt (1845–1923), possibly the world's most famous actress in her time. Bernhardt, a gifted amateur sculptor, used images of sinister women in her work. But the Divine Sarah's greatest creation was herself, as actress and as celebrity. She played the *femme fatale* on stage in her great characterization of Racine's Phaedra, who destroys the man she loves. (In this role, Bernhardt was the first actress to clutch the insides of her thighs as an expression of her desire.) She also played the *femme fatale* role in her so-called private life, which was calculated for public consumption. She took and discarded lovers, more or less publicly; she lived with a menagerie that included, from time to time, pumas, a cheetah, an exotic chameleon that she would wear attached by a little gold chain to her dress, an alligator that ate her favorite dog, and some obscene monkeys. Bernhardt also enjoyed playing with the notion of her own death. She once terrified an entire theater company by playing possum on the floor of her dressing room. When she was still a teen-ager, she purchased a coffin and had herself photographed in it. The satin-lined box was later added to her household furniture—and to the legend she had constructed for herself; for she let it be known that she used the coffin for naps when overcome by the world.

As befitted a *femme fatale*, Bernhardt was—for the times—exceedingly thin. This was an advantage to the pose, but it was a distinct drawback when she began her professional career in the 1860s. Her figure, which in photographs looks perfectly ordinary to modern eyes, was mocked as ridiculously skinny. When she auditioned to join the company of the Odéon, she read the part of a shepherdess; afterward, the senior director asked, "Whoever says a shepherdess is so thin?" But she was hired, despite his view of her as "a needle automated by four pins." A little later, when she triumphed in another role, the director praised her performance. Bernhardt reportedly smiled and asked, "You find I've grown plumper, Monsieur?"

For years, she had to put up with caustic remarks: "She has the head of a virgin and the body of a broomstick"; "Why, she's like a dried bone, this little Bernhardt!" In America, for her first tour during the winter of 1880–81, she was constantly caricatured: as a body made up of water pipes, as a cane with a sponge on top, as the narrow chimney of a factory with a bird's nest on the top, as a boa constrictor. Yet Sarah Bernhardt lived just long enough to see the day when her slender figure became not only acceptable, but stylish. In 1923, the year she died, Clara Bow made her screen debut, and two years later the skinny flapper was "It."[44]

The turn of the century was a time of incredible turbulence in attitudes toward sex, sex roles, and the status of women. The Victorian experiment with prudery had really been falling apart for decades. The hypocrisy of the double standard was increasingly criticized by men and women alike. A burgeoning women's movement was battering away at the ideology of male superiority and inexorably changing women's conceptions of themselves. It was not only the determined and courageous feminists of that era who were liberating their sisters. As influential in their own way were the great ladies of the theater and the chorus girls.

By 1890, all forms of theatrical entertainment were thriving in England and America. "Stage door johnnies" and "matinee girls"—forerunners of fan clubs—mobbed their favorite play-ers. The press was filled with pictures and stories of the reigning idols. The theater was a force in everyday life, and at all levels of society, in a way that it perhaps had never been before. Also, from mid-century onward, *fashion* had become a business; couturiers began to design dresses, not for a particular client, but for the stylish woman of the time. (And, to the extent that a garment's design became detached from the individual who would wear it, the body itself would be expected to conform to a preconceived shape.) The French led in this development, and their influence abroad became extraordinary. American middle-class women in particular, sensitive to their provincialism, be-came the slaves of French couture.

Many of the most successful designers also worked in the theater; thus, styles of costume and clothing became more alike. Actresses served both for market-testing of new designs and as one-woman promotion departments. The theatrical trend to producing classic plays in modern dress, which began around the turn of the century, was in large measure a response to the audience's avid desire to see what the actresses were *really* wear-ing, not their costumes. At the same time, costume design was much influenced by whatever style happened to be current.[45]

The actresses themselves came in several sizes and types, as befits a period of rapid transition. The buxom figure that had appealed to masculine tastes for more than two centuries was most lavishly and successfully incarnated in Lillian Russell (1861–1922). Known as the "American Beauty" and "airy, fairy Lillian," she was a tall woman and full-bodied at a maximum weight above 200 pounds. All this large-as-life sensuality, with its promise of a luxurious tumble in the hay, was carefully poured into a public image of virtue and rectitude—notwith-standing Russell's marriages to four husbands and her long-time association with Diamond Jim Brady, another gigantic figure of the Gilded Age. Lillian's appeal, which cannot be overstated, lay in her ability to combine the promise of sensual delight with a façade of utter propriety, and the attractiveness of her image was no doubt spiced by the knowledge that her real life was rather racy.

A more diminutive version of the American beauty was afforded by the famous "Florodora Girls." *Florodora* was a frothy musical comedy set in the Philippine Islands. Never mind the plot. In the second act half a dozen young women, perfectly dressed in the mode of 1900 and twirling parasols, parade slowly around the stage; they are joined by six young men who sing, "Tell me, pretty maiden, are there any more at home like you?" The Girls were selected not for talent (they didn't need any) but because they were pretty brunettes who stood five feet four inches tall and weighed 130 pounds, by no means a slender build. *Florodora* nearly flopped, until the song and the double sextette caught on, and the show went on for a near-record 505 performances. Throughout the run, women in the sextette had to be replaced. The first six all became engaged to millionaires shortly after the opening, and their successors regularly left for better acting jobs or sensational marriages. Chosen purely for physique, the Florodora Girls demonstrated the incredible power of a body type that was moving headlong into obsolescence. Its power was, to be sure, its sheer marriageability, but it was the stuff of which an American legend would be made.[46]

Counterpoised to the plump, hourglass image of Lillian Russell or the Florodora Girls was the still exotic type represented mainly by European performers who visited America. The actresses Sarah Bernhardt and Ida Rubinstein and the singer Yvette Guilbert, immortalized in Toulouse-Lautrec's acid portraits, kept the public fully conscious of the alternative woman —slender, scandalous, faintly sinister, and undeniably her *own* mistress. Then, between 1900 and 1920, in a somewhat complicated sequence of events, the slim figure of the *femme fatale* was domesticated. The sexuality that had been exotic and dangerous in the European actresses and divas became American and—almost—carefree in the flapper.

In seeking to embody the "new," that is, post-Victorian, woman, fashion had two alternatives—both derived from images of the *femme fatale*. One was the Gibson Girl, a type that dominated American fashion at the turn of the century and then gave way to the now familiar *Vogue* body. The Gibson girl retained the hour-glass outline, but emphasized independence and vitality: She was tall, with a pile of sculptured hair on her head, broad shoulders emphasized by leg-of-mutton sleeves, a prominent—and rather square—bosom, narrow waist, and wide hips under a flared skirt. In many ways, the Gibson girl was derived from a minor version of the *femme fatale*, the heroically proportioned women of Dante Gabriel Rossetti. But the heavy-lidded inscrutability of his Pandoras and Lucrezia Borgias was transmuted into sauciness, and their massive figures reduced to more conventional proportions. Rosetti's version of the *femme fatale* proved to be a dead end in art, and Charles Dana Gibson's new woman was a dead end in fashion.[47]

The slender body that has dominated twentieth-century fashion came into prominence very quickly after 1910. The rapidity of the change was undoubtedly due to one factor: the arrival of the movies as *the* main form of mass entertainment. The nature of the change was shaped by a variety of influences: Underlying all of them, however, was a single force, the liberation of women.

Women began to move with a physical vigor and exuberance that had been denied them by centuries of restraining mores and clothing. Healthy physical activity was urged on women whose bodies had been lamented as infinitely fragile vessels for a dangerous womb a mere fifty years earlier. A dance craze swept America and England, inspired by the willowy Irene Castle and her husband Vernon. To accommodate the new mobility, hemlines had to rise.

Shorter skirts revealed feet, ankles, and calves that had been concealed literally for millennia. As soon as legs became visible, the whole visual character of a woman's body began to change.

Full, flowing skirts, by concealing heavy hips and thighs, had provided a suitable pedestal for a full torso with a prominent bosom. Without such a base, the ample body began to look top-heavy, whereas the slender physique, which was lost in the yardage of an earlier era, now seemed to provide a proper balance.

Mobility in itself also makes bodies look larger, as Anne Hollander has pointed out. Standing or lying, the posed, passive body fills only a single volume, but once it begins to move, the mind's eye perceives it as filling potential spaces, and the impression of bulk is automatically increased. Film showed women in motion; candid photographs abandoned the static traditions of painting for the sense of stopped action.[48]

Women were engaged in political as well as physical movements. One of the most important of these was the birth-control effort, led by such redoubtable figures as Marie Stopes in England and Margaret Sanger in the United States. Their efforts were crucial in changing the very terms in which contraception was discussed and understood. The timid, Malthusian outlook of the men who had advocated birth control in the nineteenth century was replaced by the principle that women had the right to control their own bodies and their own reproductive potential. Contraception, which had seemed distinctly perverted in the 1880s and 1890s, had become clearly progressive after 1910. In 1921, the progress of the birth-control movement was marked by two events: Margaret Sanger organized the first American birth control conference, and Gus Kahn and Raymond B. Egan wrote a song that was on everyone's lips (including Gatsby's and Daisy's):

> Ain't we got fun?
> There's nothing surer,
> The rich get richer and the poor get—children.
> In the meantime, in between time,
> Ain't we got fun?[49]

203

In the same year, women's fashion successfully introduced the slender silhouette. (Only one year earlier, not incidentally, America had enacted women's suffrage.)

Throughout the previous decade, designers had been seeking a way to express the new temper of women, but the results were singularly awkward. Padding of the bosom and backside were largely abandoned, although the tradition of constructing dresses with many parts, each entitled to its own elaboration, continued. Dresses remained complicated, with extra material in peplums, aprons, sashes, bows, and various gathers and swags of fabric. During this period, with all its elaboration and fantasizing, clothing reflects the still powerful influence of the *femme fatale;* Middle Eastern and Oriental details and silhouettes, with their connotation of licentiousness, abound; slightly mannish features, including a feminized version of the top hat (also an echo of the Dandy), are common; feathers and exotic furs—including leopard and monkey—are everywhere.[50]

Then, around 1919, the Paris designer Vionnet invented garments made from fabric cut on the bias (diagonally across the weave). Her dresses, which draped beautifully and clung to the bodies beneath, were incompatible with fat figures. Also in 1919, for the first time the great fashion houses began to display their dresses on live models in motion; before then, customers had seen them only in sketches or on mannequins. The innovation was instantly incorporated into a Broadway musical, *Irene,* from which the song "Alice Blue Gown" became famous; fashion shows became a staple of stage and cinema.[51]

The movies disseminated the novelties in fashion and did much to establish the new standard of slenderness, but they did not *create* the new look. The first three major motion-picture actresses were a perfect array of existing types: Mary Pickford, who played "girls in that misty mid-region between sexless childhood and buxom womanliness which seems to have had a strong appeal to many American males of the early century"; Lillian Gish, as a vulnerable waif, lineal descendant of Clarissa

Harlowe and Justine; and Theda Bara, as the "Vamp," a buxom and rather comic version of the *femme fatale.* Theda Bara's career was virtually over in five years; 1919 saw her last successful movie, at least in part because the overdrawn version of the *femme fatale* that she and Pola Negri had acted temporarily lost its hold on the public's imagination.[52]

What replaced her was the "It" girl, the prototype of the flapper—an altogether new kind of woman. She was sexually free, but vibrant rather than venomous, funny rather than fatal. She was actively after a man—any man—but innocently. If her men got hurt, it was more their fault than hers. All of this insouciance was based on a tacit understanding: The flapper was not about to become a mother—not if she could help it, and she could help it. The carefree and frivolous quality of the flapper is what we are likely to think of now, but she was really more interesting than that.

Elinor Glyn, the novelist who coined "It" and defined it over and over again, once characterized It as "a strange magnetism which attracts both sexes . . . there must be a physical attraction but beauty is unnecessary." Glyn's passing reference to the androgyny of It, and the slender body which has It, should not be overlooked. The titillating possibility of disguising and interchanging girls and boys, and falling in love with the wrong person, had been a recurrent theme of the "counterculture" of the nineteenth century (as of the sixteenth century and yet earlier periods). The Victorians resisted the notion, placing great emphasis on differentiating the sexes. One aspect of this century's throwing off of Victorianism has been a tentative exploration of androgynous possibilities. Clara Bow's first screen role, in *Down to the Sea in Ships,* was that of a girl disguised as a boy. Likewise, Katharine Hepburn (whose usual screen part came to be the woman who was socially, but not sexually, threatening, a high-comic version of the *femme fatale*) played a girl masquerading as a boy in *Sylvia Scarlett.* This much undervalued movie, made in 1936, explores whether the conventions of femininity are necessarily more appealing to men than boy-ish frankness, and Hepburn's slender body is perfect for the task.

The flapper was in many ways a private and apolitical version of what feminists had been struggling for. Androgynous or not, the fact that she need not be "beautiful"—that she did not have an hourglass figure and lavish, flowing hair—was now an advantage. (In 1914, a militant feminist, Mary Richardson, had gone into London's National Gallery and axed Velazquez' "Rokeby Venus"; she was protesting the government's treatment of the suffragist Emmeline Pankhurst by trying "to destroy the picture of the most beautiful woman in mythological history." Perhaps it was no accident that she had selected virtually the first painting of a woman with the "maternal" shape.)[53] The flapper's heyday, although brief, was sufficient to establish her linear physique as that of a socially and sexually liberated woman, a free agent.

The late twenties saw a return of the *femme fatale* to American movies, notably through two extraordinary European imports, Marlene Dietrich and Greta Garbo. The physical type had changed, however; neither actress was particularly slender. Indeed, when Garbo signed her first movie contract with MGM, it was with some reluctance on the part of Louis B. Mayer, who muttered before signing, "In America men don't like fat women." It was not quite sixty years since Sarah Bernhardt, whose figure wasn't all that different from Garbo's, had nearly lost an acting contract for being too thin. History does not record whether Garbo ever produced a retort for Mayer.[54]

Mayer's remark was not, for that matter, strictly true. As movies evolved from the thirties on, the female stars tended to divide into two types. One appealed to men: Jean Harlow, Mae West, Rita Hayworth, Jane Russell, and Marilyn Monroe. The other to women: Katharine Hepburn, Joan Crawford, Bette Davis, and Rosalind Russell, among others. Men might appreciate the streamlined elegance of the great actresses, but they continued to love the women whose bodies, though slender-ized, were in the "maternal," or hour-glass, tradition of Lillian Russell and the Florodora Girls. The actresses who played to audiences predominantly made up of women were angular in physique, and their roles were more those of independent, ad-venturous women (who all too often suffered the consequences of their uppitiness).

Although the movies have continually alternated the two body types, fashion has consistently opted for the slender, lin-ear figure since 1921, except for a brief period in the 1940s and 1950s. A somewhat mannish style was cultivated in the forties, a time when women were encouraged to take jobs traditionally assigned to men. In the period of political and social reaction after the war, when women were all but driven back into the home, Dior produced his regressive "new look," with its revival of the hourglass figure and long, full skirt. In retrospect, this episode can be seen as a momentary interruption of a long-term trend.

In movies, especially of the thirties, class consciousness also played its role in the idealization of thin women. English aristo-crats were a fixture of the Depression's celluloid fantasies, and they were—except for the dowagers, who were played as "heavy" in two senses—exceedingly thin. This stereotype of the upper-crust body probably had its origins in the long, nar-row waists of the eighteenth century, when the English aristoc-racy became an international symbol of elegance (as well as loose sexuality). By the thirties, of course, the image was much softened and romanticized.

When it first appeared in art, the slender female body was a projection of male fantasies about what would happen if women's sexuality were "turned loose." Women then appro-priated the silhouette for themselves and, in doing so, took the venom out of it. For a very important period early in this cen-tury, the dominant message of the thin body was, "I am on the move, and on the make, and having a good time." In the process, thinness was also made a requirement of fashion and elegance, and the message became perverted. In 1939, when Anita Loos and George Cukor filmed "The Women," based on Clare Boothe Luce's play, they astutely chose a reducing salon for the opening scene: No other setting could have been more evocative of women in conflict with themselves, of women competing with one another for sexual and social success.

Perhaps as the notion waned that women's sexuality must be contained and controlled, a substitute form of mandatory self-control was required. The image of sexual freedom is purchased with what might be called gastronomic servitude. By not satisfying her appetite for food, a woman buys the right to sexual satisfaction.

The voluptuous figure, if the skin magazines are any evidence, still has a basic erotic appeal to men. It may also convey the message that the fleshier woman is more accessible and more submissive than her leaner sister. In the recent movie "9 to 5," which was explicitly feminist, this stereotype is partially exploited. Dabney Coleman, playing a despotic employer, makes incessant passes at Dolly Parton, whose buxom outline renders her manifestly a sex object. Jane Fonda and Lily Tomlin, with their leaner builds, are victimized in other, nonsexual ways. But the movie also departs from the traditional stereotype; Parton's character is in total control of her sexuality and is never even on the verge of giving in to her boss.

The symbolism of fatness and thinness has long since overtaken its biological importance. To be "overweight" is an aesthetic catastrophe for women, mainly owing to the meaning that has arbitrarily been assigned to it in our culture. The sheer absence of body fat is often perversely interpreted as an asset, but the underlying message is the important one. With her thin body a woman can project a statement about her character: "I am my own sexual boss; I am in control of myself; I am not a motherly, housewifely person."

Many women cannot send this message with their bodies; in spite of religious dieting, they just cannot maintain the requisite slenderness. Instead, they choose clothing that would look good on them if they *were* thin, clothing that identifies them and their outlook on life. As Anne Hollander points out, fashion has not lost its hold on us. Instead, clothing styles have come to offer a wider range of "looks," which serve to identify the person wearing them as belonging to one or another social group. If a woman wants to look like a young swinger, a rising professional, or an easygoing student, she chooses clothing that identifies her with that group—and struggles to make her body conform to her chosen style. A pair of tight blue jeans or tailored chino pants, for example, imply a certain self-possessed freedom in the woman wearing them—even though, for very many women, these garments are in fact painfully confining.[55]

What began as a symbol of liberation has, perversely, turned into a mystique that puts many women at a disadvantage. The obsessive drive to be thin serves no real purpose, except to funnel large amounts of money into the diet "industry," a dubious benefit indeed.

8

WAIST PRODUCTS

IN his preface to *The Doctor's Dilemma*, George Bernard Shaw observed:

medical practice is governed not by science but by supply and demand . . . the grossest quackery [cannot] be kept off the market if there is a demand for it. . . . By making doctors tradesmen, we compel them to learn the tricks of the trade; consequently we find that the fashions of the year include treatments, operations, and particular drugs, as well as hats, sleeves, ballads, and games.[1]

More than most others of their profession, doctors specializing in weight loss have catered to the tastes of the public. Their practices flourish, however shabby their methods, because there are no accepted medical standards for helping people lose weight. The widespread medical condemnation of overweight has not been matched by a serious, concentrated effort to understand and treat it.

Much medical attention has focused on people who are morbidly obese—that is, at least twice the average weight for their height—and whose health is endangered by their weight.

It would certainly be valuable to help these people reduce, but no safe, effective treatment for their condition has been found. Very fat people almost always regain whatever weight they lose through dieting. As a consequence, medical approaches to morbid obesity have run increasingly to desperate measures: hazardous surgery, habit-forming drugs, and grotesquely unbalanced diets.

People who are only moderately fat have also received little advice of any value from the medical profession, partly because their fatness is not in itself an illness. Weight control is acknowledged to be important in treating diabetes or hypertension, but even with these diseases treatment is likely to be more an exhortation than a workable program. The great majority of people on weight-loss regimens are being treated, or are treating themselves, for a nondisease. It is little wonder that "treatments" and "particular drugs" for weight loss change as often as the "fashions of the year"—and that none is effective.

Doctors specializing in weight loss operate on a laissez-faire basis. The American Medical Association has set no binding standards for treating overweight patients, although it does offer general recommendations and condemns particularly harmful fads from time to time. The treatment of obesity is not even a recognized medical specialty. In part, the lack of standards may reflect a moral judgment that anyone with will power should be able to lose weight on his own, with little medical help. It is also true, however, that no one, not even the best of "obesity experts," really has a good method for helping people become thinner.

When medical science is this primitive, the door is wide open for outright charlatans to try their hands. Hundreds of thousands of people are treated by "diet doctors" who do little more than dispense appetite suppressants—sometimes promoting, and maintaining, their patients' drug habits. Millions have treated themselves by following bizarre diet books—often written by physicians—that are on the whole useless, if not dangerous. The medical creed, *primum non nocere*—"first, do no harm"—is replaced by *caveat emptor.*

The most disturbing fact, perhaps, is that it can be all but impossible for a lay person to differentiate between good and bad advice. Some of the most hazardous diets and drug treatments stem directly from ideas that were first published in professional medical journals. The public is open to exploitation because medical standards for the treatment of fatness are lax on every level. In this field, anything goes because nothing works.

The American Society of Bariatric Physicians (ASBP) is the closest approximation to a professional organization of weight-loss specialists. (The name "bariatric" is taken from the Greek word for "heavy.") The society has established a clear code of guidelines for the treatment of overweight and has made creditable efforts to raise the general standards of weight-reduction clinics. But the group has gained little respect in the medical community. Because no methods of weight loss have become standard, the code of the ASBP now allows its members to try a very broad range of treatments, so long as they do not intend to harm their patients or directly lie to them.

Some of the society's leaders are pushing for firmer guidelines. Peter Lindner, chairman of its board of trustees, observes: "Anyone, today, can call himself a 'bariatrician.' There are no established, clear-cut qualifications for this title and . . . a number of unscrupulous individuals have used this title to ensnare the public." Quality control is doubly difficult because many bariatricians do not restrict themselves to treating obesity; they also dabble in faddish approaches to nutrition and health. In official presentations and informal conversations at the society's meetings, bariatricians tell each other about the benefits of megavitamin therapy, DMSO, chelation therapy (which supposedly clears debris from the body's arteries), even Laetrile. In setting guidelines for its members, the society simply ignores any aspects of a physician's practice that are not directly related to weight control.[2]

As a group, the bariatricians use a combination of science and salesmanship. These elements are embodied in Peter Lindner, who is something of a guiding presence in the society. Lindner has held virtually every important position in the group at one time or another; at ASBP meetings, wearing ribbons identifying all his past and present honors, he appears to be the four-star general of the bariatricians. A short, thin man —though he reportedly used to weight more than 200 pounds —Lindner has the manner of a driven pixie. He and his wife wear matching outfits of salmon color, or broad checked patterns—a colleague at one meeting greets them as the "Bobbsey twins"—and Lindner sports a large bow tie, half-moon glasses and pipe. His presentations, even to his professional group, are slick slideshows, full of cartoons, always beginning with a joke or even a magic trick. In spite of his flamboyant approach, however, Lindner is widely respected as a scientist and clinician, both outside the ASBP and within it; he can talk endlessly, and accurately, about the metabolic intricacies of weight loss.

In many of the other bariatricians, the show far outweighs the substance. "As far as I'm concerned, people like Peter Lindner represent the finest traditions in American medicine," says Harvard's George Blackburn, a physician who specializes in treating obesity. "But to say the same of the society would not be true. . . . You hear more weird endocrine, metabolic, nutritional gimmicks and beliefs if you talk informally to ninetenths of the people in that society—they're as close to witchcraft as you can get."[3]

"Witchcraft" or no, the society's annual meetings hardly resemble a coven; a Kiwanis meeting might be closer. The diet doctors are almost all men (though the great majority of dieters are women)—a dinner speaker welcomes the group as "doctors and their ladies." Like other American men their age, many of the bariatricians show a middle-age paunch; several are quite stout, and a few are frankly obese. They include about as many osteopaths as M.D.'s, a fact that may partly account for their low standing with the orthodox medical community.

In September 1980, the bariatricians met at the Aladdin Hotel —one of Las Vegas's more fantastic offerings, complete with "Arabian" columns and arches, and with a scale model of the Taj Mahal in the lobby. The ASBP convened in a room some-where between the Genie Buffet and the Magic Dollar Slots (rows of machines bearing pictures of alluring harem girls and the legend, "Make a Wish"). Between presentations, some of the men talked about the upcoming fight between Muhammad Ali and Larry Holmes, advertised by billboards around the city. When Ali took the worst beating of his career in that fight, he would blame his defeat on the stringent diet and thyroid hor-mone he had used to get down to fighting weight.

The glitter of the casino is almost matched by the exhibi-tors' area at the ASBP meeting. Many other medical organiza-tions screen the manufacturers who come to promote their wares; the bariatricians do not. Anyone can set up a booth here, and the exhibition hall contains the full gamut of weight-loss aids.

Pills predominate. In one corner a large poster from Sandoz, a major drug company, depicts the patient as prey. A woman, seen from the back, is wearing a bathing suit with a target on it; the outer rim says "150 lbs.," the bulls-eye, "136." "After the easy pounds," says this ad for an appetite suppressant, "come the tough ones." Many exhibitors are offering pills that can be sold without a prescription, thus saving the bariatrician the trouble of puzzling through U.S. Food and Drug Administration (FDA) regulations for controlled drugs. These remedies range from phenylpropanolamine—the basic ingredient in most over-the-counter diet pills—to this one from Nevada's Vitaline For-mulas:

STIMU-LEAN
STOPS HUNGER
AND
BOOSTS ENERGY
NATURAL SOURCE
INGREDIENTS
NO
RECORD KEEPING
NO RX
ASK FOR
FREE SAMPLE

A slim, bearded salesman, wearing a butterfly-patterned shirt and an Optimist International pin, lists Stimu-Lean's ingredients: a mixture of exotic herbal stimulants, the local anesthetic benzocaine, and, to help the patient feel full, cellulose. He is also selling L-Neur-Amine, a mixture of amino acids that is supposed to lessen hunger and fight depression all at once, by increasing levels of a brain hormone called serotonin. Asked for references, the salesman produces an article from the *National Enquirer*.

Thyroid hormone remains a hardy perennial, even though the American Medical Association has condemned its use in the treatment of overweight.[4] Many of the exhibitors compete to present the "best" version of the hormone. *"Thyroid is our specialty —not a side line,"* proclaims a leaflet from Western Research Laboratories. This company claims that its thyroid comes from "100% pure pork, from American corn-fed hogs." The leaflet continues:

Western Research Laboratories thyroid glands come from two custom packers in Iowa and Nebraska. . . . We selected Iowa and Nebraska as our gland source because the great glacier did not reach that far south; the soil in that area is rich in iodine because this essential element was not leached out.

A salesman confides that alligator thyroid is actually the best to use, for the pharmaceutical connoisseur; but, he says, it's hard to get.

Not all the exhibitors are hawking drugs, of course. Some booths promote diet foods from vegetarian meatballs to low-cal Jello. Mineralab, Inc., promises to determine patients' nutritional status by analyzing their hair. And a group called the Calorie Control Council has sent its representatives to put in a good word for saccharin.

At one booth, a new machine—the CalDetect Diet Monitor Mark IV—is promoted as a high-tech way to keep patients on their diets. The machine works much like the breath analyzer police use on drivers suppected of drinking. The Mark IV, however, detects not alcohol, but chemicals called ketones, which are produced when body fat is metabolized. This machine catches delinquent dieters; too few exhaled ketones declare that they've been eating too much food. "Excuses are unacceptable," says the brochure, "since failure to adhere to the diet readily shows on the instrument."

At the end of the last row of booths is a thin man dressed all in green—he even has a green visor—and wearing a gold spiral on a chain around his neck. This wizened Peter Pan asks a passerby, "Want a massage?," and plunks him down in a vibrating chair, complete with spinal roller. In addition to the chair, which sells for around a thousand dollars, he is selling exercise machines, tapes to cure alcoholism by subliminal suggestion, and kits for exploring "pyramid power." What does all this have to do with obesity? "It's energy," he says. "If a person has good energy he doesn't need to overindulge and become a big fat slob."

The booths mirror a deeper problem within the society as a whole. Lindner has proposed that only the most reputable manufacturers should be allowed to exhibit at the meetings. But Randall Lee, the executive director of the ASBP, explains why this advice has not been followed. The problem, in essence, is to decide what standards to use, says Lee:

If we did really tight screening, we'd be left with nobody, because there really is no single documented, proven way to treat obesity. The treatment of obesity has been compared to the treatment of diabetes before the discovery of insulin. There *is no* accepted treatment, and so everybody tries various things with various degrees of success.[5]

With so little to guide them, it is not surprising that so many bariatricians have adopted, almost as a sacrament, the symbol of medical competence: drugs. The ASBP has vigorously defended its members' "freedom to prescribe" whatever they feel is appropriate—within legal limits. Recently several states, and the FDA, have moved to tighten their regulations regarding the use of amphetamine and other stimulants in weight reduction. The society opposes these moves with the same fervor that the National Rifle Association musters against government efforts at gun control.

The predisposition to drug treatment seems to have been built into the ASBP. The society was founded some thirty years ago by Western Research Laboratories (the people who would like to bring you alligator thyroid if they could). The ASBP severed its official ties with Western in 1969, but the company's spirit is still pervasive. The society is in the process of setting up a research foundation, to be funded largely by drug companies, that will investigate the use of thyroid hormone as its first priority. At its 1980 meeting, the ASBP sponsored an all-afternoon symposium on "Thyroid in Obesity." In contrast, the therapeutic use of exercise was accorded only a single half-hour presentation—and that was before a group of physicians' assistants, not the bariatricians themselves.[6]

The society has, at least, encouraged its members to prescribe drugs safely. The ASBP guidelines stipulate, in part, that a bariatrician should take an adequate medical history for each patient, perform several specific blood and urine tests, and provide patient counseling to encourage a proper diet. Adherence to these guidelines is strictly voluntary, however. The society cannot enforce even these minimal requirements.

The ASBP's commitment to drug therapy is disappointing, but not surprising. For decades fat people have been given dangerous drugs to help them lose weight. Physicians have come to depend on these pills, and patients have come to demand them. Unfortunately, there is no sign that diet drugs will be retired from medical practice—even though there is no solid justification for using them, and never has been.

"Appetite suppressants," like most treatments for obesity, were widely used long before it was clear whether they were safe or effective. When the drugs were discovered, by accident, they were prescribed enthusiastically. Potential dangers were minimized and benefits exaggerated. As hazards became obvious, new remedies were sought, found, and prescribed, even though there was little evidence that they were much safer than the drugs they replaced. It is only recently that the rationale for using *any* drug to suppress appetite has finally come under close scrutiny.

The amphetamines, a family of drugs known on the street as "speed," were discovered in the early 1930s and were used to treat obese patients by the end of that decade. Several investigators noticed that people of normal weight who were given the drugs for other reasons—such as depression and narcolepsy—happened to become thinner. In 1938, two Boston psychiatrists reported that benzedrine sulfate, a type of amphetamine, also helped the obese to lose weight. They thought that the effect was largely psychological. In their view, many people overate because of "anhedonia"—a kind of depressed state that led to "a restless seeking for stimulation" and was alleviated by amphetamine. They noticed that the drug also seemed to have a direct appetite-suppressing effect.[7]

By the late forties, it was clear that the effect of amphetamine was probably more physiological than psychological. A team of physiologists at the University of Chicago found that benzedrine caused dogs as well as people to eat less—and the dogs, as far as they could tell, had not been particularly moody. But although the action of the drug was better understood, these investigators totally misjudged its safety. They anticipated no adverse effects "in view of the relatively low toxicity of amphetamine," and wrote that "no evidence of deleterious effects of the drug was observed."[8]

In fact, amphetamines are powerful, habit-forming drugs with serious side effects, including gastrointestinal disturbances, insomnia, hyptertension—and, in some cases, psychosis. Nevertheless, when the drugs were first seized on as a remedy for overweight, their danger was largely ignored. In 1948, drug company statistics showed that two-thirds of patients treated for overweight were given amphetamines. At about this time, one clinician wrote that "dexedrine sulfate [amphetamine] is a nontoxic safe drug which may safely be used in obstetric patients to aid them in preventing excessive gain of weight." Apart from potential harm to the mother, amphetamines taken in pregnancy could certainly not have been considered "nontoxic" or "safe" for the fetus.[9]

These early, regrettable errors might be put down to a lack of experience with relatively new drugs. But appetite suppressants have continued to be widely prescribed, although their hazards are now well known and their usefulness has been increasingly questioned. As early as 1972, the FDA found that "all anorectic [appetite-suppressing] drugs are of limited usefulness and that their use for prolonged periods in the treatment of obesity can lead to drug dependence and abuse and must be avoided." In an extensive review of the literature, the federal agency found that people taking the drugs lost weight only marginally faster than those who only dieted; the difference was a fraction of a pound per week. Moreover, any boost from the drugs seemed to be short-lived, with the greatest effect seen in the first few weeks.[10]

This pattern is precisely what would be expected if the drugs act to lower setpoint—as Albert Stunkard's work, described in chapter 4, suggests. The setpoint of a person who takes an "appetite suppressant" may fall by ten pounds or so. The drug is not lowering "appetite" per se, but coercing the body into maintaining a smaller store of fat. Weight is lost until the new setting is reached—a process that takes a few weeks—and then it stabilizes.

It then appears that the drug has stopped working, inasmuch as weight loss has tapered off. In fact, the drug is still active, but now only maintaining the lowered setpoint. As soon as the drug is discontinued, the setpoint rises to its previous level, and weight is regained. Only a lifetime course of these drugs would keep a person's weight down—and then only by ten to twenty pounds, it appears. The chemicals are far too dangerous, and the weight loss too small, to justify using them this way.

In spite of the clear case against appetite suppressants, the Food and Drug Administration has been only moderately successful in regulating even the most hazardous of them. Although amphetamines were reclassified as even more dangerous in 1972, and the Justice Department ordered their production cut, a large number still remained on the market. In July 1979, the FDA announced that it intended to ban the use of amphetamines in weight control. As we write, the proposed ban is still being contested by the manufacturers, which stand to lose a large and, thanks to the amphetamines' addictive potential, reliable income from the agency's action. By some estimates, the ban would decrease national production of the drugs from 290 million pills a year to about 35 million.

Even if it stands, the FDA's action would still leave physicians free to prescribe several "amphetaminelike drugs" that have similar effects, only in lesser degree. As the FDA noted in its own 1972 report, these drugs are no more effective in weight control than true amphetamines. They are also probably not much safer; they seem to have a high potential for abuse. Amphetaminelike drugs have been popular on the black market in Sweden, where true amphetamines have been tightly controlled since the 1940s, and they have been sold extensively as street drugs in the southeastern United States.[11]

Although a drug's chemical nature is important from a regulatory viewpoint, it may have relatively little to do with the agent's effectiveness in promoting weight loss. Several factors, including the physician's relationship with the patient and the way a drug is administered, can affect the ease of reducing. Overall, the placebo effect—the emotional response to receiving a pill that is *supposed* to make dieting easier—may be at least as important as the actual physiological effect of a drug. This effect is best exemplified by the response to human chorionic gonadotropin (HCG), a sex hormone made by the placenta and extracted from the urine of pregnant women. HCG was part of a weight-loss system developed in the 1950s by Albert T. Simeons, who claimed that the hormone would virtually dissolve body fat. Even Simeons admitted that people who received shots of HCG would not lose weight unless they also followed his 500-calorie-a-day diet. He claimed nevertheless that the hormone made dieting easier by ensuring that weight was lost only from "abnormal fat deposits"—a claim unsupported by any evidence.[12]

Patients who followed Simeons's system readily lost weight. The explanation, though, was not in the hormone's action, but in the way it was presented. Simeons's patients received daily shots of HCG, and the act of going to a clinic every day for a "fat-dissolving" injection proved to be a powerful reinforcer. Several controlled studies have now shown that patients who receive placebo injections on this schedule do about as well as those who receive HCG. Further, both groups lose more weight than people receiving most conventional treatments.[13]

The placebo effect has been central to the practice of many "diet doctors," who have made fortunes while offering the moral equivalent of snake oil. A drug-oriented weight-loss clinic is a perfect setup for assembly-line treatment, since fat patients change little from month to month and rarely ask to see the physician. Because the patients are likely to regain any weight they lose, and because they may become dependent on the drugs they are given, they stand a good chance of becoming repeat customers. Properly managed, the weight-loss business can be as reliable as undertaking.

A quintessential diet doctor was Alfred Ferriss, who ran what may have been the largest weight-loss operation in the state of California. If Hollywood ever filmed "The Alfred Ferriss Story", the lead would have to be played by Dabney Coleman (the tyrannical boss in the film *9 to 5*), who bears a striking physical resemblance to Ferriss and conveys the physician's almost frightening drive and intensity.

Ferriss entered the weight-loss business from an unrelated specialty, radiology. Around 1970, he became dissatisfied with medicine and dropped out of practice for a year or two. Then one day, a friend called to tell him about a special injection being given at some weight-loss clinics. As Ferriss recalls, it was supposed to be a "magical bullet that people could stick in their arms . . . and see the fat melt away." As one might expect, the secret ingredient turned out to be HCG.

When Ferriss himself first heard about HCG's alleged fat-dissolving properties, he recalls, "I said, that can't be anything but a shuck and a jive; and sure enough it wasn't true." What was true, however, was that people were so eager to lose weight that they would subject themselves to repeated injections at expensive clinics. Ferriss set out to deliver the same product to more people at a lower price. He started with HCG, but supplemented it with other drugs to help patients stick to his drastic 500-calorie diet: amphetaminelike drugs; then tranquilizers to counteract overstimulation; and a diuretic to produce loss of fluid (and thus of pounds). He threw in Vitamin B-12 injections for good measure, and the pharmacy was complete.

Ferriss soon realized that this routine had the makings of a "mechanical system" that could be run by nurses and other staff members in his absence. He started a chain of clinics, leaving much of the daily care of patients to his employees. As he later admitted to the state medical board, pills were handed out by his staff, who had no legal authority to dispense drugs, and for a time patients were even taught to give themselves shots. At one point, Ferriss managed some seventy clinics around the state with no other physicians to assist him.

Things ran more smoothly, and more conventionally, after Ferriss brought other doctors into his practice. Even so, California's Board of Medical Quality Assurance still found fault with the doctor's system, claiming that medical supervision of the regimen was insufficient. In 1981, the board found that Ferriss had "aided and abetted the unlicensed practice of medicine," and that his clinics "promoted the prescribing of excessive amounts of a dangerous drug and controlled substance." After several years of legal wrangling, Ferriss lost his license to practice medicine in California. However, the board quarreled only with the way Ferriss dispensed appetite suppressants, not with his prescribing the drugs. An unknown number of weight-loss clinics may use similar drugs in a regimen that is little better than Ferriss's—but avoid prosecution by staying within the letter of the law.[14]

The use of prescribed appetite suppressants has gone hand-in-hand with a growing market for over-the-counter versions. These products are displayed prominently in most drugstores and are advertised flamboyantly in newspapers. Some are promoted with claims that, if true, would make them powerful metabolic napalm in the war against fat. An ad for Thera-Thin capsules is headlined: "Doctor's program featuring crash-burn diet and amazing capsule forces your body to burn away fat as it . . . *Neutralizes All The Calories In The Food You Eat!*"

Another product, called Maxi-Slim, is billed as an "Explosive New Fat Burn-Off System . . . the Ultimate weapon against Fat." This advertisement includes testimonials from anonymous doctors—such as "M.D. Top Obesity Specialist, important Long Island Hospital"; moreover, the product's ingredients are unnamed.[15]

The mail-order diet formulas, like those sold over the counter, are rather prosaic in composition. Common ingredients are methylcellulose, a bulking agent that is supposed to induce a feeling of fullness, and benzocaine, a local anesthetic included to dull the taste buds. The key ingredient in most of them, however, is a drug called phenylpropanolamine, or PPA for short. This nonprescription decongestant is chemically similar to amphetamine—it differs from the more powerful drug by a single oxygen atom—and is a stimulant. Although there is a great difference in potency, PPA is qualitatively similar to amphetamine, a poor man's speed, so to speak. Recently, drug dealers have exploited the resemblance by selling pills containing PPA, caffeine, and other legal stimulants as the real thing. Some manufacturers have even produced PPA pills to resemble well-known brands of amphetamine, apparently to encourage the deception.[16]

The FDA has taken a relatively tolerant view of phenylpropanolamine, although it limits the concentration that can be sold in nonprescription pills. In May 1979, an FDA advisory panel of physicians found that the drug could help people lose weight safely. Recent evidence, however, suggests that phenylpropanolamine may share some of amphetamine's unpleasant side effects, making it less safe than was originally thought. PPA can induce hypertension in people with normal blood pressure. And in 1981, the *Journal of the American Medical Association* published a report showing that the drug could affect the central nervous system to produce anxiety, agitation, dizziness and, in rare cases, hallucinations. Ironically, some headshops have started to warn their customers that instead of true speed, they may be buying a dangerous substitute: PPA.[17]

Today, the majority of dieters must at least know that they should steer clear of appetite suppressants. The potential side effects are scary enough to minimize their attractiveness. But a dieter who avoids the Scylla of speed may still be sucked in by Charybdis: the diet books.

The first rule for writing a diet book is simple: Find a gimmick. Tom Cooper, a doctor from Marietta, Georgia, knows this. An affable man, who dresses informally and cracks jokes with a slight Southern accent, Cooper has been popular with both his patients and his colleagues. He treats his patients sympathetically, since he once weighed 240 pounds himself (and is still rather plump). He is well respected in the American Society of Bariatric Physicians, where he has served as president and educational director. He is also one of the country's more successful authors of diet books; 1979 saw the publication of *Dr. Cooper's Fabulous Fructose Diet.* Fructose, the sugar found in fruit, according to Cooper, was supposed to satisfy the dieter's hunger for sweets without the adverse physiological effects of table sugar. The advertisements gave a simple lesson in biochemistry:

Ordinary . . . diets can unbalance the body's energy system, creating up-and-down swings in blood sugar levels. Low blood sugar triggers the hunger alarm in your brain, turns on your appetite, and forces you off your diet. . . . Fructose is absorbed into the bloodstream slowly and smoothly, without creating the roller-coaster blood sugar response.

The claim makes no sense; fructose is merely a component of table sugar—somewhat sweeter, weight for weight, but otherwise similar in character. Nevertheless, the book sold well, and the next year Cooper published a new one: *Dr. Cooper's South American Diet.*[18]

In the introduction to this latter book, Cooper says that his diet plan was derived from methods used in Peru and Venezuela, where obesity is endemic. He writes:

This author was able to get the basic formula and regimen in the original Spanish. After careful translation and the equivalent substitution for foodstuffs popular in this country, *The South American Diet* was introduced to my patients with what conservatively could be termed "fantastic" results.

When one finally comes to the diet plan, it seems to have lost something in the translation. It is, like dozens of other diets, a simple low-calorie, low-carbohydrate menu, offering the reader limited amounts of such foods as grapefruit and cantaloupe, Kraft cheese and Special K cereal (hardly staples of traditional Peruvian cuisine). The only exotic component of the diet is an herbal tea, which Cooper suggests should be taken as a diuretic —along with nutritional supplements, and, if they are needed, tranquilizers.[19]

Do these diets really work? Well, yes and no. Cooper claims that German and Finnish research backs up his ideas about fructose, although he concedes that "a lot of people have disputed this" and that fructose "may be a placebo." At least fruit sugar and a "South American" regimen can't hurt, he says, and they may even help wean a patient from harmful drugs. Herbal teas are presumably safer than diuretic pills, and Cooper says some of his own patients stopped taking amphetamine when they started on fructose.

But even Cooper admits that his diets may owe their success more to psychology than to biochemistry. "If you're going to have a child take a dose of medicine that's bitter," says Cooper, "you have to sugar-coat it"—presumably with fructose.

If you don't give the overweight patients at least some gimmick to begin with, they won't stay with you. All my diets are a little bit different than what they would get if they went to a hospital nutritionist. But by the time I'm through with them and they're ready for weight maintenance, almost all of them are on the middle-of-the-road approach.[20]

Every successful diet book relies on some trick to give readers the appearance of novelty. It would be impossible to review all the different diet plans here. That arduous task is admirably accomplished by *Rating the Diets,* a book periodically updated by *Chicago Sun-Times* columnist Theodore Berland and the editors of *Consumer Guide.* (Even Berland has not resisted the temptations of commercialism, we regret to report. He is co-author of a book called *Lose Weight the Acupuncture Way.*) After reading a score of diet books—and reaching our limit of tolerance—we have discerned some of their guiding principles.[21]

When we began this book, we planned to avoid writing a self-help manual. There are already more than enough books telling "how to" lose weight and stay thin—most of them packed with misinformation. This once, we shall depart from our rule, to offer some advice that we hope no one will follow: a set of rules, as best we can formulate them, for becoming the author of a successful diet book.

How to Write Your Own Diet Book

1. *Say what you are.* Needless to say, it helps to be a physician or an osteopath. But no special knowledge of weight control is needed. Some of the most popular diet books have been written by cardiologists and obstetricians. Lay people, too, can cut themselves into the deal. Consider *The Amazing Diet Secret of a Desperate Housewife* and *The Hollywood Emergency Diet.* (The actor who wrote the latter, the advertisement boasts, "is not a scientist or doctor. He's not even a college graduate.") Nathan Priti-

kin has made a fortune on his diet-and-exercise plan, originally promoted for heart patients, yet he has no formal medical training; before he devised his system, he was an inventor.

Pritikin and other lay authors have profited from the dieter's distrust of physicians, who, after all, have done relatively little to help people lose weight. Judy Mazel, author of *The Beverly Hills Diet*—which identifies her as a "nutrition magician and diet guru"—explains herself thus: "I do not purport to be a medical doctor. . . . Granted, my ideas are revolutionary, but isn't it about time we found a cure for fat? If medical experts had conclusively proven the causes of fat, we'd all be thin. I have simply pulled together scattered facts and synthesized them." Anyone can do the same.[22]

2. *Pick a catchy title.* This is essential. In 1958, Richard Mackarness published a high-fat, low-carbohydrate diet with the rather bland title, *Eat Fat and Grow Slim.* It went nowhere. Just two years later, Herman Taller published a similar diet plan, but it was dramatically titled, *Calories Don't Count.* It stayed on the best-seller lists for the better part of a year. Drama is everything. Robert Linn's liquid protein plan sold well over a million copies under the title, *The Last Chance Diet*—even though the title became funereally appropriate when deaths from liquid protein were reported. As a last resort, choose a famous name like the Mayo Diet or the Rice Diet. Or name the diet after an exotic locale—South America, Scarsdale, Beverly Hills.[23]

3. *Get them into the tent.* Dieting is no fun, and your readers need motivation. Tell them, as usual, that extra weight increases the risk of heart disease, cancer, diabetes, gout, arthritis, but add one or two diseases they've never heard of. Then turn around and play the sympathetic friend. *You* know that it's not their fault that they are fat; they have a metabolic problem that medical science has failed to recognize. Promise to help them with a plan, based on newly discovered scientific principles, that will allow them to lose weight with no hunger and boundless energy—and improve their sex lives into the bargain.

4. *Present the Master Plan.* This takes some ingenuity. As a general rule of thumb, the diet should be as unnatural and unbalanced as possible; there is, by now, no other way to make it seem special. A tried-and-true method is to tell readers to eat only certain food groups and exclude others. The most common version is low in carbohydrates—bread, sugar, even fruits and vegetables—which many authors paint as the villains of weight gain. Sidney Petrie's book, *Fat Destroyer Foods: The Magic Metabolizer Diet,* is one of the purest examples of this approach. Petrie (who is a hypnotherapist, not a nutritionist) writes that "proteins, and even fats, are fat destroyer foods. Put them in the company of carbohydrate and they switch roles. *A protein or fat calorie, paired with a carbohydrate calorie, makes two fat producing calories.* One carbohydrate calorie can change the life style of ten and even twenty protein calories." And so on. Cutting out carbohydrates, says Petrie, enables a person to stay thin while consuming Martinis and Whipped Cream—the title of another of his books.[24]

A bolder approach is to base a diet on a single food. Eggs and grapefruit are now traditional; a recent count turned up no less than fifty-one diets based on these two staples. One can eat only so many eggs or grapefruits, so diets like these turn out to be low in calories, and people do lose weight on them. The hitch, though, is that single-food diets may be too obviously simple-minded, threatening the dieter with early boredom.[25]

Judy Mazel has cleverly surmounted this obstacle in *The Beverly Hills Diet.* Her rigid six-week diet plan is based largely on single-food days, but the food-of-the-day *varies* in a programmed way. Watermelon, grapes, pineapples, and other fruits predominate (although she does include an all-chicken extravaganza). Her diet can, of course, lead to diarrhea, which Mazel applauds. "If you have loose bowel movements, hooray! Keep in mind that pounds leave your body two main ways— bowel movements and urination. The more time you spend on the toilet, the better. On watermelon days especially, you can expect to urinate a lot. That's the idea."[26]

5. *Break out the textbooks.* Every diet plan needs some scientific-sounding justification. Old diet books are a good place to look; the dieting public has a short memory. Low-carbohydrate diets have been recycled, with essentially the same rationale, for a century. If you can't find a ready-made reason for your gimmick, look through some articles on nutrition and metabolism, take a few quotes out of context, and make something up. Mazel found her inspiration in a book she found in a health-food store, where she went to buy cashews. Borrowing some ideas about enzymes, digestion, and the interaction of foods in the body, Mazel decided that "it's not *what* you eat or *how much* you eat but *when* you eat and what you eat together that counts." The reason to eat only one food at a time, she says, is that "most enzymes can't work simultaneously and that many cancel one another out in our digestive systems."[27]

Don't be shy about theorizing. Remember to claim that human nutrition is still very poorly understood.

6. *Pad, pad, pad.* You may not have much to tell the reader; in some books, the diet plan is only a page long. So fill up the book with recipes, anecdotes, homilies, and reprints of government nutrition tables (which are not copyrighted). You could also follow one famous author's example and break up your book into twenty-five short chapters. Some are only a page long, but each gets its own separate title page. Like dietary fiber, this adds bulk.[28]

7. *Foretell the future.* Your readers know that, like paradise, weight lost is also regained. Tell them that you know this, too, and have designed your diet to help them change their eating habits for life. If the plan is thoroughly unnatural—a liquid protein diet, for instance—tell them that their abstinence from a normal diet will allow them to rethink their eating patterns. If the diet includes fairly balanced menus of real food, tell them that the transition from the diet to regular eating will be smooth and simple. Tell them anything, and round out the picture with some common-sense advice on behavior modification.

You can, of course, do what Robert Atkins does in his *Diet Revolution*. Tell your readers that they must stay on a slightly modified version of the diet—in this case, a high-fat, low-carbohydrate regimen—for the rest of their lives. This approach, however, takes some guts.[29]

8. *Contemplate exercise.* But ignore it as much as possible. If the subject must come up, you're for it.

9. *Blame the victim.* Some of your readers—in fact the great majority—will get nothing whatever from your book. Absolve yourself of any responsibility. Proponents of fasting, for example, claim that hunger disappears during a fast; but this may not be every faster's judgment. Thus, *Fasting as a Way of Life* includes this caveat: "Any so-called hunger 'pangs' are simply normal gastric contractions or stomach spasms. They represent the *sensation* of hunger rather than true hunger." In *The Last Chance Diet,* Linn claims, "The program cannot fail. Only you can fail." End of discussion.[30]

10. *Cover yourself.* Somewhere, in large type or small, advise the reader to consult his or her physician before going on your diet.

The mechanics of diet books are easy to understand. But where do their authors get their ideas? The answer is disturbing. Many fad diets capitalize on ideas that are originally published in professional medical journals—and that are, nevertheless, ill-conceived and potentially dangerous.

Two fundamental facts about dieting are well known. First, all reducing diets work by restricting caloric intake. And second, the way that a diet allocates calories to carbohydrates, fats, and proteins is virtually irrelevant. The facts are simple—and, to many physicians and their patients, unacceptable. Because the attempt to cut calories presents the dieter with the Sisyphean task of pushing against his setpoint, the search for the perfect reducing drug has been paralleled by the search for the perfect diet, one that would somehow circumvent reality and give dieters an easier time of it. A variety of speculative approaches has been developed through medical research, often using carefully selected, hospitalized subjects. The results of these experiments have then been distorted and commercialized irresponsibly. Sometimes, however, the original ideas—as well as their commercial incarnations—are deeply flawed.

Since World War II, the most perennial and popular diets have been those that reduce carbohydrate intake. These diets descend from the regimen that William Banting publicized in his famous *Letter on Corpulence Addressed to the Public*. Banting, a corpulent cabinet-maker, had consulted the physician William Harvey for treatment of an earache; and Harvey, for reasons that remain obscure, treated the condition by putting Banting on a diet. When Banting lost weight, he enthusiastically promoted Harvey's method. As he described it:

Certain articles of ordinary diet, however beneficial in youth, are prejudicial in advanced life, like beans to a horse, whose common ordinary food is hay and corn. . . . I will, therefore, adopt the analogy, and call such food human beans. The items from which I was advised to abstain as much as possible were:—Bread, butter, milk, sugar, beer, and potatoes, which had been the main (and, I thought, innocent) elements of my existence. . . . These, said my excellent adviser, contain starch and saccharine matter, tending to create fat, and should be avoided altogether.[31]

Harvey's advice, through Banting, won many adherents, and the *Letter* went through several printings. A century later, shortly after 1950, his ideas were rediscovered, and the low-carbohydrate diet was presented as if it were new.

Low-carbohydrate formulas have been the most popular of diets for the last twenty years. The secret of their success is almost certainly a side effect. Because they alter mineral metabolism, these diets bring about diuresis—a rapid loss of body water, and hence of weight. The dehydrated dieter soon sees as much as a ten-pound loss on the bathroom scale and is encouraged to continue the effort a bit longer.

After two or three days, as stores of carbohydrate are depleted, fat begins to break down. In the process, chemicals called ketones are released. The claim that ketones decrease appetite has attracted many dieters to low-carbohydrate regimens, even though the claim is unsupported by evidence. The most recent low-carbohydrate success was the Scarsdale diet, which became even more popular after its author, Herman Tarnower, was killed.[32]

The scientific basis for the low-carbohydrate diet, such as it is, derives from the work of Alfred W. Pennington, who was an internist with the E. I. du Pont Company, in Wilmington, Delaware. Pennington, believing that obesity resulted from a defect in the body's ability to burn carbohydrates, proposed a low-carbohydrate diet to remedy the condition. In 1953, Pennington outlined his recommendations in the *New England Journal of Medicine.*

First, said Pennington, low-calorie diets per se could not be expected to help overweight people in the long term. He thought ketones were necessary for weight loss, that they would promote breakdown of the body's fat stores. And production of ketones is encouraged by a low-carbohydrate diet. In fact, Pennington had the story a little garbled; ketones are the product of fat breakdown, not its cause. But he was adamant in damning carbohydrates. "The type of treatment to which these considerations logically lead," he wrote, "is that of a diet in which carbohydrate, alone, is restricted and protein and fat are allowed ad libitum."[33]

Pennington's recommendations defied the laws of chemistry and physics. He was implying, for example, that a person who ate only an apple and two bananas a day would not lose weight, whereas someone who ate two dozen hamburgers (without the buns) would. Pennington did test his diet on du Pont employees and reported good results. But others, predictably, had less success with his regimen. In 1955, Sidney Werner of Columbia University put the theory to the test, and it failed. Werner found that hospitalized patients lost as much weight on a high-carbohydrate diet as on a high-fat diet, except for the early loss of water that the high-fat diet caused in some people.[34]

Pennington's ideas were briefly forgotten. Then, in 1960, Herman Taller, a Rumanian-born obstetrician, published the first modern, best-selling diet book, *Calories Don't Count*. Taller fully acknowledged Pennington, from whom he borrowed freely. He presented a diet plan that allowed unrestricted intake of protein and fat but cut back heavily on carbohydrates. Taller put forth his idea with enthusiastic salesmanship, and added some odd touches of his own; he proposed, for example, that drinking safflower oil would speed the fat-burning process. Even so, the essence of his program was quite close to Pennington's.[35]

Taller's book raised howls from the medical establishment—he was far more harshly criticized than Pennington himself had been. Harvard's Fredrick Stare characterized *Calories Don't Count* as "trash," adding, "There is hardly a word of sense in the whole book." According to Philip L. White of the AMA Council on Foods and Nutrition, "This book is a grave injustice to the intelligent public and can only result in considerable damage to the prestige of the medical profession." Despite their protests, the book sold some two million copies. Only when Taller turned out to have financial connections with a manufacturer of safflower-oil capsules, endorsed in his book, did the ensuing bad publicity lead to a decline in his popularity. Ultimately, Taller was convicted of mail fraud, conspiracy, and violation of federal drug regulations.[36]

The jacket copy for *Calories Don't Count* billed it as "Unbelievable—but true!" The description was only half-right. Calories *do* count, of course. In 1964, as an implicit response to Taller, metabolic specialists in California showed that changing the diet of people on a weight-reducing regimen made no difference in the speed of weight loss, as long as the number of calories remained constant. (Even adding a shot of safflower oil to the diet made no difference.)[37]

It turns out, too, that a *high-*carbohydrate diet may be more healthful than a low-carbohydrate diet, and at least as effective for weight loss. Dietary fiber can help diabetics get by with less insulin and may help prevent cancer of the colon. Fiber may also help people feel full while they eat relatively few calories. Although this possibility is still controversial, Olaf Mickelsen and his colleagues at Michigan State University have shown that college students reduced fairly quickly by eating twelve slices of low-calorie, high-fiber bread each day, along with whatever else they wanted. Apparently the bread reduced their hunger for other foods.[38]

The continuing prejudice against carbohydrates is wholly irrational; they contain only half as many calories, ounce for ounce, as fats do. But for one reason or another, generations of diet doctors have condemned carbohydrates while telling people, perversely, to eat as much fat as they liked. A decade after Taller, Robert Atkins, a cardiologist, resurrected the high-fat diet with his *Diet Revolution.*

As Taller had done before him, Atkins drew on the work of Pennington, as well as later experiments by British scientists. He praised ketosis even more highly than Taller had. Atkins wrote that "ketosis is a state devoutly to be desired, because while you are in this happy state (and I mean that literally, for an elevation of mood accompanies it as a rule) your fat is being burned off with *maximum* efficiency and *minimum* deprivation (since in ketosis your hunger disappears!)."[39]

Atkins capitalized on the durable idea that ketones have anti-hunger properties—an assumption that pervades the medical and popular literature, but that has yet to be proved. The idea seems to have come from observations of fasting people, who often experience decreased hunger. Fasters do enter a state of ketosis, but their digestive machinery also shuts down, and it may be this change, rather than the ketones, that causes the loss of appetite. As a group of Yale physicians have pointed out, "There are no controlled studies demonstrating that ketosis either protects against hunger or enhances a sense of well-being in human beings. Such teaching is based on anecdotal accounts rather than scientific fact."[40]

Atkins's theories were neither particularly new, nor particularly good. But to hear him tell it, his ideas were socially as well as scientifically revolutionary. At the close of his book, he wrote:

Martin Luther King had a dream. I, too, have one. I dream of a world where no one has to diet. A world where the fattening refined carbohydrates have been excluded from the diet. . . . Write your senators and congressman. . . . Help see that school cafeterias stop filling up our children on a cheap diet of mainly refined carbohydrates. . . . And lobby for laws that require diet foods to be *low in carbohydrates as well as calories.* With your help, there truly can be a Diet Revolution![41]

Atkins did come to the attention of the U.S. Senate, but not in the way he had hoped. On April 12, 1973, he was called to appear before Senator George McGovern's Select Committee on Nutrition and Human Needs. The American Medical Association had already publicly condemned the Atkins diet, and the Senate committee called several expert witnesses to add their disapproval.

The hearings appear to have had little effect. At this writing, Atkins still maintains a healthy practice and has come out with a new book, *Dr. Atkins' Nutrition Breakthrough.* Nevertheless, the hearings did raise an important issue. Medical experts called before the committee testified that Atkins's plan was not only fraudulent, but potentially harmful. The high-fat regimen he recommended could increase cholesterol levels in the blood. The Atkins plan also posed a special danger to pregnant women, inasmuch as ketosis might harm the fetus.[42]

These charges of harm were largely hypothetical. No one is known to have died from following Atkins's diet. The first clearly fatal plan was one that came along a few years later: the liquid protein diet.

This disastrous approach was based on an experimental program, called the "protein-sparing modified fast," that was considered the biggest advance in obesity therapy during the 1970s. The concept was developed by several investigators in the United States and France, but is generally credited to George Blackburn, a surgeon at Harvard Medical School, who began by studying the nutritional needs of post-surgical patients. In the process, Blackburn sought a way to ensure optimal nutrition on a low intake of calories. He developed a "modified fast" and used it to treat obese patients, because conventional diets had proved "an abysmal, disastrous failure."[43]

It is clearly not healthful to fast completely for any length of time; to acquire the necessary nutrients to survive, the body soon starts breaking down muscle protein as well as fat. But what if a person ate just enough protein to protect the muscle? Blackburn and his colleagues had tried this approach and claimed it worked. Patients lost weight, but appeared to lose only fat, not lean tissue. In addition, the protein-only diet raised their ketone levels and lowered levels of insulin—biochemical changes that Blackburn thought would be helpful in weight loss. Because this semifast was designed to save the body's protein, it was called the "protein-sparing modified fast," or PSMF for short.

Blackburn's group gave its patients real food, such as breast of chicken, in carefully measured doses. But another physician, Victor Vertes in Cleveland, favored a high-protein liquid for his obese patients. Liquid portions are easier to measure, and they have the added advantage, supposedly, of weaning a patient from attachment to real food. Blackburn and his colleagues tried the liquid protein approach for a time, but rejected it in favor of lean meat. Nonetheless, protein formulas caught on with several practitioners of the PSMF.[44]

To their credit, the inventors of this new type of fasting sounded a note of caution as they introduced it. In their first paper, Vertes and his colleagues emphasized that they had given liquid protein only to very obese patients, and acknowledged that "this therapeutic approach is drastic and runs counter to conventional nutritional wisdom and dietary counseling." Within a few years, however, clinicians became more sanguine about the PSMF and were using it with an increasing number of patients. The dangers of the approach first became clear when it was commercialized in the most infamous of diet books, *The Last Chance Diet*.[45]

Written by osteopath Robert Linn, this book promoted the author's own "Prolinn" formula—an implicit advertisement that led to some legal trouble:

It's not as thick as Jell-O, but it doesn't run like water. It has the full-pink tint of a Beaujolais, but even the most uneducated of wine drinkers would not be fooled. It contains no fats, no carbohydrates, only a few calories, and an abundance of protein. And it's what you will be substituting for the sustenance you're used to. It will provide your body with all the protein it needs. I call it Prolinn.[46]

Linn's book made liquid protein a huge success; *Newsweek* reported that an estimated four million Americans tried Prolinn or some other liquid protein preparation. Linn, of course, had been reassuring. "It's safe: there has not been a reported case of any permanent bad effects although thousands of patients have completed the fast successfully." The guarantee soon rang hollow. By 1978, the FDA and the Center for Disease Control were investigating some fifty-eight cases in which people had died while using the liquid protein diet. For once, bad publicity actually helped end a dangerous diet fad; sales of liquid protein plummeted.[47]

Proponents of the PSMF took pains to dissociate themselves from Linn's liquid protein plan. Commercial liquid protein preparations, unlike those used in the clinics, were produced from cattle hides and thus contained low-quality protein; they may not have been "as thick as Jell-O," but they were essentially based on gelatin. The preparations may have lacked some of the amino acids necessary for life, and they did not contain enough of such essential minerals as potassium, phosphorus, and magnesium. The deaths from liquid protein diets had resulted from heart failure, presumably from nutritional deficiencies—although the precise cause remains unknown.[48]

Blackburn repeatedly cautioned that the PSMF should only be an adjunct to a comprehensive weight-control program, and should be administered by a knowledgeable physician: "It was fine as long as it was in the physicians' hands, because they could talk people into taking vitamins and minerals," said Blackburn in 1979. "But the exploiters just carried on with the connective tissue protein without the co-factors. . . . A gullible public and exploiting industry added up to disaster."[49]

Now it appears, however, that even medical supervision is no guarantee that a low-calorie protein diet will be safe. Rafael Lantigua and his colleagues, at the University of Rochester, placed six patients on a liquid protein diet under very close supervision. As they reported in 1980, fully half of this random sample showed "potentially life-threatening arrhythmias"—irregularities of the heartbeat that presumably had been the main cause of the reported deaths from liquid protein. Worse, the problems only showed up under a sophisticated system of around-the-clock heart monitoring, and the causes of the abnormalities remained impossible to determine. In other words, even an assiduous clinician would not be able to detect these arrhythmias in normal clinical practice. The authors had a firm conclusion: "We recommend that the use of liquid protein diets should be terminated pending further investigation of the causes and of prevention of the cardiac toxicity."[50]

The Rochester physicians had used a commercial liquid protein preparation, which provided the minimum daily requirements of amino acids to their subjects. Their patients also received potassium supplements and vitamins. It is likely that giving their subjects more nutritional supplements—especially minerals—would have prevented the arrhythmias. However, the treatment these patients received was as good as the treatment most competent physicians would provide—and they were observed with unusual care. If more precautions are needed, then highly restricted, all-protein diets should be regarded as experimental treatments at best, not established methods of weight loss.[51]

Zero-carbohydrate diets may offer no real benefits to offset their risks. In February 1980, an article in the *New England Journal of Medicine* reported a Yale study of seven obese patients. Each subject was placed on two different diets in succession: a 400-calorie all-protein diet, and a 400-calorie mixture of protein and carbohydrate. "Low calorie protein diets," the investigators concluded, "cannot be viewed as more efficacious than mixed diets in the management of obesity and may, in fact, result in adverse effects not observed with carbohydrate-containing diets." The all-protein diet offered no advantage in speeding true weight loss (though it produced a loss of water) or in preventing the breakdown of body protein.[52]

The Yale findings are controversial; both diets were unusually low in calories, and were not supplemented as the PSMF is. But the benefits of an all-protein diet still appear to be largely hypothetical. J. S. Garrow, a British authority on obesity, has noted the confusion around the protein-sparing modified fast: "Virtually every statement on the subject is contradicted by some other investigator," he writes.[53]

This uncertainty reflects a defect of the PSMF and, in fact, all stringent diet plans. The goal has been to devise a diet that would contain all necessary nutrients within a minimum number of calories, to produce weight loss as quickly and safely as possible. But no one yet knows enough about human nutrition to be able to say what the necessary nutrients are, or how much of them is needed. Moreover, the biochemical rationale for the PSMF, which is essentially the same as for other low-carbohydrate diets, is a poorly tested hypothesis that may turn out to be simply incorrect.

In treating fatness, physicians have not only conformed to prevailing styles, as Shaw noted—they have become trendsetters. Medical approaches to weight control have been emulated by lay entrepreneurs. The prescription of appetite suppressants is echoed in the over-the-counter market for phenylpropanolamine. Stringent, unbalanced diets, devised in metabolic research wards, are popularized in best sellers.

Unfortunately, by themselves, neither diets nor drugs work in the long term, whether they are prescribed or self-administered. Their failure has led to a new, and grim, medical fashion in the treatment of the morbidly obese. Increasingly, physicians are looking to surgery and restraint to help these patients lose weight. Intestinal-bypass surgery is so hazardous that it is largely being abandoned. But new methods of stapling the stomach, or even wrapping it in a kind of mesh to shrink it, are being enthusiastically tried; and jaw wiring appears to be making a comeback.

These approaches, of course, will always remain in the hands of physicians; and surgeons will only treat those who are dangerously overweight. But the attitude embodied in surgery may be reflected on a wide scale. The surgical approach holds that weight cannot be lost through will power, special diets, or even drugs; rather, the body itself must be cut, shaped, manipulated.

This philosophy is expressed in several commercial novelties designed to shape the client's body while she remains completely passive. "Body-wrapping," a French import, has recently become available on the East Coast. The areas to be reduced are smeared with a cream—which may contain such ingredients as sea salt, herbs, and cod liver oil—and then wrapped in special bandages. (One *Boston Globe* reporter who tried the treatment said she felt like a roast packaged in Saran Wrap.) The goal is to "melt" fat areas—especially the puckered, orange-peel fat modishly termed "cellulite"—right off the body.[54]

Other French techniques for fighting cellulite are more aggressive, and some are potentially dangerous. Machines massage a woman's legs with powerful jets of air, or administer a barrage of "fat-dispersing" injections. These methods are utterly unrealistic: So-called cellulite is no different from the rest of the body's adipose tissue, and the puckered skin associated with it is produced by connective tissue, which cannot be removed or altered by any known technique. Still, these bogus therapies for a nonexistent malady have a firm foothold in Europe and may yet be exported to the United States.[55]

Another kind of reducing machine—the "passive exercise" device—has already found a new popularity in America. These machines deliver slight electrical shocks to selected muscles, cause them to contract, and supposedly do the client some good. In the fall of 1980, *Health & Diet Times*—a New York publication that covers such things—reported that a Tone-N-Trim Center using these devices had opened next door to Bloomingdale's. The publication reported credulously that "a 35-minute session is equivalent to 1,500 push-ups or sit-ups without the unpleasant aches and pains that are required from such strenuous exercise." There is clear evidence that these devices, used as surrogates for exercise, do not help people get into shape or lose weight.[56]

The very concept of "passive exercise" is a classic of doublethink; along with "working on a suntan," it makes about as much sense as "foodless meal." Its popularity lies in the false promise of fitness without effort.

Anyone who seriously wants to become thinner should consider a program of physical activity. Exercise does take work, even a certain amount of will power; but unlike dieting, it repays the effort. Perhaps more important, exercise transforms the body from a fleshy object, which must be pummeled or starved for its own good, into an independent and self-regulating organism.

9

EAT AND RUN:
THE IMPORTANCE
OF EXERCISE

IN the summer of 1981, an American of our acquaintance returned home after four years of living in sub-Saharan Africa. "The biggest change I found on coming back," he volunteered, "and it's very conspicuous, is the number of people out exercising. If I remember correctly, when I left it still seemed a little strange to see people go running down a city street in the colorful equivalent of underwear. It *still* looks odd to me, but nobody else seems to notice."

You didn't have to spend a few years out of circulation to perceive the difference. City parks had become clogged with joggers. Health clubs were proliferating almost as rapidly as fast-food franchises. Running shoes had been transformed from a sporting-goods oddity into a major item of commerce and an acceptable form of footwear for all but the most formal occasions. The statistically minded could record the change by counting the number of entrants in the New York Marathon; from a few hundred in 1975, it went to 16,005 in 1980.[1]

Indeed, the change has been obvious, and it has arrived in tandem with so many other fads, styles, and marketing revolutions that it has not seemed to require much in the way of explanation. Jogging just seems to go with granola, "light" beverages and cigarettes, environmentalist politics, weekend therapy sessions, and sexual self-expression. Only the most naïve could attribute this vogue for exercise to health education, although health benefits have often been cited, *ex post facto.* The real reason for the boom in recreational exertion, however, cuts much deeper than fashion, or even politics. The burst of jogging, swimming, stationary bicycling, and working out on weight machines was almost certainly a reaction to the fact that Americans had been *reducing* their activity levels for many years. Evidently they had reached the lower limit of their ability to tolerate inactivity.

The drop in energy output was measured indirectly by the Human Nutrition Center of the United States Department of Agriculture (USDA). From large, careful surveys conducted in 1965 and 1977, the USDA discovered that Americans had reduced their per capita intake of calories by 10 percent; children and young adult males, especially, were eating less. And if they were eating less, they had to be *doing* less, for they certainly were not losing weight. Another government survey compared Americans in the early 1970s with those living a decade earlier. Men of average height were four to six pounds heavier in the middle-age groups; women had gained somewhat less.[2]

We have dropped our caloric intake precisely because living in America has required less and less energy; by eating a sparser diet people have unconsciously compensated for an increasingly sedentary life. The USDA statistics imply that by the late 1970s the nation was becoming, if not immobile, exceedingly sedentary. The change even from the 1960s was dramatic. Consider this example: Young men took in about 2,950 calories a day in 1965; twelve years later they consumed only 2,500. A man who cuts his daily intake by 450 calories, *without* becoming less active, can expect to lose almost a pound a week—though the loss may taper off as the metabolic rate slows to compensate for caloric deprivation. Men did not become thinner, so they must have been moving less.

The change in American activity patterns has not been brought on by a decay in moral fiber, but by broad social and economic developments. The nature of work has changed markedly in the last few decades. Really heavy labor has become almost nonexistent. In the 1950s, when the Stanford epidemiologist Ralph Paffenbarger began a study of San Francisco longshoremen, he found that 40 percent of them were doing "heavy" work (above 5 calories a minute, or roughly 2,300 a day, in lifting and carrying). Just ten years later, thanks to mechanization, only 15 percent of longshoremen remained in that category—and by 1972, when containerized shipping was introduced, just 5 percent were doing heavy labor.[3]

The majority of the workforce shifted from farming and industrial work to service jobs after World War II, and production was rapidly automated in the 1960s and 1970s. Meanwhile, suburbanization required ever greater dependence on automobiles. Television provided a strong incentive to immobility, and increasing use of television as a babysitter may explain why the energy turnover of preschool children fell proportionately more than that of any other group in the population, according to the USDA.

It appears that by 1977 Americans had reached activity levels that were approaching an all-time minimum for the human species. Only women in purdah and a few other, exceptional classes of people could have maintained such a low output. By eating less to compensate, Americans were beginning to risk nutritional deficiencies. For example, calcium intake of children declined between 1965 and 1977, and several groups fell below the recommended amount.

The drift to inactivity could not have continued at the same rate; if it had, a large portion of the population would literally be confined to bed twenty-four hours a day by the year 2000. Clearly, that is not going to happen. As the 1970s closed, the trend seemed to be reversing itself. Faced with a world that no longer demanded physical effort to work, play, or get around town, citizens began to take matters into their own hands. More accurately, they voted with their feet—and began the kind of conspicuous exercising that now characterizes the American landscape.

The year 1977 may well have marked a transition between the phase of declining involuntary activity and the rise of voluntary exercise. In that year, a Gallup Poll found that 47 percent of Americans claimed to perform some kind of daily recreational exercise—twice the percentage of 1961. This was, according to George Gallup, "one of the most dramatic changes in American lifestyles to have taken place in recent decades." Of all the people interviewed, 12 percent claimed to jog every day; among young adults the figure approached 30 percent. Results from a poll taken in 1980 showed no further increase in the proportion of people exercising.[4]

Jogging has been the principal form of voluntary, regular exercise, probably because it is the least elaborate. But as the movement, so to speak, began, it hardly seemed to be a spontaneous reaction to excessive ease. It was perceived as an aggressive, obnoxious fad in some quarters, even as its prophets proclaimed it the key to longevity, a better sex life, and spiritual peace. Although rather comic claims and counterclaims as to the benefits and hazards of jogging appeared in the medical and lay press, the relationship of activity to caloric balance attracted surprisingly little attention.

As the government studies showed, cutting calories does not help people lose weight if they also become less active. On the other hand, people who begin to exercise can become thinner without consciously dieting.

This fact was hardly appreciated until recently. It had been a well-established myth, supported from time to time by medical pronouncements, that exercising makes people hungrier and consequently works against efforts to lose weight. Another, often repeated argument is that the calories spent in exercise are so few that they cannot conceivably matter. By one estimate, a person would have to walk up and down stairs for four solid hours—time enough to scale the Empire State Building—just to lose a single pound of fat.[5] Anything less ambitious—say, jogging half a mile to a mile—burns off only the calories from a single apple. On the face of it, it seems easier to skip the apple, stay home, and watch television.

Confronted by these figures, a determined individual could still attempt to balance every bite of food with the activity required to burn it off. But as we pointed out at the beginning of this book, no one can estimate the calories in food and exercise accurately enough to pull off the required juggling act. And the effort to do the impossible is sure to be frustrating. It is difficult, for example, to imagine anyone sticking with *The Eat Anything Exercise Diet* by Frank Konishi, Judi Kesselman, and Franklynn Peterson. "John noted that a twelve-minute walk would work off the calories in a cup of coffee with cream and sugar," the authors write of a client who followed their plan. "So for his usual four cups a day, he could walk an extra forty-eight minutes. His glass of milk required thirty-one minutes of walking. And to save the butter on his sandwich, he could add another seven minutes, for a total of eighty-six minutes of walking." "John" compromised by giving up some of his little indulgences as well as walking more.[6]

Such obsessive calorie-counting is not only futile but unnecessary; the body responds to exercise in a way that can promote weight-loss automatically. As we saw in chapter 4, the setpoint appears to be altered by activity. If a person is truly sedentary—as most Americans probably are unless they make a special effort—then the setpoint adjusts to an abnormally high level. Regular activity can bring it back down. Although only a few calories are burned *during* a run around the local track, the effects of jogging, rapid walking, or any kind of regular endurance exercise, are long-lasting. An active body is "set" to be thinner than an inactive one.

In general, any animal should adapt in two ways as its setpoint is lowered: It should adjust its intake of food appropriately, and it should burn calories at a higher rate. Both of these effects are seen when a person exercises. Jean Mayer's pioneering studies, described in chapter 4, showed that moderately active people (and rats) ate less and weighed less than those who were inactive. As the activity level rose further, the setpoint held constant, and subjects ate enough extra to supply the calories needed for their output.

There is some indication that exercise also increases the metabolic burning of calories, as well as regulating appetite. In 1935, a study of Harvard football players showed that athletic activity could raise the metabolic rate considerably. Work at the Fatigue Laboratory and the Department of Hygiene at Harvard's Medical School showed "that even fifteen hours after a game or a strenuous practice . . . the metabolic rate is in general distinctly elevated . . . it may be twenty-five percent above normal."[7]

Half a century later, this finding remains controversial. The effects of exercise on the production of metabolic heat are still not entirely clear. What is clear, however, is that running several miles a week, for example, does more than burn up a hundred calories per mile; the exercise can work in other ways to help the body stabilize at a lower weight. People who begin an exercise training program often lose more weight than can be accounted for by calories burned during the actual activity. As the Swedish physiologist and obesity researcher Per Björntorp has written,

The famous Vasaloppet, an eighty-five-kilometer long ski race in Sweden, takes about ten hours for a nonathlete to finish. Provided that nothing is eaten during this day of hard labor, the loss of calories will still be less than one kilogram [2.2 pounds] of adipose tissue. Such calculations indicate that other mechanisms have to be responsible for the weight decrease during a training program, and the most likely candidates are effects on appetite regulation or on thermogenesis.[8]

If exercise, or the lack of it, can affect the setpoint, then we might expect that many people become fat as a result of lowering their activity levels. A survey from 1939 (described in Chapter 4) did find that a majority of obese people had first gained weight during a period of forced inactivity, such as an illness or long convalescence. Since the 1960s, Jean Mayer and others have systematically studied groups of fat people to see whether they move less than thin people.

In one of the most objective (and impressive) studies, Beverly Bullen, Robert Reed, and Mayer made sixteen-millimeter movies of girls at two summer camps—an obese group at Cape Cod's Camp Seascape and a group of normal weight at nearby Camp Wono. At both Seascape and Wono, campers participated in supervised sports—volleyball, swimming, and tennis. When films from the two camps were analyzed in detail, the obese girls were found to be far less active while participating in all three sports.[9]

Subsequent studies, perhaps influenced by the powerful conclusion of Bullen, Reed, and Mayer, have also reported that fat children are relatively inactive, but the methods have rarely been so painstaking. Several have based their assessment of activity on parents' reports. A dissenting study, conducted by Marjorie Waxman and Albert Stunkard, was based on observations of children both at home and on the school playground. The children were seen to be inactive at home, but they got a normal amount of exercise at school and, because of their extra weight, presumably were burning more calories than their leaner schoolmates.[10]

Earlier, working with Anna-Marie Chirico, Stunkard had attempted to compare the overall activity levels of obese and lean adults. In 1960, the investigators supplied pedometers to obese and lean subjects and requested that they wear the devices through their waking hours. When the mechanical counters were read and compared, they showed that the lean women had walked more than twice as far as the fat ones. The pedometers revealed a smaller difference between the two groups of men.[11] Fat children and adults may differ in their patterns of eating and exercising. Waxman and Stunkard suggested that obese children may be normally active, at least in some situations, but eat unusually large amounts, whereas fat adults seem to eat less than average and to be less active than their lean contemporaries.

The various studies of activity have, individually, yielded intriguing and plausible results, yet they have not added up to a consistent or airtight case proving inactivity to be the major reason for weight gain. So many variables affect both fatness and fitness that their relationship is hard to pin down.

Just as the eating behavior of fat people is altered by their attempts to restrain intake and by the situations in which they find themselves, so also their levels of activity may be influenced by their emotions and surroundings. Chirico and Stunkard discovered that the fat women in their study were more depressed than the lean ones, as well as less active, and suggested that the emotional state of the fat might well account for a certain sluggishness. The children who were different at home and at school are another warning against facile interpretations. Likewise, in some circumstances, fat girls and women may be loath to exercise simply because they are self-conscious. The fat girls at Camp Seascape displayed a "distinctly negative" attitude toward swimming, according to the observers, and participated in the sport with more than their usual lethargy. This finding might seem paradoxical; the buoyancy of fat people makes swimming an easier sport for them than for the very lean. Indeed, some of the most successful swimmers of the English Channel have been distinctly stout. But for an adolescent girl living in mid-century America, branded as fat enough to be sent away to a weight-loss camp and then asked to put on a swimsuit and display her body, somehow a "distinctly negative" attitude seems altogether comprehensible.

The caloric cost of activity may also differ in fat and thin people. In many activities, the caloric expenditure of a fat person is greater than normal, for the obvious reason that it takes more work to move a heavy weight. For example, if a man weighs 160 pounds, it costs him a hundred calories to run a mile in ten minutes. If he gained sixty pounds, it would cost him 136 calories. But if he remained the same weight and ran the mile in six minutes instead of ten, he would add only nine calories to his output. In other words, a heavy person moving relatively slowly may in fact be working far harder than a slender person who is moving much faster.[12]

Further, of course, it is a perennial temptation—and a pitfall —to assume that fat people, like happy families, are all alike. Not only does the notion arise from our habit of stereotyping, but it oversimplifies research: A group of fat people can be compared with a group of thin ones, and if by a stroke of luck some difference shows up, the results can be reported. But fat and thin people are equally diverse in their habits and patterns of living. It should come as no surprise that attempts to find consistent differences between the two groups—with respect to their metabolic rates, eating patterns, or exercise habits—have produced uncertain and often conflicting results.

Whether or not inactivity produces obesity, exercise does appear to be an effective remedy—at least for some people. Because exercise can lower the setpoint, a training program has many advantages over a reducing diet. A stringent diet can lead to a loss of both muscle and fat; the right kind of exercise, however, will burn fat preferentially while it builds up muscle. The metabolic rate drops during a long-term diet, but simultaneous exercising can compensate for this effect. Moreover, exercise can be pleasurable, as a diet never is.

Overweight subjects, in a program at the University of California at Davis, showed that exercise would counteract some of the drawbacks of dieting, particularly the fall in metabolic rate, and thus promote weight loss. Judith Stern—a nutritionist and avid skier—collaborated with exercise physiologists Edward Bernauer and Paul Mole to study six people they put on a low-calorie diet. As expected, metabolic rates fell after two weeks—the typical "starvation" reaction. Then the subjects began an exercise program. Over the next two weeks, metabolic rates returned to normal in half the dieters, who then lost weight more rapidly. One of them, in fact, lost thirty pounds within a month.

Stern cautions that these findings are still preliminary, and that other investigators have failed to find a similar effect. Yet she is confident that "exercise, certainly for adults, is really key in preventing weight gain as you get older." Basal metabolic rate, she points out, decreases by 2 percent to 5 percent with every decade past the age of thirty. Activity, by offsetting this effect, may help to diminish the accumulation of fat that seems virtually inevitable with aging. Really vigorous exercise can be very potent. Norwegian woodcutters, for example, do not grow fat with age; they maintain about 15 percent body fat, and an average weight of around 160 pounds, for forty years.[13]

Diet in combination with exercise worked well for Stern's subjects. But if exercise alone helps maintain a relatively low setpoint, then sedentary people should lose weight spontaneously if they undertake an exercise program and ignore dieting. This hypothesis has been tested by several investigators. At the University of California campus in Irvine, Grant Gwinup worked with a group of obese men and women who had been discouraged by repeated failures at dieting. He told them to forget about controlling what they ate and to begin a program of physical activity. The exercise was carefully adjusted to the capacity of each individual, and for most of them it began as brisk walking for ten or fifteen minutes daily. Although most subjects dropped out of the program fairly early, anyone who reached the point of walking briskly for at least thirty minutes, five days a week, began to lose weight spontaneously, with no reported effort to resume dieting.

The eleven women who stayed with the program generally found that they wanted to increase their activity above the minimum level, and several became virtual addicts, spending upwards of an hour a day in brisk walking or an equivalent activity. A year and a half after they began, the women had each lost twenty-two pounds on average and were continuing a steady, slow loss. Moreover, as Gwinup has written, they "frequently commented that weight loss through exercise, unlike that previously achieved through dieting, was not accompanied by feelings of weakness and increased nervousness, but rather by feelings of increased strength and relaxation."[14]

Other investigators have demonstrated the same effect that Gwinup reported. Dorothy L. Moody and her colleagues, at Pennsylvania State University, put eleven college women struggling with their weight on an eight-week program of walking and jogging, again with no special diet. The women lost an average of more than five pounds each. And Arthur Leon and his colleagues, at the University of Minnesota, showed that the approach works at least as well with men. After sixteen weeks of vigorous walking—again with no limitation on food intake —half a dozen obese young men lost an average of thirteen pounds each. The question that remains to be answered is whether exercise programs can achieve long-term adherence without a high rate of dropping out.[15]

Exercise alone is typically a slow route to weight loss. According to a review of the reported data, exercise initially takes off no more than one-third of a pound each week from fat people and about one-tenth of a pound from people of essentially normal weight.[16]

Progress during an exercise program, however, may be faster than it appears. Studies of animals and people—including those of Gwinup, Moody, and Leon—have established that exercise actually produces the loss of fat at the same time that it is building up muscle. Moody's subjects, for example, lost almost twelve pounds of fat but only half as much weight because they simultaneously gained six pounds of muscle. Conversely, more than a third of the weight lost through dieting alone—and some two-thirds of the weight lost on a total fast—can reflect loss of muscle, not fat.[17]

Because muscle is denser than fat, a muscular person is leaner, as well as stronger, than a fat person of the same weight. Fat loss—not weight loss—is what most dieters truly seek. But the confusion between "overweight" and "overfat" has been with us for years. To take one famous example, in 1942 two United States Navy physicians took careful measurements of twenty-five professional football players. Seventeen of the athletes could have been classified as unfit for military service because they were more than 15 percent above the "average weight for height" determined from insurance company tables. But the doctors found that, for eleven of these seventeen men, only a small percentage of their weight was actually fat. They were in "prime physical condition"; their weight came from big muscles, which presumably would have been an asset in the military. The Defense Department has yet to clear up its confusion. In 1981, the Navy announced that a three-year study had shown that heavy people—including many who would be rejected as overweight—were stronger than lighter individuals. For such chores as opening hatches and unlocking watertight doors, heavy people proved superior.[18]

Compulsive scale-watchers are especially inclined to confuse weight with fat. Joan Ullyot—an exercise physiologist in San Francisco, and author of several popular books on running— describes one woman jogger who turned to liquid protein for quick weight loss:

She was 132 pounds and five feet eight inches—which is not bad—and in her forties. When she went on the liquid protein diet, she soon was so weak that she couldn't keep running; so she stopped running, but she kept losing weight on her diet and got down to 112 pounds. She felt very happy, but she looked just horrible—with skinfolds hanging off her—and very weak.

Tests showed that the woman had lost virtually no fat, but twenty pounds of muscle. "No wonder she couldn't move," Ullyot adds. The physician herself weighs the same—135 pounds—as she did before she began running ten years ago. "I'm just the same as I've always been," she says. "I usually fluctuate up or down ten pounds, mainly depending on how much wine I drink and how many desserts I eat. But I've lost twenty pounds of fat since I started running and put on twenty pounds of muscle—and I've gone down two dress sizes."[19]

The activity that burns fat is "aerobic," or oxygen-utilizing, exercise. Muscles rely on two different kinds of fuel to power them. One, sugar, is used for short bursts, as in an all-out sprint or in weight lifting; here the muscles depend on a rapid breakdown of glycogen, a form of sugar stored in the muscle and continually replenished by the bloodstream. A spurt of intense effort—for as long as, say, sixty seconds—can draw solely on the body's glycogen reserves. During such activity, energy is extracted from the sugar by processes that require no oxygen; thus this type of work is known as "anaerobic." Any more sustained effort (which uses the muscle at far less than its maximum capacity), draws on fatty acids released from adipose tissue, combining them with oxygen to derive a steady supply of the needed energy. Because it consumes oxygen, this second process is termed "aerobic."

This dual system exists because glycogen can supply a good deal of energy very rapidly. However, not only is glycogen bulky to store, but also the anaerobic process quickly builds up a load of lactic acid, which must be dissipated and burned or else it will injure the muscle. On the other hand, fat stores energy in a very compact way, and muscles readily metabolize it during aerobic effort; thus, they can continue activity for a very long time in this mode. So-called aerobic exercises are those that push muscles to work moderately for a long enough time to shift them from a relatively heavy dependence on glycogen to predominant dependence on fatty acids. About 90 percent of the energy for a 100-yard dash comes from anaerobic processes, whereas 99 percent of the energy for a two-hour jog is aerobic.

In addition to the difference in the kinds of fuel they burn, the two kinds of exercise have very different consequences over the long term. Repeatedly pushing a muscle to near its maximum capacity causes it to add contractile tissue; it becomes stronger as a result. But this anaerobic process seems to have rather little effect on the rest of the body. Aerobic exercise, on the other hand, adds a rather small amount of contractile protein to the muscle, but it markedly increases the components of muscle needed for energy metabolism, and it stimulates growth of the local circulation. It also causes the heart to work harder and thus to grow stronger. As part of the body-wide changes that seem to go along with this kind of "conditioning," fat stores are reduced.[20]

The form of exercise required to bring about conditioning need not be conspicuously athletic. What is necessary is continuous exertion. Breathing and heart rate must accelerate, to a level that depends on the individual's age and previous condition, for at least twenty minutes at a time. Jogging is, for many people, an effective way to reach this goal. It has the virtue of simplicity and at this point is so common that one need not feel conspicuous. People who see themselves as fat, however, may justifiably feel daunted by the prospect. Indeed, for them jogging may not even be a desirable way to begin.

Rapid walking can be very effective as a form of conditioning, especially for people who are heavy. Although the human frame is so designed that a casual stroll is extremely efficient and requires a minimum of power, the body functions far less efficiently as the pace gets faster. This means that a very rapid walk can become quite strenuous—even more so than jogging at the same speed. In fact, we tend naturally to break into a run at precisely the speed that makes walking less efficient than jogging. Thus, pushing a walking pace to the upper limit of ease and continuing for twenty minutes can be excellent conditioning, or "aerobic" exercise.[21]

Swimming, of course, is a superb alternative to walking or jogging, especially for people who have joint problems. However, facilities may be hard to reach, expensive to use, or crowded. Travel time also adds to the total amount of time spent in exercise—a drawback for busy people. For all these reasons, Howard Knuttgen, an exercise physiologist at Boston University, observes, "swimming tends not to be a lifetime sport."[22]

Bicycles can also be used for aerobic exercise, but getting a workout can be deceptively difficult, according to Knuttgen. Because bicycles are so efficiently designed, they require only about one-sixth the energy of running at any given speed. Consequently, with a light bicycle on a level surface, one must pedal very fast—almost dangerously so on most roads—to achieve the required effect. Even riding ten to fifteen miles on a bicycle may produce relatively little conditioning for the effort, unless one has a heavy bike and sets a course that includes long uphill stretches. Stationary bicycles can serve the purpose rather better than a regular bicycle because resistance can be set high enough to mimic the effect of a long hill. Good ones are expensive, but the cheaper models can usually be adjusted, with some care, to make the required workout possible. People with disabilities affecting their legs can sometimes find the equivalent of a stationary bicycle for the arms, but these devices are found mainly in laboratories and rehabilitation clinics.[23]

Whatever form of suitably taxing effort is found—and, unfortunately, it has to feel like effort to be of any use—it must be repeated fairly frequently to lower fat stores. In 1978, the American College of Sports Medicine outlined its recommendations for slenderizing exercise. They prescribed a program of continuous aerobic exercise for at least twenty minutes at a time, burning 300 calories or more each session, with at least three sessions a week.[24]

Two years later, Leonard Epstein and Rena Wing of the Western Psychiatric Institute and Clinic, in Pittsburgh, analyzed all the published studies that provided reliable data on the subject. They found that the frequency of exercise mattered a good deal. People who exercised four or five times a week lost weight three times faster than those who only exercised three days a week, and one or two weekly sessions were completely ineffective. Likewise, people who burned over a thousand calories a week in exercise had twice the benefit of those who exercised with less intensity. Epstein and Wing's summary of the field suggests one reason why Gwinup's group of eleven women did so well. They exercised *daily.* Obviously, no guidelines can be absolute, and individuals respond idiosyncratically to physical activity. Indeed, we all know some very lean people who echo Robert Maynard Hutchins's famous remark that, whenever he felt like exercising, he would lie down until the impulse had passed.[25]

The type of diet, as well as the type and frequency of exercise, is an important consideration in starting any training program. Combining an exercise plan with a very low carbohydrate diet is generally a bad idea, because carbohydrates are needed to replenish the body's store of glycogen. Recently, Ethan Sims's colleagues, at the University of Vermont, have shown that the body can adapt to long periods of carbohydrate deprivation, such as a protein-sparing modified fast. After six weeks, obese subjects on a no-carbohydrate diet—with adequate vitamin and mineral supplements—can endure moderate aerobic exercise as well as others on a more balanced regimen can. But the PSMF does *not* provide the necessary fuel for more strenuous aerobic exercise intense enough to be useful in weight reduction. And such anaerobic activities as weight-lifting, which depend heavily on glycogen stores, become all but impossible.[26]

Short-term, low-carbohydrate plans, of the type popularized in many "nine-day wonder" diets, are simply incompatible with strenuous exertion. This was stunningly demonstrated in the early 1940s, when Canadian troops were experimentally fed pemmican—cured meat composed of 70 percent fat and 30 percent protein—while on maneuvers in subarctic conditions. The Royal Canadian Army wanted to learn whether pemmican could be used as an emergency ration in combat. It could not. By the fourth day, examination "revealed a group of listless, dehydrated men with drawn faces and sunken eyeballs whose breath smelled strongly of acetone." The authors of the report acknowledged that the infantrymen might have adapted to their strange diet over a longer period of time. But they pointed out that "troops in combat would probably be killed during this period if they were trying to use pemmican alone as their ration."[27]

Often, people not only want to lose fat, they want to lose it from particular places. It is a widespread superstition that muscle-building exercise can achieve this goal of "spot" reducing. Sometimes, the concept of spot reduction is supported by repeating the old maxim that "fat doesn't form over a working muscle." And it is intuitively appealing that exercising the hips, thighs, or stomach would melt away the covering fat. Unfortunately, maxim and intuition are wrong, as anyone who has looked at pictures of champion weightlifters should realize. Fat lies under the skin and has nothing to do with muscles. Tennis players, for example, have larger muscles—but absolutely no less fat—on their playing arms. Gwinup and his colleagues, who made the measurements, take them as "direct evidence against the validity of the concept of 'spot reduction.' "[28] The point has been expressed somewhat more vividly by Covert

Bailey, author of the popular book *Fit or Fat?* "I was starting to get a little roll around my midsection," he writes, "so I did what anyone would do. Sit-ups. I did three hundred sit-ups a day. I did sit-ups first thing in the morning. I did sit-ups on my coffee break. . . . Within three months, my stomach muscles were like cast iron . . . but with three inches of marshmallow on top of the muscles."[29]

The distribution of fat under the skin appears to be under rather strong genetic control, and it changes with age. Some people have more in one place, some in another. There is no known way to alter that pattern and no point in buying any of the devices or programs advertised for the purpose. However, generalized weight loss, through diet or exercise, does seem to remove fat from the largest deposits more than the smaller ones. Maja Schade and her colleagues, at the University of Wisconsin, compared spot reduction with whole-body exercise in a group of young women on a weight-reduction program, by measuring the thickness of their subcutaneous fat at several sites before and after. They found that weight loss, regardless of the type of exercise, produced the same effect: Most fat was lost from the most prominent deposits.[30]

Despite the evidence that spot reduction does not occur, it is the promise of the newest weight-loss mania: Richard Simmons's exercise plan. Through an increasingly popular daytime television show and a best-selling book (the *Never-Say-Diet Book*), Simmons has become "America's most successful professional ectomorph," in the words of *People* magazine. Simmons deserves some credit for emphasizing exercise instead of faddish dieting (although he has proffered dietetic banana splits made with cottage cheese to his television audience). But, in his evangelical zeal, he encourages his audience of three or four million faithful viewers to forget aerobic exercise—which is actually the form of exercise that aids in weight control—and to engage in a spot-reducing regimen that, of itself, is bound to be ineffective for sustained weight loss.

Simmons says little about the physiology of exercise in his book—which is just as well, because when he does he makes silly mistakes. He claims, for example, that "If you exercise but continue to eat like a horse . . . the fat surrounding your muscles will just become firm and solid," and that deep breathing is essential to weight loss because "carbon dioxide lives in all those cute little fat cells you're trying to get rid of and just helps them puff up and fill out." These fanciful bits of physiology might be excused, but not his statements about aerobic exercise: "Unfortunately, walking and related strides don't do a great deal for many other body areas that need alteration," he writes. "The hips, the double chins, the saggy arms don't benefit from all that huffing and puffing. . . . Walking, running, jogging are partial exercises, not complete ones. If you have twenty pounds to lose I'd hate to be the one who pays for your shoes."

Perhaps, but if you are planning to lose weight through Simmons's "body-correcting exercises," we'd hate to pay for your leotards. Simmons does not acknowledge, or does not know, that aerobic exercise in fairly long, frequent bouts—of jogging or fast walking, for example—is the only form of exercise known to speed fat loss from *any* part of the body. Simmons's regimen of bending and stretching exercises (including sit-ups) is promoted as correcting "various problem areas from bags under the eyes to fat thighs, buttocks, stomach, and arms," but is nothing more than the old spot-reduction pitch. The five-minute sessions that he recommends, one in the morning, another in the evening, are simply not long enough to yield the minimal benefit of aerobic exercise. (Indeed, the Simmons plan seems designed to interrupt one's television viewing as little as possible.)[31]

Does *any* form of exercise provide the magic formula for weight loss that diet books have promised but never delivered? As we have outlined, there is some reason to believe that, in the past, enforced activity has been a major means of weight control. Exercise, moreover, has both physiologic and nutritional advantages over semistarvation. But once activity ceases to be an inevitable part of life and becomes something that the individual must elect to do, as it now is for the vast majority of Americans, then will power becomes a limiting factor. For some people, keeping up an exercise program can be as hard as sticking to a diet. Although Gwinup showed that increasing physical activity could very effectively produce weight loss in people who had failed at dieting, his experiment also illustrated a limitation of the approach. Only eleven women completed his program, whereas thirty-nine men and women had begun it. All the men, and the working women, dropped out—most of them with the excuse that they simply did not have time. The women who stayed with the program were, by and large, not working. They had the time to get started, and once they were involved, they evidently got hooked on the sense of well-being that regular activity generally produces.

At Pennsylvania State University, twenty-eight women in middle age went through a twelve-week conditioning program, during which they lost weight and gained in physical fitness. Then they went out on their own with plans to continue the schedule they had learned. Eighteen months later, when Patricia MacKeen checked up on them, she found that the lost weight had been regained and levels of fitness had almost completely receded to their former level. Only eight of the women were still jogging, but too infrequently to maintain their improved condition. As a sign in the research laboratory summarizes, "It is hard to be good."[32]

It *can* be hard, but it can be very worthwhile, particularly for people affected by diabetes or hypertension, the two disorders that have been especially associated with obesity. Evidence is accumulating quite rapidly that aerobic conditioning can significantly improve these very common conditions and also

262

lower the risk of heart disease, which is often a result of diabetes or high blood pressure.

When jogging was first coming into vogue, the main rationale offered by its advocates was that it offered protection from heart disease. In 1975, Thomas J. Bassler, a California pathologist, asserted that any nonsmoker who could run a marathon was *ipso facto* "immune" to fatal heart attacks. His statement, dubious on its face, elicited some extreme counterclaims. George E. Burch, of Tulane University, called jogging "a dangerous fad," and stressed the risk of injury to bones, joints, tendons, and muscles—including the heart muscle. He also suggested that joggers were more liable than nonjoggers to be run over in traffic, but later recanted with the admission that no data proved joggers to be more accident-prone than other pedestrians. At about the same time, Christiaan Barnard, the South African pioneer of heart transplantation, expressed his contempt for jogging: "I see no difference in this form of masochism and that bought for a simple fee from the ladies who specialize in leather pants and whips." Historically minded advocates of the sedentary life could also quote the story of Pheidippides. The first man to run a course of 26 miles plus 385 yards, he arrived at Athens in 490 B.C. with news that the Greeks had defeated the Persians at Marathon. Having delivered his message, the runner thereupon collapsed and died.[33]

Modern marathon runners have not suffered this fate in significant numbers, but in 1979 Stanford physicians reported on a series of eighteen people who had died during or just after jogging—most of them from established coronary heart disease. They found that the victims were inclined to be fanatic exercisers and had ignored clear symptoms in order to continue with a scheduled run. A subsequent statistical analysis pointed out that up to 104 "jogging deaths" a year would occur if joggers as a group were inclined to drop dead with the same frequency during running as comparably lean, nonsmoking individuals during an equivalent period of inactivity.[34]

The hypothesis that physical activity is a major means of preventing heart attacks has not been proved, but a great deal of suggestive evidence makes it seem very likely. In the past three decades or so, reports on groups as diverse as London bus drivers and Israeli kibbutz workers have shown that the more active people had lower rates of heart disease. Most of the studies, however, failed to account for possible differences in diet, personality, or stress levels that might have been associated with the different levels of activity, and thus might have confused the results. None, moreover, has been able to disprove the possibility that naturally healthier people gravitate to the more active jobs.

Even the most impressive of recent research, that conducted by Stanford's Paffenbarger, has not completely resolved the quandary. In 1951, he began his study of more than six thousand longshoremen in the San Francisco Bay Area. Twenty-four years later he could report that men whose jobs required heavy physical labor had significantly fewer deaths from heart disease than those in lighter work. Some three years after that, he also reported the results of a long-term observation of Harvard alumni. The men who burned less than 2,000 calories a week in voluntary physical activity—the equivalent of running about twenty miles a week—had 64 percent more heart attacks than their more active classmates. In these studies, Paffenbarger controlled for such confounding variables as blood pressure and smoking, but it is still possible that the survivors had healthier hearts to begin with, or that they had healthier diets or less demanding jobs.[35]

The Framingham Study did attempt to unravel the possible association of exercise with other risk factors for heart disease. They found no correlation, except that the more active people weighed less and had lower blood pressure. The citizens of Framingham were not a ferociously active lot, and unfortunately the data tell us little about the influence of activity on health. The most sedentary people appeared to have a higher risk of heart disease and stroke than moderately active people, but too few people were more than moderately active to allow any conclusions regarding intense exertion.[36]

This limitation was nicely circumvented by a group of Framingham statisticians, who compared the data from the Massachusetts town with similar information obtained in Honolulu and San Juan, Puerto Rico. Early in 1981 they reported that, in all three cities, the men who *ate* the most had the lowest risk of heart disease. The big eaters were not above average weight; they therefore were the most *active* subjects in the study. Again, the suggestive constellation appears: high activity, low weight, and low risk of heart disease.[37]

Paffenbarger's study of Harvard alumni has sometimes been thought to imply that protection from heart disease requires at least 2,000 calories' worth of exercise a week. The Framingham results, on the other hand, implied that moderate activity has a modest benefit, and left unanswered the question of more intense exertion. All in all, people who are unwilling to run twenty miles a week—a substantial commitment of time and energy—might be inclined to assume a stoic, and supine, position. However, Paffenbarger's data have been misinterpreted because he used the 2,000-calorie mark for dramatic effect in presenting his data. At that level of exertion, his subjects seemed to be getting the maximum protection. But his data actually showed that heart attack rates declined with *all* levels of activity up to that level. And the three-city study essentially supports this notion: Some activity is better than none, and more is better than some. There is no need to become obsessed —or crippled with athletic injuries—to benefit from exercise.

How does activity reduce the risk of heart disease? For one thing, the heart responds to exercise by increasing its capacity for work, and it may thus acquire a reserve that protects it at an age when circulation is becoming compromised. Beyond

265

that, the critical effect of exercise could well be a change in the way fats—and particularly cholesterol—are transported in the blood.

Cholesterol, a complex, relatively small molecule, is an absolutely essential structural component of the body. Most people produce a substantial amount of this fatty (or waxy) substance in their own bodies; the amount in the food they consume seems of little importance. (On the other hand, the total amount of so-called saturated fat in the diet may be important to the way cholesterol is handled by the body.) Cholesterol does not readily dissolve in water; it must, therefore, be attached to a protein carrier for transport through the bloodstream. As it happens, there are two major classes of these protein carriers. One class—now commonly known as LDL's, for "low-density lipoproteins"—delivers cholesterol, along with other fats, to various sites in the body for either immediate use or storage. Unfortunately, if an artery becomes slightly injured, as may occur from time to time simply as a result of turbulent blood flow near a branching point, a series of reactions stimulated by the injury can cause the LDL's to begin unloading cholesterol in the artery's wall. Once begun, this process tends to perpetuate itself, and atherosclerosis is the result.

Another set of blood proteins, however—the HDL's or "high-density lipoproteins"—apparently serves as a removal system. The HDL's pick up cholesterol and other fats from many sites and carry them to the liver for excretion. These scavenger proteins, if they are present in a sufficiently large quantity, may even be able to remove cholesterol from a damaged portion of artery, at least during the early stages of deposition.[38]

It is now clear that physical conditioning leads to an increase in the proportion of HDL's to LDL's and therefore favors removal of excess cholesterol. In 1977, Peter Wood, William Haskell, and their colleagues, at Stanford, reported that male and female runners who averaged at least fifteen miles a week had markedly higher HDL levels than did sedentary controls. Their results were later confirmed at Houston's Baylor College of Medicine, where it was found that the elevated HDL levels were a true effect of exercise and not of diet, even though runners in their study did eat less meat than the general public. Finnish investigators also reported that HDL levels could be raised in middle-aged men, selected at random, who were put on a four-month exercise program. (This experiment was possible because the Finns in the study area were known to have a phenomenally high rate of heart attacks. After a blitz of public education on the subject, they were inclined to be cooperative.) The Finnish results indicated that runners have no special initial advantage that makes them respond to exercise with elevated levels of HDL; rather, anyone who exercises aerobically can expect the benefit.[39]

As usual, however, the picture is less clear than one would like, and it is probable that populations and individuals respond in distinctive ways to exercise. Runners in New Zealand seemingly increase their HDL's only if they run at least thirty-five miles a week, whereas, in Texas, a more moderate program was sufficient. Certainly, the type of exercise is important. Soccer players, whose training is largely aerobic, have higher HDL levels than hockey players, who put out the same amount of energy, but less of it aerobically.[40]

The major medical reason for advocating weight loss is to help control two very common conditions, diabetes and high blood pressure. The vast majority of adults who become diabetic are unmistakably overweight. (Although obesity may be caused by the same process that leads to diabetes, the chain of causation is not clear.) The long-term damage produced by diabetes is apparently caused by high glucose (sugar) levels in the blood; for some reason, the excess glucose damages capillaries, including those of the heart, kidney, retina, and nervous system. Normally, insulin, secreted by the pancreas, lowers blood sugar, but in the common type of diabetes that begins in maturity, insulin levels are quite high. The problem, then, is not a lack of insulin but a generalized insensitivity to it.

Jesse Roth, who has studied insulin levels in obesity at the National Institutes of Health, points out that the chain of cause and effect is not yet established. Insulin levels may rise to compensate for insensitive tissues, or the tissues may decrease their sensitivity when an excess of the hormone is in the blood. Roth compares the situation to a mother yelling at her children. Does she yell louder because they don't listen, or do they ignore her because she yells so much? But the outlines are now firmly in place, and there is no dispute that fat people do indeed have higher than normal levels of insulin, along with a reduced sensitivity to it, whether or not they have reached the stage of high blood sugar. Further, this situation seems to be a potential effect of any gain in fat: Sims's prisoner volunteers experienced a rising level of insulin along with diminished sensitivity (although the actual values remained within the normal range). Conversely, starvation leads to an increased sensitivity to insulin, as is seen in patients with anorexia nervosa.[41]

Because sensitivity to insulin is the problem, the traditional treatment of diabetes in this group of patients may only exacerbate matters. Sims observes:

When you treat your patients with insulin, they frequently begin a cycle of increased weight, increased insulin resistance, and higher blood-sugar levels—all of which may lead to cardiovascular problems. . . . Many, and probably most of these people are spending large amounts of money for medication that is counterproductive to their health.[42]

For reasons that are still completely unclear, lowering the body's stores of fat leads to a generalized increase in its sensitivity to insulin. For this reason, diabetics should make every effort to reduce and may have to diet to achieve a suitable weight loss. However, the traditional low-carbohydrate diet has no more to recommend it for diabetes than it does for simple obesity. As long as the overall intake of calories is low enough to produce weight loss, and large amounts of refined sugar are excluded, carbohydrates—in the form of whole grain foods, especially—are even a desirable component of a diabetic's diet.[43]

Exercise has long been advocated for diabetics, but only recently has the reason for it begun to become clear. Exercise, in and of itself, increases insulin sensitivity. The effect is most pronounced in muscles, which are a major customer for the circulating blood sugar. As muscles are conditioned, they seek to increase their stores of glycogen, and thus, it would appear, call for more sugar from the bloodstream. After a bout of exercise, insulin and glucose levels fall for a day or so, and this effect can be seen before any loss of weight or fat.[44]

Insulin sensitivity depends on the presence of receptors that recognize the hormone and also on the eagerness with which they attach themselves to it. Brief periods of exercise rapidly increase the avidity with which receptors hold onto insulin (and thus prolong the effect of the hormone). More sustained conditioning induces the cells, chiefly muscle cells, to increase the number of their receptors and thus enables them to respond to a higher proportion of the hormone molecules than before.[45]

The damage caused by high blood sugar appears to be at least partially a result of its ability to distort the normal response of platelets—spheroid bodies in the blood that participate in the process of clotting. The excess glucose seems to make platelets stickier than they should be, thus leading to spontaneous clotting of small vessels. Exercising appears to reduce the abnormal stickiness of platelets in diabetics, and so may help to prevent the complications of the disease by more than one means. This same effect—reducing the stickiness of platelets—could also play a role in preventing heart disease in nondiabetics.[46]

By now, a few studies on the effect of exercise in patients with high blood pressure have been reported, and they, too, indicate a potential for benefit. The Chicago Coronary Prevention Evaluation Program was one of the most ambitious efforts to reduce hypertension—as well as other risk factors for heart disease—through a program of diet and exercise. From 1958 to 1968, more than 500 middle-aged men were recruited in the Chicago area. More than 300 were still in the program when it ended in 1973; a third of these had entered the program with high blood pressure, and another third were in the "high normal" range when they enlisted. The average blood pressure of the subjects dropped significantly after they entered the program, and often it remained low for as long as a decade of observation. These men may have succeeded in part because they became somewhat thinner; weight loss was correlated with the drop in blood pressure. And the exercise aspect of the program—light exercise at least three times a week—presumably helped them maintain the weight loss.[47]

In any case, exercise can act directly to lower blood pressure, whether or not it eliminates fat from the body. Björntorp and his colleagues, in Sweden, found that a six-month training program consistently lowered blood pressure in twenty-seven overweight women. Yet these women, on average, did *not* lose weight or body fat when they became active. Apparently, exercise was acting in some other way to alter the physiological systems that regulate blood pressure.[48] The greatest drop in blood pressure was seen in women with initially high insulin levels. Insulin may raise blood pressure by promoting sodium retention in the kidney; a drop in insulin levels caused by activity, conversely, could lower blood pressure.

This effect is still poorly understood, but it is encouraging. It suggests that hypertensive people who have failed in the attempt to lose weight—or who are lean to begin with—may be able to improve their condition by exercise rather than diet. Up to now, such people have had to turn to medications that can be unpleasant to take or have unwanted side effects. As Sims points out, exercise—and, where appropriate, weight loss—could provide an alternative prescription, the value of which has been underestimated. "We can no longer afford to recommend the use of medication for the overweight, mildly hypertensive segment of the population," he writes, "when it carries with it the potentiality for long-term hazards and expense, and when it has not been determined whether safe, non-pharmacologic measures may not be equally effective and truly rehabilitative."[49]

Exercise is unlikely to be a panacea, or even to produce dramatic weight loss in everyone who tries it. Its benefits are no doubt real, but how great they are remains to be established. The current popularity of exercise may even bias the interpretation of research results. "It's difficult to separate out what's fact, what's fiction, and what's fashionable," says cardiologist Richard Kahler of La Jolla's Scripps Clinic. "Exercise is very fashionable these days, and there are a lot of people, including physicians, who are stressing it very heavily." Yet, he argues, "we don't know if regular exercise prevents coronary disease. We just don't know that."[50]

Prevention may be too strong a word. Taken as a whole, however, the evidence suggests that frequent, aerobic exercise produces a complex of physiological changes that are likely to diminish cardiovascular illness. Certain critical changes, such as increased sensitivity to insulin, a shift to HDL cholesterol, and lowered blood pressure, occur whether or not weight is lost. The fat person who exercises may come to look biochemically "thin."

Dieting, which has been advocated for the same purposes, may actually be less effective than exercise in the long run, and for most people it produces discomfort or overt depression. Physical activity, at least after the first phases, usually enhances the participant's sense of well-being. Why, then, have weight-conscious people paid so little attention to the role of conditioning? Partly, no doubt, because of the prejudice that overeating, not inactivity, is the primary cause of weight gain.

Even more important may be the belief that it takes no real effort to diet. Somehow, it should be a simple matter just to control the inward flow of calories. Exercise, on the other hand, takes time and trouble; it can be seen as threatening to reduce a person's productivity or to rob time from other, preferred forms of recreation. In fact, there is some truth to these feelings; work is increasingly incompatible with physical activity.

The principles of behavioral psychology provide another reason for people's preference for dieting over exercise, although the latter is potentially more effective. Dieting offers rapid reinforcement, even if it is in the form of a deceptive loss of fluid weight, whereas conditioning may not confer obvious rewards (or become actively enjoyable) for a matter of weeks.

And finally, many people think of exercise as something requiring violent activity in public while wearing a minimum of clothing. Understandably, individuals who are unhappy about their appearance might prefer to diet at home rather than puff down a city street wearing track shorts.

Self-consciousness is a dominant force in the lives of fat people and, indeed, of all people who *think* they are overweight. It is tragic that embarrassment prevents them from following a course that could help them feel better about their appearance, combat depression, and improve their health. That they avoid exercise, then, is one more symptom of a social as well as an individual problem: Stigmatization of fat people leads to unwarranted shame and a distorted self-image. The natural response of the person affected only perpetuates the injury.

10

BODY AND SOUL

ON April 12, 1979, at least 16 million Americans ceased to be overweight. Those lucky individuals may not have known what happened to them; they were the unwitting beneficiaries of a statistical finding announced by the Society of Actuaries, which had just raised its estimate of "desirable" weight. The new standards marked a much smaller fraction of the nation as overnourished than the earlier standards had decreed. The news media dutifully reported this actuarial revolution, and its significance was widely debated. And yet, as we showed in chapter 5, the revision taught only one clear lesson: Standards of obesity have been, and still are, arbitrary.[1]

Americans have long struggled to embody an illusory ideal—the perfect weight for everyone of the same sex, height, and "frame" size. Conveniently called "desirable" by actuaries, this exceedingly lean figure has been promoted in the literature of both public health and high fashion. Yet despite a dogged and costly national effort, Americans have remained a population of diverse sizes and shapes.

We have sought in the preceding chapters to explain and

celebrate this aspect of human diversity. "Desirable" weight tables are invidious precisely because each person has a characteristic weight, which is determined by many factors, not merely the intersection of height and "frame size." Each person comes equipped with a private ideal, in the form of a setpoint, which prescribes his or her most comfortable weight. Within rather broad limits, the amount of fat that is comfortable is also perfectly compatible with good health and long life. Rejecting or resisting it leads at best to a lot of misery; at worst it makes people ready victims of hazardous drugs, bizarre diets, and pointless gimmicks.

There is as yet no safe, practical way to discern an individual's setpoint—no convenient meter with wires and a dial that might give a reading. Measuring changes in metabolic rate or estimating the size and number of fat cells may give some clue, but both of these procedures are elaborate (and to some degree unpleasant) laboratory procedures, and in any case they aren't really necessary. Most people can establish for themselves what amount of body fat is natural for them—it is reflected in a stable weight that is maintained without conscious attention, the weight to which one returns after dieting or overeating.

Most people have no medical reason to become thinner than their natural, "set" weight. But there are important exceptions: Fat people with high blood pressure, and those who become diabetic as adults, can benefit from weight loss. Even these people, however, should not consider reducing diets as the only choice; like other dieters, they will usually find themselves regaining the lost weight, unless they are exceedingly conscientious. Combining a moderate diet with a regular exercise program—which can be as simple as frequent, brisk walking—may be the best prescription for diabetics and hypertensives. Exercise, which often lowers the setpoint of formerly sedentary people, also works directly to lower blood pressure and ameliorate diabetes.

People who are extremely, or "morbidly" obese—like those

who are exceedingly thin—do have higher-than-average rates of disease and death and presumably would benefit from weight loss. But adequate reduction by dieting alone is virtually impossible for the morbidly obese, and some of the other methods they have been subjected to, notably intestinal-bypass surgery and the variants of the liquid protein diet, are themselves hazardous.

In a more nearly rational world, relatively few people would feel compelled to try losing weight; from a medical standpoint, reducing would simply not be in their best interests. But the myth persists that fatness is dangerous, and that "overweight" people are willfully, and perversely, injuring themselves. Health care providers have bolstered this image. Insurance vendors, notably Blue Cross, have used the image of a "fat slob" in advertising which asserts that the overweight are driving up the costs of health insurance. Physicians, too, tend to be prejudiced against fat people in ways that may affect their advice to patients and the quality of their care. Most physicians responding to one questionnaire characterized obese patients as "weak-willed," "ugly," and "awkward."[2]

The medical condemnation of obesity has been based more on emotion than on evidence. Physicians and public health officials, along with most people, have acted as if individuals become fat because they are lazy gluttons—not because it is their biological destiny. Fatness has thus been taken as a symbol of flawed character, an affront to the rest of society.

Academic scientists and health professionals have produced some arguments against fatness that are little more than pseudoscientific, moralistic tracts. Late in 1978, two scholars at the University of Illinois—Bruce Hannon and Timothy Lohman—published the following remarkable calculation: If all overweight Americans were to diet down to their "ideal" weights, enough energy would be saved in food production to fuel 900,000 automobiles for a year, or to meet the annual residential need for electricity in Boston, Chicago, San Francisco, and

Washington, D.C. The authors were content to blame a portion of the energy crisis on fat people; they stopped short of recommending that the overweight be hauled off to rendering plants for recycling.

The American Journal of Public Health, to its discredit, published the paper, even though the argument had nothing to do with health and was based on simplistic, incorrect assumptions. There is no evidence that fat people, on average, eat more than thin ones do. In fact, thin marathon runners probably eat more food than anyone, but Hannon and Lohman did not suggest that they save the country's energy reserves by giving up their training schedules. The authors' definition of "ideal body fatness," too, was arbitrary; they simply used the range found in trained athletes as the norm. Unfortunately, enhanced by the *Journal's* cachet, this unsound paper was widely and uncritically quoted in the lay press.[3]

It was, however, only an egregious example. Fatness is routinely and stridently condemned by people who might be expected to know better. Why? The answer, perhaps, is that fatness has been seen as a symbolic rejection of basic American values: self-discipline and self-control. When Republican Congressman John LeBoutillier accused the Speaker of the House, Tip O'Neill, of being "big, fat and out of control"—much to the embarrassment of his senior colleagues—he was voicing a widespread assumption about the character of fat people. Fatness is seen as a mark of weakness, whereas thinness has been taken, totally without evidence, as visible proof of self-mastery.[4]

Margaret Mackenzie, an anthropologist at the University of California, has provocatively explored the prejudice against fatness in *Fear of Fat: The Politics of Body Size.* She points out that the concept of self-control is integral to our notions of both economic and personal success. The quest for thinness has become a symbolic way of applying the Protestant ethic and the spirit of capitalism to one's own body. Dieters, counting pounds or calories, deal in a currency of carefully measured inputs and outputs. "One manages the body as one should manage property: economically, efficiently, and prudently," writes Mackenzie, who continues:

[T]he ideas . . . of self-discipline and self-denial, of the mastery of the will . . . of success through effort, of perfectibility through constant striving to improve oneself . . . of the distrust of excessive pleasure . . . all are indispensable in developing capitalistic private enterprise. This is the morality that also pervades the discourse on fatness.[5]

The prototype of the successful manager—one who can balance both money and calories—is Jean Nidetch, the founder of Weight Watchers. Her autobiography, *The Story of Weight Watchers,* is a classic of rags-to-riches literature. Through perseverance, hard work, and sublime self-control, she managed both to transform her body and at the same time to build an international business.

In 1961, when she weighed 214 pounds, Nidetch obtained a diet plan from the Obesity Clinic of New York City's Department of Health. Feeling that she would lose more weight with support from other fat women, she invited six friends to come to her modest apartment and share in the diet. They met regularly. The other women began bringing their friends. Soon, Nidetch organized regular classes in a small room above a movie theater; then other branches opened up; and, by the end of the decade, Weight Watchers had gone from a kaffeeklatsch to a hugely successful—and profitable—organization. Nidetch lost seventy-two pounds and gained an empire. She kept her weight down and invested the money, but she never forgot her roots. As she tells her readers, she is still Jean Slutsky Nidetch, a Formerly Fat Housewife from Brooklyn, New York.[6]

It is a dazzling success story, but what is the moral? Is it that anyone can permanently lose "excess" weight? Or that any ordinary American can build an international conglomerate from scratch? We have largely discarded the Horatio Alger

277

myth that anyone with enough gumption can strike it rich in America. But we seem to have replaced it with an equally false belief that anyone with a little moral fiber can remake his or her body to suit the current thin ideal.

The myth of caloric self-control is a major reason for the tenacity of prejudice against fat people. Racism, sexism, and religious discrimination are embarrassments in a supposedly egalitarian and pluralistic society. But if people could *choose* whether to be fat or thin, then everyone would have an equal opportunity to be the "right" size. If fat people did not exist, American society might have to invent them: They have become virtually the last target of guilt-free discrimination.

Since the 1960s there has been ample evidence that fat people are a stigmatized minority group. Jean Mayer showed in 1966 that the admissions committees of Ivy League universities discriminate against fat applicants, especially women. Upper-class women tend to be far thinner than lower-class women—in part because they are under greater pressure to diet, but also because slender women have greater opportunities in education, business, and marriage.

For men, body size is not clearly linked to social class. But fat people of both sexes do suffer employment discrimination. A stock newspaper item is that the police department in Orange, Connecticut, the school department in Los Angeles, or the command at Fort Eustis, Virginia, is forcing its employees to lose weight. Although the employers are obliged to cite health reasons for this enforced dieting, an aesthetic principle is clearly the basis for their punitive action. In a study of employers' attitudes, Maryland's Human Relations Commission found that fat workers were characterized as "lazy, lacking in self-discipline, sloppy, not well motivated, unclean, and, in one instance, smelly."[7]

The stigma applies not only to the morbidly obese—although they are especially hurt by it—but to anyone who is weighed in the balance and found "too fat." Women, especially, may be

278

penalized for exceeding the arbitrarily thin standard that has been defined as acceptable. In 1979, for example, National Airlines fired a flight attendant, Ingrid Fee, for being overweight. At five feet seven inches, Fee weighed 143 pounds; the airline's maximum for her height was 139 (which was the upper limit allowed by Metropolitan Life's now obsolete 1959 tables for women of "medium frame"). Fee hired a lawyer, who asked, rhetorically, "How can you say four pounds overweight makes a terrible stewardess?"[8]

The strict definition of an "acceptable" body size has made American women distrustful of their bodies and distorted their self-images. Many women of normal weight overestimate their own size and proceed to diet frantically—or simply end up hating themselves. In 1980, 69 percent of the women in a sample of New York college students saw themselves as "slightly overweight" or "overweight." But only 39 percent of the women actually weighed more than "normal," according to measurements of height, weight, and fat folds on the arm. "More than half the women in all weight categories appeared to have mildly distorted body images," the investigators concluded. For anorexics, who literally starve themselves to become thin, the distortion can be profound. Even at the point of malnutrition, these extreme dieters may still see themselves, perversely, as "too fat."[9]

The prejudice against fatness is cruel, destructive, and unfair. Many people who are pressured to lose weight—by friends, relatives, or physicians—are not overly fat to begin with. Even for the few people who are morbidly obese, fatness is not a matter of choice, and it is certainly not a measure of character. Body size may not be quite as immutable as skin color, but it is surely far more difficult to change than clothing style. And "size-ism" is a prejudice no more defensible than racism or sexism.

As leanness has been increasingly prized, Americans have actually become fatter. (No doubt this trend alone makes thinness ever more appealing as a mark of status and privilege.) The weight gain has been taken as a sign of a national malaise, of weakness and self-indulgence. In fact, Americans are gaining weight because their environment has changed irrevocably in ways that encourage fatness. These changes have been largely ignored, while the nation continues stubbornly to treat fatness in moralistic terms.

Three specific factors are likely to be responsible for the trend. The most important, almost certainly, is a decline in levels of physical activity. A more speculative possibility is that a reduced burden of infectious disease—thanks to the development of immunization and antibiotics since World War II—has allowed people to fatten. Dietary changes may also have played a role, although not in any obvious fashion.

If people react as rats do by raising their setpoint in response to certain features of the available food, then recent trends in dietary history may have contributed to the national weight gain. Most conspicuous is the increased per capita consumption of sugar. It is not the sugar in itself that "makes people fat." Sugar is perfectly acceptable as an energy source—although by itself it brings only calories and no other nutrients, such as vitamins—and it is not intrinsically more "fattening" than fat or protein. But it does induce the setpoint in rats to rise a little, and could conceivably have a similar effect in human beings. The effect is not strong in rats and may not be in people. But, since Americans do consume massive amounts of soft drinks and other sweetened foods, if there is an effect they are likely to be showing it.

Whether artificial sweeteners are of any use at all in weight control has not been established. If they also act to raise the setpoint, then they would act as an inducement to fatten, even though the sweeteners themselves lack calories. Sheer variety in food might also act to raise the setpoint, as does a high fat content.

At the same time that food has been increasing in richness

and variety, daily life has become easier—and so has burned fewer and fewer calories. As we showed in chapter 9, the caloric demands of work have been decreased by mechanization and automation, even for such active laborers as longshoremen. Activity levels have fallen so drastically that the average American would easily have gained twenty pounds in the last two decades, if caloric intake had not been cut during the same period. The government, industry, and health organizations are beginning to urge Americans to exercise more. If they are successful, we will probably become somewhat thinner as a nation. But we will never again *have* to be as active as people were at the turn of the century.

Even if everyone begins to jog a mile a day, which is never likely to happen, some people will still remain quite a bit fatter than others. If attitudes do not also change these individuals will still be regarded as fat and will still be discriminated against. What is needed, more urgently than changes in diet or exercise patterns, is the understanding that there need be nothing shameful about fatness.

Several feminist therapists have come to this realization, and have started groups to offer alternatives to the obsessive goal of weight loss. These groups help women get out of the binge-and-diet trap by helping them figure out what they really *want* to eat. Losing weight is a secondary goal. If women are told that they can eat any food they want—even rich desserts—then they should lose the urge to binge in private while they diet in public. Susie Orbach (author of *Fat is a Feminist Issue*), social worker Melody Marks, in San Francisco, and others have developed this method with some success. Even when women in these groups do not lose much weight, they tend to feel better about themselves and more in control of their eating habits.[10]

Susan and Wayne Wooley, who direct the Clinic for Eating Disorders at the University of Cincinnati Medical College, have been leaders in developing this approach. Susan Wooley, who has learned to be comfortable at 200 pounds herself, says that patients are told from the start:

Our goal for treatment is different from other kinds of programs. If what they're interested in is solely a weight-loss program, they shouldn't come to us. The only thing that we can promise is to help them get off the seesaw of dieting, off the misery of the way they feel about themselves. We'll help each person try to get a very accurate picture of exactly what's involved in losing weight and maintaining that lower weight, and then really examine the question of whether or not it's worth it to them.

The Wooleys believe that fatness is biologically determined, to a large extent, and is generally not caused by overeating. When women in their groups learn this, the effect can be liberating. "We really think that the one thing we're successful at is changing people's view of themselves. Very few people leave here feeling that there's something intrinsically wrong with them, or that they're gluttons, or that they're bad."[11]

In their practice, the Wooleys have applied the philosophy of the "fat liberation" movement, which is growing rapidly and becoming increasingly militant. The National Association to Aid Fat Americans, founded in 1969, has been largely a social club for fat women, and for men who are self-proclaimed "fat admirers." Now, some of its members are becoming involved in fighting legal battles over size discrimination. A more overtly political group, the Fat Underground, has been working since the early 1970s to educate women about the biological nature of fatness and the oppression of the diet industry. (Their arguments, in many ways, have anticipated our own.)

Although discrimination in jobs and education remains, the American look, at least, is changing. Clothing in large sizes has become the latest discovery of the fashion industry, and promises to be one of the most profitable. Large models are increasingly sought after, and a magazine called *BBW*—for Big Beautiful Women—has built a circulation of several hundred thousand. The vogue for thinness has been perpetuated by the fashion industry; perhaps these changes signal its end.

The leaders of fat liberation have been people who are significantly heavier than the average, such as the women in *BBW*. If fat people are a minority group, these pioneers are the ones who cannot pass as members of the thin majority, and they would stand to benefit the most from a change in attitudes toward fatness. But their efforts may also help people who weigh far less, yet are also obsessed with their size, to accept themselves.

We hope so. The endless quest for thinness has done far more harm than good. For many people, it has represented an expensive, unnecessary, and unsuccessful war against the body. A truce is long overdue.

Notes

Chapter 1

1. Eleanor Pao, "Nutrient Consumption Patterns of Individuals in 1977 and 1965," *Outlook '80*, U.S. Department of Agriculture, 6 November 1979; Sidney Abraham, *Weight by Height and Age for Adults 18–74 Years: United States, 1971–74* (Hyattsville, Md.: U.S. Department of Health, Education and Welfare, 1979).

2. Reuel A. Stallones, "The Rise and Fall of Ischemic Heart Disease," *Scientific American* 243(5, 1980):53–59; U.S. Department of Commerce, Bureau of the Census, *Statistical Abstract of the United States*, 101st ed. (Washington, D.C.: Government Printing Office, 1980), p. 72; see also discussion, chapter 5 herein.

3. Norris McWhirter, ed., *Guinness Book of World Records*, 1979 ed. (New York: Sterling, 1978), p. 20.

4. Caloric estimates are taken from Frank Katch and William McArdle, *Nutrition, Weight Control and Exercise* (Boston: Houghton Mifflin, 1977), passim.

5. Rena R. Wing and Leonard H. Epstein, "Prescribed Level of Caloric Restriction in Behavioral Weight Loss Programs," *Addictive Behaviors* 6(1981):139–44.

6. Ancel Keys et al., *The Biology of Human Starvation*, 2 vols. (Minneapolis: University of Minnesota Press, 1950), p. 843.

7. Our account is summarized from Keys, *Human Starvation*, pp. 63–78, 117, 119, 175–83, 819–63, 892–98.

8. Ethan A. H. Sims, "Studies in Human Hyperphagia," in George Bray and John Bethune, *Treatment and Management of Obesity* (New York: Harper and Row, 1974), p. 29.

9.——— et al., "Experimental Obesity in Man," *Transactions of the Association of American Physicians* 81 (1968):153–70; Sims, interview (14 September 1979).

10. O. G. Edholm et al., "The Energy Expenditure and Food Intake of Individual Men," *British Journal of Nutrition* 9 (1955):286–300; idem, "Food Intake and Energy Expenditure of Army Recruits," *British Journal of Nutrition* 24 (1970): 1091–1107.

11. Theresa A. Spiegel, "Caloric Regulation of Food Intake in Man," *Journal of Comparative and Physiological Psychology* 84 (1973):24–37.

Chapter 2

1. Susan Deri, "A Problem in Obesity," in Arthur Burton and Robert Harris, eds., *Clinical Studies of Personality*, 2 vols. (New York: Harper & Brothers, 1955), 2:525–81.

2. S. Rado, "Ueber die Psychische Wirkung der Rauschgifte," *Internationale Zeitschrift für Psychoanalyse* 12 (1926), cited ibid., p. 577.

3. Stanley Conrad, "The Problem of Weight Reduction in the Obese Woman," *American Practitioner and Digest of Treatment* 5 (1954):38–47.

4. Susie Orbach, *Fat is a Feminist Issue* (New York: Paddington Press, Ltd., 1978), p. 60.

5. Colleen Rand, "Obesity and Human Sexuality," *Medical Aspects of Human Sexuality* 13 (January 1979):140–52; Thomas Wise and Jacqueline Gordon, "Sexual Functioning in the Hyperobese," *Obesity and Bariatric Medicine* 6 (1977):84–87; Henry Jordan and Leonard Levitz, "Sex and Obesity," *Medical Aspects of Human Sexuality* 13 (October 1979):104–17.

6. John Neill, John Marshall, and Charles Yale, "Marital Changes after Intestinal Bypass Surgery," *Journal of the American Medical Association* 240 (1978): 447–50.

7. Harold Kaplan and Helen Singer Kaplan, "The Psychosomatic Concept of Obesity," *Journal of Nervous and Mental Disease* 125 (1957):181–201.

8. Norris Weinberg, Myer Mendelson, and Albert Stunkard, "A Failure to Find Distinctive Personality Features in a Group of Obese Men," *American Journal of Psychiatry* 117 (1961):1035–37.

9. Mary Moore, Albert Stunkard, and Leo Srole, "Obesity, Social Class and Mental Illness," *Journal of the American Medical Association* 181 (1962):962–66.

10. Albert Stunkard, *The Pain of Obesity* (Palo Alto: Bull Publishing Co., 1976), p. 145.

11. Ibid., p. 146.

12. A. H. Crisp and B. McGuiness, "Jolly Fat," *British Medical Journal* 1 (1976): 7–9.

13. Robert Simon, "Obesity as a Depressive Equivalent," *Journal of the American Medical Association* 183 (1963):208–10.

14. *Diagnostic and Statistical Manual of Mental Disorders,* 3rd ed. (Washington, D.C.: American Psychiatric Association, 1980), p. 67; Colleen Rand, "Treatment of Obese Patients in Psychoanalysis," *Psychiatric Clinics of North America* 1 (1978): 661–72.

15. Hilde Bruch, "Transformation of Oral Impulses in Eating Disorders," *Psychiatric Quarterly* 35 (1961):458–81.

16. Ibid., pp. 461–62.

17. Hilde Bruch, "Conceptual Confusion in Eating Disorders," *Journal of Nervous and Mental Disease* 133 (1961):46–54.

18. Hilde Bruch, *Eating Disorders* (New York: Basic Books, 1973), p. 132.

19. Albert Stunkard, "Obesity and the Denial of Hunger," *Psychosomatic Medicine* 21 (1959):281–89; Albert Stunkard and Sonja Fox, "The Relationship of Gastric Motility and Hunger," *Psychosomatic Medicine* 33 (1971):123–34.

20. Background reviewed in Stanley Schachter, "Some Extraordinary Facts about Obese Humans and Rats," *American Psychologist* 26 (1971):129–44.

21. Stanley Schachter, Ronald Goldman, and Andrew Gordon, "Effects of Fear, Food Deprivation, and Obesity on Eating," *Journal of Personality and Social Psychology* 10 (1968):91–97.

22. Stanley Schachter and Larry Gross, "Manipulated Time and Eating Behavior," ibid.:98–106.

23. Richard Nisbett, "Determinants of Food Intake in Obesity," *Science* 159 (1968):1254–55.

285

24. Ronald Goldman, Melvyn Jaffa, and Stanley Schachter, "Yom Kippur, Air France, Dormitory Food, and the Eating Behavior of Obese and Normal Persons," *Journal of Personality and Social Psychology* 10 (1968):117–23.

25. Judith Rodin, "The Externality Theory Today," in Albert Stunkard, ed., *Obesity* (Philadelphia: W. B. Saunders Co., 1980), pp. 226–39.

26. Richard Nisbett, "Hunger, Obesity, and the Ventromedial Hypothalamus," *Psychological Review* 79 (1972):433–53.

27. Herman, interview (14 April 1981).

28. C. Peter Herman and Janet Polivy, "Restrained Eating," in Stunkard, *Obesity,* pp. 208–25.

29. C. Peter Herman and Deborah Mack, "Restrained and Unrestrained Eating," *Journal of Personality* 43 (1975):647–60.

30. Herman, interview (14 April 1981).

31. Schachter, interview (21 September 1979).

32. Janet Polivy and C. Peter Herman, "Effects of Alcohol on Eating Behavior," *Journal of Abnormal Psychology* 85 (1976):601–6.

33. C. Peter Herman and Janet Polivy, "Anxiety, Restraint, and Eating Behavior," ibid. 84 (1975):666–72; Polivy and Herman, "Clinical Depression and Weight Change," ibid. 85 (1976):338–40.

34. Albert Stunkard, "Restrained Eating: What It Is and a New Scale to Measure It," in Luigi Cioffi, ed., *The Body Weight Regulatory System* (New York: Raven Press, 1981).

35. Herman, interview (14 April 1981).

36. Albert Stunkard, "The 'Dieting Depression,' " *American Journal of Medicine* 23 (1957):77–86; Bruch, *Eating Disorders,* pp. 186–93.

37. Myron Glucksman et al., "The Response of Obese Patients to Weight Reduction," *Psychosomatic Medicine* 30 (1968):359–73; Albert Stunkard and John Rush, "Dieting and Depression Reexamined," *Annals of Internal Medicine* 81 (1974):526–33; Patrick O'Neil et al., "Restraint and Age at Onset of Obesity," *Addictive Behaviors* 6 (1981):135–38.

38. Bruch, *Eating Disorders,* pp. 197–98.

39. Herman and Polivy, "Restrained Eating," pp. 223–4; Regina Casper et al., "Bulimia," *Archives of General Psychiatry* 37 (1980):1030–35; Paul Garfinkel, Harvey Moldofsky, and David Garner, "The Heterogeneity of Anorexia Nervosa," ibid.:1036–40.

40. Herman and Polivy, "Restrained Eating," p. 221.

41. Bruch, *Eating Disorders,* p. 198.

42. C. B. Ferster, J. I. Nurnberger, and E. B. Levitt, "The Control of Eating," *Journal of Mathetics* 1 (1962):87–109.

43. C. B. Ferster, personal communication, cited in Sydnor Penick et al., "Behavior Modification in the Treatment of Obesity," *Psychosomatic Medicine* 33 (1971):49–55.

44. Richard Stuart, "Behavioral Control of Overeating," *Behaviour Research and Therapy* 5 (1967):357–65.

45. Penick, "Behavior Modification."

46. Michael LeBow, "Can Lighter Become Thinner?" *Addictive Behaviors* 2 (1977):87–93.

47. *Countdown Guide Book to Permanent Weight Loss* (Fort Collins, Colorado: Teledyne Water Pik, 1977); "How to Lose Weight, Or Go Crazy, Or Both," *Consumer Reports,* May 1978, p. 253.

48. John Foreyt and Richard Frohwirth, "Introduction," in John Paul Foreyt, ed., *Behavioral Treatments of Obesity* (New York: Pergamon Press, 1977), p. 2.

49. Joel Gurin, "Learning to Hate What You Love Most," *San Francisco Chronicle*, 30 November 1977, p. BB–1.

50. Albert Stunkard, "Presidential Address—1974," *Psychosomatic Medicine* 37 (1975):195–236; Hilde Bruch, "The Treatment of Eating Disorders," *Mayo Clinic Proceedings* 51 (1976):266–72.

51. Michael Mahoney, "The Obese Eating Style," *Addictive Behaviors* 1 (1975): 47–53; Albert Stunkard et al., "Obesity and Eating Style," *Archives of General Psychiatry* 37 (1980):1127–29.

52. K. S. Kissileff, H. A. Jordan, and L. S. Levitz, "Eating Habits of Obese and Normal Weight Humans," *International Journal of Obesity* 2 (1978):379.

53. Barbara Rosenthal and Robert Marx, "Differences in Eating Patterns of Successful and Unsuccessful Dieters, Untreated Overweight and Normal Weight Individuals," *Addictive Behaviors* 3 (1978):129–34.

54. Ferguson, interview (23 February 1979).

55. Rena Wing and Robert Jeffery, "Outpatient Treatments of Obesity," *International Journal of Obesity* 3 (1979):261–79.

56. Albert Stunkard and Sydnor Penick, "Behavior Modification in the Treatment of Obesity," *Archives of General Psychiatry* 36 (1979):801–806.

57. K. D. Brownell and Albert Stunkard, "Behavior Therapy and Behavior Change," *Behaviour Research and Therapy* 16 (1978):301.

58. Stunkard, interview (1 October 1979).

59. Colleen Rand and Albert Stunkard, "Obesity and Psychoanalysis," *American Journal of Psychiatry* 135 (1978):547–51.

60. Susan Sontag, *Illness as Metaphor* (New York: Farrar, Straus & Giroux, 1978), p. 57.

Chapter 3

1. Wooley, interview (10 October 1979).

2. Milton Coll, Andrew Meyer, and Albert Stunkard, "Obesity and Food Choices in Public Places," *Archives of General Psychiatry* 36 (1979):795–97.

3. Susan Wooley, Orland W. Wooley, and Susan Dyrenforth, "Theoretical, Practical, and Social Issues in Behavioral Treatments of Obesity," *Journal of Applied Behavior Analysis* 12 (1979):3–25; J. S. Garrow, *Energy Balance and Obesity in Man* (New York: American Elsevier, 1974), pp. 84–85.

4. Chandler McCuskey Brooks and E. F. Lambert, "A Study of the Effect of Limitation of Food Intake and the Method of Feeding on the Rate of Weight Gain During Hypothalamic Obesity in the Albino Rat," *American Journal of Physiology* 147 (1946):695–707.

5. J. G. V. A. Durnin, "Energy Balance in Man with Particular Reference to Low Intakes," *Bibliotheca Nutritionis et Dieta* 27 (1979):1–10.

6. David A. Booth, "Acquired Behavior Controlling Energy Intake and Output," in Albert Stunkard, ed., *Obesity* (Philadelphia: W. B. Saunders Co., 1980), pp. 101–43; David Wirtshafter and John D. Davis, "Set Points, Settling Points, and the Control of Body Weight," *Physiology and Behavior* 19 (1977):75–78; Philip R. Payne and Alan E. Dugdale, "A Model for the Prediction of Energy Balance

Notes

and Body Weight," *Annals of Human Biology* 4 (1977):525–35; P. V. Sukhatme and Sheldon Margen, "Auto-Regulatory Homeostatic Nature of Energy Balance," *American Journal of Clinical Nutrition,* in press; Nicholas Mrosovsky and Terry L. Powley, "Set Points for Body Weight and Fat," *Behavioral Biology* 20 (1977): 205–23; Theodore B. Van Itallie, Nicole Schupf Smith, and David Quartermain, "Short-Term and Long-Term Components in the Regulation of Food Intake," *American Journal of Clinical Nutrition* 30 (1977):742–57; Nancy J. Rothwell and Michael J. Stock, "Regulation of Energy Balance in Two Models of Reversible Obesity in the Rat," *Journal of Comparative and Physiological Psychology* 93 (1979):-1024–34; Richard E. Keesey, "A Set-Point Analysis of the Regulation of Body Weight," in Stunkard, *Obesity,* pp. 144–65.

7. D. Johnson and E. J. Drenick, "Therapeutic Fasting in Morbid Obesity," *Archives of Internal Medicine* 137 (1977):1381–82.

8. Calvin Trillin, "U.S. Journal," *The New Yorker* 47 (3 July 1971):57–63.

9. Albert D. Loro, Jr., and Carole S. Orleans, "Binge Eating in Obesity," *Addictive Behaviors* 6 (1981):155–66.

10. Burr Snider, "Fat City," *Esquire* 79 (March 1973):112–14, 174–82.

11. Lars Sjöström, "Fat Cells and Body Weight," in Stunkard, *Obesity,* pp. 72–100.

12. Jules Hirsch and P. W. Han, "Cellularity of Rat Adipose Tissue," *Journal of Lipid Research* 10 (1969):77–82; Irving Faust et al., "Diet-Induced Adipocyte Number Increase in Adult Rats," *American Journal of Physiology* 235 (1978): E279–E286; Judith S. Stern and Patricia R. Johnson, "Size and Number of Adipocytes and Their Implications," in Howard M. Katzen and Richard J. Jahler, eds., *Diabetes, Obesity, and Vascular Disease,* vol. 2, pt. 1 (New York: Wiley, 1978), pp. 303–40.

13. Hirsch, interview (20 September 1979); Knittle, interview (29 September 1979); Sjöström, "Fat Cells and Body Weight"; G. Berglund et al., "The Effects of Early Malnutrition in Men on Body Composition and Adipose Tissue Cellularity at an Adult Age," *Acta Medica Scandinavica* 195 (1974):213–16; Per Björntorp et al., "The Effect of Maternal Diabetes on Adipose Tissue Cellularity in Man and Rat," *Diabetologia* 10 (1974):205–209.

14. William H. Mueller and Russell M. Reid, "A Multivariate Analysis of Fatness and Relative Fat Patterning," *American Journal of Physical Anthropology* 50 (1979):199–208; D. W. Harsha, A. W. Voors, and G. S. Berenson, "Racial Differences in Subcutaneous Fat Patterns in Children Aged 7–15 Years," *American Journal of Physical Anthropology* 53 (1980):333–37.

15. Lois M. Zucker and T. F. Zucker, " 'Fatty,' a New Mutation in the Rat," *Journal of Heredity* 52 (1961):275–78; Keesey, "Set-Point Analysis."

16. James E. Cox and Terry L. Powley, "Development of Obesity in Diabetic Mice Pair-Fed with Lean Siblings," *Journal of Comparative and Physiological Psychology* 91 (1977):347–58.

17. J. F. Hayes and J. C. McCarthy, "The Effects of Selection at Different Ages for High and Low Body Weight on the Pattern of Fat Deposition in Mice," *Genetics Research* 27 (1976):389–403.

18. Stanley M. Garn and Diane C. Clark, "Trends in Fatness and the Origins of Obesity," *Pediatrics* 57 (1976):443–56; Stanley M. Garn, Patricia E. Cole, and Stephen M. Bailey, "Effect of Parental Fatness Levels on the Fatness of Biological and Adoptive Children," *Ecology of Food and Nutrition* 7 (1977):91–93; Stanley M. Garn et al., "Evidence for the Social Inheritance of Obesity in Childhood

and Adolescence," in L. Gedda and P. Parisi, eds., *Auxology* (New York: Academic Press, 1978), pp. 217–23; Terryl T. Foch and Gerald E. McClearn, "Genetics, Body Weight, and Obesity," in Stunkard, *Obesity,* pp. 48–71.

19. Foch and McClearn, "Genetics, Body Weight, and Obesity," pp. 63–64.

20. William C. Knowler et al., "Diabetes Incidence in Pima Indians: Contributions of Obesity and Parental Diabetes," *American Journal of Epidemiology* 113 (1981):144–56.

21. John D. Davis et al., "Sustained Intracerebroventricular Infusion of Brain Fuels Reduced Body Weight and Food Intake in Rats," *Science* 212 (1981):81–83.

22. Albert Stunkard, "Satiety Is a Conditioned Reflex," *Psychosomatic Medicine* 37 (1975):383–87.

23. R. O. Neumann, "Experimentelle Beiträge zur Lehre von dem täglichen Nahrungsbedarf des Menschen unter besonderer Berücksichtigung der notwendigen Eiweissmenge (Selbstversuche.)," *Archiv für Hygiene,* 45 (1901):1–87.

24. Addison Gulick, "A Study of Weight Regulation in the Adult Human Body during Over-nutrition," *American Journal of Physiology* 60 (1922):371–95.

25. F. H. Wiley and L. H. Newburgh, "The Doubtful Nature of 'Luxuskonsumption,'" *Journal of Clinical Investigation* 10 (1931):733–44.

26. J. S. Garrow, "The Regulation of Energy Expenditure in Man," in George Bray, ed., *Recent Advances in Obesity Research* (London: Newman, 1978), 2:200–10.

27. Sims, interview (14 September 1979).

28. David O. Foster and M. Lorraine Frydman, "Nonshivering Thermogenesis in the Rat," *Canadian Journal of Physiology and Pharmacology* 56 (1978):110–22.

29. Nancy Rothwell and Michael Stock, "A Role for Brown Adipose Tissue in Diet-induced Thermogenesis," *Nature* 281 (1979):31–35; P. Trayhurn, P. L. Thurlby, and W. P. T. James, "Thermogenic Defect in Pre-obese *ob/ob* Mice," *Nature* 266 (1977):60–61; Jean Himms-Hagen and Michel Desautels, "A Mitochondrial Defect in Brown Adipose Tissue of the Obese *(ob/ob)* Mouse," *Biochemical and Biophysical Research Communications* 83 (1978):628–34.

30. "Do the Lucky Ones Burn off Their Dietary Excesses?," *Lancet* 2 (1979): 1115–16.

31. George Bray, "Effect of Caloric Restriction on Energy Expenditure in Obese Patients," *Lancet* 2 (1969):397–98.

32. D. S. Miller and Sally Parsonage, "Resistance to Slimming," *Lancet* 1 (1975):773–75.

33. P. C. Boyle, L. H. Storlien, and R. E. Keesey, "Increased Efficiency of Food Utilization Following Weight Loss," *Physiology and Behavior* 21(1978):261–64.

34. Wooley, interview (10 October 1979).

Chapter 4

1. Nicholas Mrosovsky and David F. Sherry, "Animal Anorexias," *Science* 207 (1980):837–42.

2. David A. Levitsky, Barbara J. Strupp, and Janet Lupoli, "Tolerance to Anorectic Drugs," *Pharmacology, Biochemistry, and Behavior* 14 (1981):661–67.

3. Albert Stunkard, "The Development of Tolerance to Appetite Suppressant Medication," *Journal of Psychedelic Drugs* 10 (1978):331–41; Linda Wilcoxon

Notes

Craighead, Albert Stunkard, and Richard M. O'Brien, "Behavior Therapy and Pharmacotherapy for Obesity," *Archives of General Psychiatry* 38 (1981):763–68; Albert Stunkard, "Anorectic Agents," in Silvio Garattini and Rosario Samanin, eds., *Anorectic Agents* (New York: Raven Press, 1981).

4. David R. Jacobs, Jr., and Sara Gottenborg, "Smoking and Weight," *American Journal of Public Health* 71 (1981):391–96; idem, "Smokers Eat More, Weigh Less than Nonsmokers," *American Journal of Public Health* 71 (1981):859–60.

5. J. S. Garrow, "Dental Splinting in the Treatment of Hyperphagic Obesity," *Proceedings of the Nutrition Society* 33 (1974):29A; George Bray, *The Obese Patient* (Philadelphia: W. B. Saunders Co., 1976), p. 438; E. J. Drenick and H. W. Hargis, "Jaw Wiring for Weight Reduction," *Obesity and Bariatric Medicine* 7 (1978): 210–13.

6. Theodore B. Van Itallie and John G. Kral, "The Dilemma of Morbid Obesity," *Journal of the American Medical Association* 246 (1981):999–1003; M. R. Mills and Albert Stunkard, "Behavioral Changes Following Surgery for Obesity," *American Journal of Psychiatry* 133 (1976):527–31; George Bray, "Jejunoileal Bypass, Jaw Wiring, and Vagotomy for Massive Obesity," in Albert Stunkard, ed., *Obesity* (Philadelphia: W. B. Saunders Co., 1980), pp. 369–87.

7. Albert Stunkard and Sydnor Penick, "Behavior Modification in the Treatment of Obesity," *Archives of General Psychiatry* 36 (1979):801–806.

8. Richard E. Keesey, "A Set-Point Analysis of the Regulation of Body Weight," in Stunkard, *Obesity*, pp. 144–65.

9. Terry L. Powley, "The Ventromedial Hypothalamic Syndrome, Satiety, and a Cephalic Phase Hypothesis," *Psychological Review* 84 (1977):89–126; G. C. Kennedy, "The Role of Depot Fat in the Hypothalamic Control of Food Intake in the Rat," *Proceedings of the Royal Society (London), Series B* 140 (1953):578–92; Bartley G. Hoebel and Philip Teitelbaum, "Weight Regulation in Normal and Hypothalamic Hyperphagic Rats," *Journal of Comparative and Physiological Psychology* 61 (1966):189–93; K. B. J. Franklin and L. J. Herberg, "Ventromedial Syndrome," *Journal of Comparative and Physiological Psychology* 87(1974):410–14; Anthony Sclafani, Deleri Springer, and Lawrence Kluge, "Effects of Quinine Adulterated Diets on the Food Intake and Body Weight of Obese and Non-Obese Hypothalamic Hyperphagic Rats," *Physiology and Behavior* 16 (1976):631–40.

10. Jeffrey W. Peck, "Rats Defend Different Body Weights Depending on Palatability and Accessibility of Their Food," *Journal of Comparative and Physiological Psychology* 92 (1978):555–70.

11. Anthony Sclafani and Deleri Springer, "Dietary Obesity in Adult Rats," *Physiology and Behavior* 17 (1976):461–71; Anthony Sclafani, "Dietary Obesity," in Stunkard, *Obesity*, pp. 166–81.

12. Howard Haines, D. B. Hackel, and Knut Schmidt-Nielsen, "Experimental Diabetes Mellitus Induced by Diet in the Sand Rat," *American Journal of Physiology* 208 (1965):297–300; D. L. Coleman, "Genetics of Obesity in Rodents," in George Bray, ed., *Recent Advances in Obesity Research*, 2 vols. (London: Newman, 1978), vol. 2.: 142–52.

13. Douglas G. Mook, "Saccharin Preference in the Rat," *Psychological Review* 81 (1974):475–90; Elena O. Nightingale and Frederick C. Robbins, "Saccharine and Society," *American Journal of Medicine* 71 (1981):9–12.

14. Joel Grinker, "Obesity and Sweet Taste," *American Journal of Clinical Nutrition*

31 (1978):1078–87; idem, interview (27 September 1979); M. Cabanac, R. Duclaux, and N. H. Spector, "Sensory Feedback in Regulation of Body Weight," *Nature* 229 (1971):125–27.

15. James A. Greene, "Clinical Study of the Etiology of Obesity," *Annals of Internal Medicine* 12 (1939):1797–1803.

16. Jean Mayer et al., "Exercise, Food Intake and Body Weight in Normal Rats and Genetically Obese Adult Mice," *American Journal of Physiology* 177 (1954): 544–48; Jean Mayer, "Decreased Activity and Energy Balance in the Hereditary Obesity-Diabetes Syndrome of Mice," *Science* 117 (1953):504–505.

17. M. L. Johnson, B. S. Burke, and J. Mayer, "Relative Importance of Inactivity and Overeating in the Energy Balance of Obese High School Girls," *American Journal of Clinical Nutrition* 4 (1956):37–44.

18. Jean Mayer, Purnima Roy, and Kamakhya Prasad Mitra, "Relation between Caloric Intake, Body Weight, and Physical Work," *American Journal of Clinical Nutrition* 4 (1956):169–75.

19. P. D. Wood et al., "Comparison of Nutrient Intake in Sedentary and Active Middle-aged Men and Women," *Medicine and Science in Sports and Exercise,* in press.

20. Wood, interview (1 September 1981).

Chapter 5

1. Society of Actuaries, Committee on Mortality, *Build and Blood Pressure Study,* 2 vols. (Chicago: Society of Actuaries, 1979) 1:45–68.

2. "New Weight Standards for Men and Women," *Statistical Bulletin of the Metropolitan Life Insurance Company* 40 (November–December, 1959):1–4; Sidney Abraham, "Weight by Height and Age for Adults 18–74 Years, United States, 1971–74," U.S. Department of Health, Education and Welfare, *Vital and Health Statistics: Series 11, Data from the National Health Survey,* no. 208 (DHEW Publication no. PHS 79–1656), 1979.

3. Frederick H. Epstein, "Estimating the Effect of Preventing Obesity on Total Mortality and Hypertension," *International Journal of Obesity* 3(1979):163–66.

4. Abraham, "Weight by Height and Age"; U.S. Department of Commerce, Bureau of the Census, *Statistical Abstract of the United States,* 101st ed. (Washington, D.C.: Government Printing Office, 1980), p. 72.

5. Thomas Royle Dawber, *The Framingham Study: The Epidemiology of Atherosclerotic Disease* (Cambridge, Mass.: Harvard University Press, 1980), pp. 142–59; William B. Kannel et al., "Relation of Body Weight to Development of Coronary Heart Disease," *Circulation* 35 (1967):734–44.

6. Paul Sorlie, Tavia Gordon, and William B. Kannel, "Body Build and Mortality," *Journal of the American Medical Association* 243 (1980):1828–31.

7. Reubin Andres, "Influence of Obesity on Longevity in the Aged," in Carmia Borek, Cecilia M. Fenoglio, and Donald West King, eds., *Aging, Cancer and Cell Membranes* (New York: Thieme-Stratton, 1980), pp. 238–46; N. B. Belloc, "Relationship of Health Practices and Mortality," *Preventive Medicine* 2 (1973): 67–81; A. R. Dyer et al., "Relationship of Relative Weight and Body Mass Index

Notes

to 14-Year Mortality in Chicago Peoples Gas Company Study," *Journal of Chronic Diseases* 28 (1975):109–23; T. J. Cole, J. C. Gibson, and H. C. Olsen, "Bronchitis, Smoking and Obesity in an English and Danish Town," *Bulletin of the Physiopathology of Respiration* 10 (1974):657–79.

8. Arnold Engel, *Osteoarthritis and body measurements,* U. S. Public Health Service Publication no. 1000, ser. 11, no. 29, April 1970; Paul D. Saville and Jessie Dickson, "Age and Weight in Osteoarthritis of the Hip," *Arthritis and Rheumatism* 11 (1968):635–51; Lars G. Danielsson, "Incidence and Prognosis of Coxarthrosis," *Acta Orthopaedica Scandinavica,* suppl. 66, 1964, pp. 42–44.

9. Reuel A. Stallones, "The Rise and Fall of Ischemic Heart Disease," *Scientific American* 243 (May 1980):53–59.

10. Ancel Keys, "Overweight, Obesity, Coronary Heart Disease and Mortality," *Nutrition Reviews* 38 (1980):297–307; Ancel Keys, *Seven Countries: A Multivariate Analysis of Death and Coronary Heart Disease* (Cambridge, Mass.: Harvard University Press, 1980), p. 194.

11. Geoffrey Rose et al., "Myocardial Ischemia, Risk Factors and Death from Coronary Heart Disease," *Lancet* 1 (1977):105–109.

12. Roland L. Weinsier et al., "Body Fat," *American Journal of Medicine* 61 (1976):815–24.

13. Benjamin N. Chiang, Lawrence V. Perlman, and Frederick H. Epstein, "Overweight and Hypertension," *Circulation* 39 (1969):403–21; George V. Mann, "The Influence of Obesity on Health," *New England Journal of Medicine* 291 (1974): 178–85, 226–32; Harriet P. Dustan, "Obesity and Hypertension," *Comprehensive Therapy* 6 (March 1980):29–35; Michael Tuck et al., "The Effect of Weight Reduction on Blood Pressure, Plasma Renin Activity, and Plasma Aldosterone Levels in Obese Patients," *New England Journal of Medicine* 304 (1981):930–33; Ethan A. H. Sims, "Mechanisms of Hypertension in the Syndromes of Obesity," *International Journal of Obesity,* 5 (1981):9–18; Ethan A. H. Sims and Peter Berchtold, "Obesity and Hypertension: Mechanisms and Implications for Management," *Journal of the American Medical Association* 247 (1982): 49–52.

14. M. Berger, W. A. Muller, and A. E. Renold, "Relationship of Obesity to Diabetes," in Howard M. Katzen and Richard J. Mahler, eds., *Diabetes, Obesity, and Vascular Disease,* Advances in Modern Nutrition, 2 vols. (New York: Wiley, 1978), 2: 211–28; Gerald M. Reaven and Jerrold M. Olefsky, "Role of Insulin Resistance in the Pathogenesis of Hyperglycemia," ibid., pp. 229–66; Lester B. Salans and Samuel W. Cushman, "Relationship of Adiposity and Diet to the Abnormalities of Carbohydrate Metabolism in Obesity," ibid., pp. 267–301.

15. Theodore B. Van Itallie and John G. Kral, "The Dilemma of Morbid Obesity," *Journal of the American Medical Association* 246 (1981):999–1003.

16. Charles B. Clayman and Daniel J. O'Reilly, "Jejunoileal Bypass," ibid.:988.

17. Society of Actuaries and Association of Life Insurance Medical Directors of America, *Build Study 1979* (Chicago: Society of Actuaries and Association of Life Insurance Medical Directors of America, 1980), pp. 119–22.

18. Thomas McKeown, *The Role of Medicine* (London: Nuffield Provincial Hospitals Trust, 1976), pp. 61–94.

19. William Wadd, *Cursory Remarks on Corpulence* (London: Callow, 1810); William Banting, *Letter on Corpulence* (London: Harrison, 1863).

20. Banting, *Letter on Corpulence*, 3rd ed. (1864), pp. 36–37.

21. Julie Ann Miller, "Making Old Age Measure Up," *Science News* 120(1981): 74–76.

22. Morton Keller, *The Life Insurance Enterprise, 1885–1910* (Cambridge, Mass.: Harvard University Press, Belknap Press, 1963), pp. 6–9, 157–84, 265–92.

23. Harold M. Frost, "History and Philosophy of Life Insurance Medicine," in Harry E. Ungerleider and Richard S. Gubner, eds., *Life Insurance and Medicine* (Springfield, Ill.: Charles C. Thomas, 1958), pp. 201–34; Oscar H. Rogers, "Medical Selection and Substandard Business" (Address Delivered at the Eighteenth Annual Meeting of Life Insurance Medical Directors, New York, N.Y., 23 October 1907), pamphlet, n.p.

24. Oscar H. Rogers, "Build as a Factor Influencing Longevity," *Abstract of the Proceedings of the Association of Life Insurance Medical Directors of America from Organization to and Including the Sixteenth Annual Meeting,* 29 May 1901 (New York: Knickerbocker Press, 1906), pp. 280–88.

25. Ancel Keys, "Is Overweight a Risk Factor for Coronary Heart Disease?" *Cardiovascular Medicine* 4 (1979):1233–43.

26. John K. Gore, "Should Life Companies Discriminate Against Women?" *Papers and Transactions of the Actuarial Society of America* 6 (1900):380–88; Ingrid Waldron, "Why Do Women Live Longer Than Men?" *Journal of Human Stress* (March 1976):2–13; Ingrid Waldron and Susan Johnston, "Why Do Women Live Longer Than Men?" *Journal of Human Stress* (June 1976):19–30; Robert D. Retherford, *The Changing Sex Differential in Mortality,* Studies in Population and Urban Demography, no. 1 (Westport, Conn.: Greenwood, 1975), pp. 78–82.

27. Frost, "History and Philosophy," p. 217.

28. Margaret Ashwell, W. R. S. North, and T. W. Meade, "Social Class, Smoking, and Obesity," *British Medical Journal* 2, no. 6150 (25 November 1978): 1466–67.

29. Louis I. Dublin, "The Influence of Weight on Certain Causes of Death," *Human Biology* 2 (1930):159–84.

30. Louis I. Dublin, *After Eighty Years* (Gainesville: University of Florida Press, 1966), pp. 1–33; Edmund B. Wilson, "Studies on Chromosomes," *Journal of Experimental Zoology* 2 (1905):371–405.

31. Dublin, *After Eighty Years,* pp. 37–49; idem, "Benefits of Reducing," *American Journal of Public Health* 43 (1953):993–96; idem, "Overweight—America's No. 1 Health Problem," *Today's Health* 30 (1952):18–21; idem, "Do Husbands Like Plump Wives?" *McCall's* 78 (March 1951):6,8; idem, "Stop Killing Your Husband," *Reader's Digest* 61 (July 1952):107–9.

32. Louis I. Dublin, "The Insurability of Women" (Address delivered at the Medical Section of the American Life Convention, 1913) 10 pp., pamphlet, n.p.; idem, *After Eighty Years,* pp. 47–49.

33. Dublin, "The Influence of Weight," p. 167.

34. Donald B. Armstrong et al., "Obesity and Its Relation to Health and Disease," *Journal of the American Medical Association* 147 (1951):1007–14; Louis I. Dublin and Herbert H. Marks, "Mortality among Insured Overweights in Recent Years," *Transactions of the Association of Life Insurance Medical Directors* 35 (1951): 235–66; Dublin, "Benefits of Reducing"; idem, "Fat People Who Lose Weight

Notes

Live Longer," in David P. Barr, ed., *Overeating, Overweight, and Obesity,* Nutrition Symposium Series, no. 6, 1953, pp. 106–22; idem, "Relation of Obesity to Longevity," *New England Journal of Medicine* 248 (1953):971–74; Herbert H. Marks, "Influence of Obesity on Morbidity and Mortality," *Bulletin of the New York Academy of Medicine* 36 (1960):296–312.

35. "New Weight Standards for Men and Women," Statistical Bulletin.

36. M. H. Ross, "Length of Life and Caloric Intake," *American Journal of Clinical Nutrition* 25 (1972):834–38.

37. Alex Comfort, "Eat Less, Live Longer," *New Scientist* 53 (1972):689; Richard Conniff, "Living Longer," *Next* (May/June, 1981), pp. 38–48.

38. Leaf, interview (1 February 1980).

39. Myron Winick, "Food and the Fetus," *Natural History* 90 (January, 1981): 76–81.

Chapter 6

1. Robert E. Ricklefs, *Ecology* (Newton, Mass.: Chiron, 1973), pp. 461–501.

2. Caroline M. Pond, "Morphological Aspects and the Ecological and Mechanical Consequences of Fat Deposition in Wild Vertebrates," *Annual Review of Ecology and Systematics* 9 (1978):519–70.

3. E. P. Odum, "Premigratory Hyperphagia in Birds," *American Journal of Clinical Nutrition* 8 (1960):621–29.

4. Claude-Marcel Hladik, "Diet and the Evolution of Feeding Strategies among Forest Primates," in Robert S. O. Harding and Geza Teleki, eds., *Omnivorous Primates* (New York: Columbia University Press, 1981), pp. 231–32.

5. Steven J. C. Gaulin and Melvin Konner, "On the Natural Diet of Primates, Including Humans," in R. J. Wurtman and J. J. Wurtman, eds., *Nutrition and the Brain,* vol. 1 (New York: Raven Press, 1977), pp. 1–86; Alan E. Mann, "Diet and Human Evolution," in Harding and Teleki, *Omnivorous Primates,* pp. 10–36.

6. Pond, "Morphological Aspects," pp. 552–53.

7. Paul Colinvaux, *Why Big Fierce Animals Are Rare* (Princeton: Princeton University Press, 1978), pp. 136–49.

8. Ricklefs, *Ecology,* pp. 488–501.

9. Richard Borshay Lee, *The !Kung San* (Cambridge, England: Cambridge University Press, 1979), pp. 250–306; Gaulin and Konner, "On the Natural Diet," pp. 60–69.

10. Hladik, "Diet and the Evolution," pp. 243–44.

11. Brian Hayden, "Subsistence and Ecological Adaptations of Modern Hunter/Gatherers," in Harding and Teleki, *Omnivorous Primates,* pp. 394–98.

12. Glynn Isaac, "The Diet of Early Man," *World Archaeology* 2 (1970):278–99; Glynn Ll. Isaac and Diana C. Crader, "To What Extent Were Early Hominids Carnivorous?," in Harding and Teleki, *Omnivorous Primates,* pp. 37–103.

13. Pond, "Morphological Aspects," p. 553.

14. Lee, *The !Kung San,* p. 314.

15. Rose E. Frisch, "Food Intake, Fatness, and Reproductive Ability," in R. A. Vigersky, ed., *Anorexia Nervosa* (New York: Raven Press, 1977), pp. 149–61; idem, "Population, Food Intake, and Fertility," *Science* 199 (1978):22–30.

16. Pond, "Morphological Aspects," 558–60; D. A. W. Edwards, "Differ-

ences in the Distribution of Subcutaneous Fat with Sex and Maturity," *Clinical Science* 10 (1951):305–15; Božo Škerlj et al., "Subcutaneous Fat and Age Changes in Body Build and Body Form in Women," *American Journal of Physical Anthropology* 11 (n.s., 1953):577–600; Stanley M. Garn, "Fat Patterning and Fat Intercorrelations in the Adult Male," *Human Biology* 26 (1954):59–69; William H. Mueller and Russell M. Reid, "A Multivariate Analysis of Fatness and Relative Fat Patterning," *American Journal of Physical Anthropology* 50 (1979):199–208.

17. Pond, "Morphological Aspects," p. 559.

18. W. F. Bodmer and L. L. Cavalli-Sforza, *Genetics, Evolution, and Man* (San Francisco: W. H. Freeman, 1976), pp. 527–55.

19. Anne Scott Beller, *Fat and Thin* (New York: Farrar, Straus & Giroux, 1978), pp. 19–36.

20. O. Schaefer, "Are Eskimos More or Less Obese Than Other Canadians?" *American Journal of Clinical Nutrition* 30 (1977):1623–28.

21. Pond, "Morphological Aspects," pp. 551–53.

22. Cahill, interview (19 September 1979); Ivan G. Pawson and Craig Janes, "Massive Obesity in a Migrant Samoan Population," *American Journal of Public Health* 71 (1981):508–13; Peter T. Boag and Peter R. Grant, "Intense Natural Selection in a Population of Darwin's Finches (Geospizinae) in the Galápagos," *Science* 214 (1981):82–84.

23. R. E. Wright-St. Clair, "Diet of the Maoris of New Zealand," *Ecology of Food and Nutrition* 1 (1972):213–23.

24. C. M. Cassidy, "Nutrition and Health in Agriculturists and Hunter-Gatherers: A Case Study of Two Prehistoric Populations," in Norge W. Jerome et al., eds., *Nutritional Anthropology: Contemporary Approaches to Diet and Culture* (Pleasantville, N. Y.: Redgrave, 1980), pp. 117–45; Jack Harlan, *Crops and Man* (Madison, Wisc.: American Society of Agronomy and the Crop Science Society of America, 1975), pp. 48–51.

25. Charles A. Reed, "Origins of Agriculture," in Charles A. Reed, ed., *Origins of Agriculture* (The Hague: Mouton, 1977), pp. 879–953.

26. Carlo M. Cipolla, *The Economic History of World Population,* 7th ed. (Harmondsworth: Penguin, 1978), pp. 86–90.

27. William C. Knowler et al., "Diabetes Incidence in Pima Indians: Contributions of Obesity and Parental Diabetes,"*American Journal of Epidemiology* 113 (1981): 144–56; W. Bruce Masse, "Prehistoric Irrigation Systems in the Salt River Valley, Arizona," *Science* 214 (1981):408–15.

28. James V. Neel, "Diabetes Mellitus," *American Journal of Human Genetics* 14 (1962):353–62; D. L. Coleman, "Diabetes and Obesity," *Nutrition Reviews* 36 (1978):129–32; idem, "Obesity Genes," *Science* 203 (1979):663–65; A. E. Dugdale and P. R. Payne, "Pattern of Lean and Fat Deposition in Adults," *Nature* 266 (1977):349–51.

29. William H. McNeill, *Plagues and Peoples* (New York: Doubleday/Anchor, 1976), pp. 35–76.

30. Quoted in Leslie A. Marchand, *Byron* (New York: Alfred A. Knopf, 1970), p. 399.

Notes

Chapter 7

1. *Boston Globe,* 22 February 1979, p. 14.
2. Margaret Walters, *The Nude Male* (New York: Penguin Books, 1979), pp. 290–91.
3. Kenneth Clark, *The Nude,* Bollingen ser. 35, no. 2 (Princeton: Princeton University Press, 1956), p. 14.
4. Anne Hollander, *Seeing through Clothes* (New York: Viking Press, 1978), pp. xiv, 90.
5. Walters, *The Nude Male,* p. 13.
6. Carol M. Cipolla, *The Economic History of World Population* (New York: Penguin Books, 1978), p. 115; Emily R. Coleman, "Medieval Marriage Characteristics," *Journal of Interdisciplinary History* 2 (1971):205–19; Lawrence Stone, *The Family, Sex and Marriage: In England 1500–1800* (New York: Harper & Row, 1977), pp. 483–91; Emmanuel LeRoy Ladurice, *Montaillou: The Promised Land of Error,* trans. Barbara Bray (New York: George Braziller, Inc., 1978), pp. 139–68.
7. Clark, *The Nude,* p. 319; Hollander, *Seeing through Clothes,* p. 110.
8. Clark, *The Nude,* pp. 318–20; Hollander, *Seeing through Clothes,* pp. 94, 109, 111.
9. Hollander, *Seeing through Clothes,* p. 98.
10. Ibid., p. 106.
11. Stone, *Family, Sex and Marriage,* p. 63.
12. Jo Ann McNamara and Suzanne Wemple, "The Power of Women through the Family in Medieval Europe," in Mary S. Hartman and Lois Banner, eds., *Clio's Consciousness Raised* (New York: Harper & Row, Harper Torchbooks, 1974), pp. 103–18.
13. Stone, *Family, Sex and Marriage,* pp. 83–91.
14. Robert V. Schnucker, "Elizabethan Birth Control and Puritan Attitudes," *Journal of Interdisciplinary History* 5 (1975):655–67; Johan Huizinga, *The Waning of the Middle Ages,* (London: Edward Arnold, 1924), p. 114; Stone, *Family, Sex and Marriage,* pp. 66, 135–42.
15. Philippe Ariès, *Centuries of Childhood,* trans. Robert Baldick (New York: Alfred A. Knopf, 1962), pp. 38, 40; Stone, *Family, Sex and Marriage,* pp. 63–81, 105–14; Barbara A. Hanawalt, "Childrearing among the Lower Classes of Late Medieval England," *Journal of Interdisciplinary History* 8 (1977):1–22.
16. Clark, *The Nude,* pp. 2, 343; Hollander, *Seeing through Clothes,* pp. 55, 92.
17. Hollander, *Seeing through Clothes,* pp. 148–52; E. E. Rich and C. H. Wilson, eds., *The Cambridge Economic History* (Cambridge: Cambridge University Press, 1977), 5:9–10; Pierre Goubert, *The Ancient Régime,* trans. Steve Cox (London: Weidenfeld & Nicolson, 1973), pp. 36–42.
18. Michel Foucault, *The History of Sexuality,* trans. Robert Hurley (1978; New York: Random House, Vintage Books, 1980), 1:17–35; Stone, *Family, Sex and Marriage,* pp. 288–324.
19. Steven Marcus, *The Other Victorians* (1966; New York: New American Library, Meridian, 1974), p. 282; David Foxon, *Libertine Literature in England, 1660–1745.* Reprinted, with revisions, from *The Book Collector* (London: The Book Collector, 1964), pp. 4–10; Stone, *Family, Sex and Marriage,* pp. 537–40.
20. Stone, *Family, Sex and Marriage,* pp. 444–47, 536.
21. Natalie Zemon Davis, *Society and Culture in Early Modern France* (Stanford: Stanford University Press), pp. 124–51.

22. Louise A. Tilly, Joan W. Scott, and Miriam Cohen, "Women's Work and European Fertility Patterns," *Journal of Interdisciplinary History* 6 (1976):447–76; Stone, *Family, Sex and Marriage*, p. 550.

23. Mario Praz, *The Romantic Agony*, trans. Angus Davidson, 2nd ed. (London: Oxford University Press, 1951), pp. 74–79; Susan Sontag, *Illness as Metaphor* (New York: Farrar, Straus & Giroux, 1978), pp. 29–31.

24. Richard Jenkyns, *The Victorians and Ancient Greece* (Cambridge, Mass.: Harvard University Press, 1980), pp. 1–20, 133–54; Walters, *The Nude Male*, pp. 45, 48–53, 62; Clark, *The Nude*, pp. 10, 23–24.

25. George Gordon, Lord Byron, *The Corsair* (1814) lines 197–98; Sontag, *Illness*, p. 29.

26. Leslie A. Marchand, *Byron* (New York: Alfred A. Knopf, 1970), pp. 2–10, 43, 109, 243, 386, 397.

27. William Shakespeare, *Hamlet*, act 5, sc. 2, line 287; Hollander, *Seeing through Clothes*, pp. 123–24.

28. Byron, *The Waltz* (1812), lines 192–99.

29. Ellen Moers, *The Dandy* (New York: Viking Press, 1960), pp. 27–28.

30. William Acton, *The Functions and Disorders of the Reproductive Organs in Childhood, Youth, Adult Age, and Advanced Life Considered in Their Physiological, Social, and Moral Relations*, 4th ed. (London: John Churchill and Sons, 1865), pp. 11, 71–72. (The latter two quotations are from Acton's summary of a pamphlet by Dr. Ritchie, "An enquiry into a frequent cause of insanity in young men.")

31. Stone, *Family, Sex and Marriage*, p. 495.

32. Bruce Haley, *The Healthy Body and Victorian Culture* (Cambridge, Mass.: Harvard University Press, 1978), pp. 205–10.

33. Henry F. Pringle, *The Life and Times of William Howard Taft* 2 vols. (New York: Farrar & Rinehart, 1939), 1:286–88, 2:1072–74.

34. Daniel Scott Smith, "Family Limitation, Sexual Control, and Domestic Feminism in Victorian America," in Hartman and Banner, eds., *Clio's Consciousness Raised*, pp. 119–36; Acton, *Functions and Disorders*, p. 112; Carroll Smith-Rosenberg and Charles Rosenberg, "The Female Animal," *Journal of American History* 60 (1973):332–56; Marcus, *The Other Victorians*, pp. 197–251.

35. Ruth H. Bloch, "Untangling the Roots of Modern Sex Roles," *Signs* 4 (1978):237–52; Nancy F. Cott, "Passionlessness," ibid.:219–36.

36. William L. Langer, "The Origins of the Birth Control Movement in England in the Early Nineteenth Century," *Journal of Interdisciplinary History* 5 (1975):669–86; Marcus, *The Other Victorians*, pp. 218, 234–35.

37. Patrick Bade, *Femme Fatale* (New York: Mayflower Books, 1979), pp. 6–39.

38. Charles Neilson Gattey, *A Bird of Curious Plumage* (London: Constable, 1971), pp. 1–6.

39. Praz, *Romantic Agony*, pp. 122, 398; Gattey, *Bird*, p. 22.

40. Gattey, *Bird*, passim.

41. Henry James, *William Wetmore Story and His Friends: From Letters, Diaries, and Recollections*, 2 vols. (Boston: Houghton, Mifflin, 1903), 2:162–63.

42. Bade, *Femme Fatale*, pp. 19, 25, 36.

43. August Strindberg, *The Father*, 1887; Bade, *Femme Fatale*, p. 24.

44. Cornelia Otis Skinner, *Madame Sarah* (Boston: Houghton Mifflin, 1967), pp. 53, 54, 56, 92, 156, and passim.

45. Hollander, *Seeing through Clothes*, pp. 353–55; Lois W. Banner, *"Being Beautiful*

in America (New York: Knopf) in press; Quentin Bell, "The Riddle of Fashion," *Human Nature* 1 (1978):60–68.

46. Banner, *Being Beautiful;* Gerald Bordman, *American Musical Theatre* (New York: Oxford University Press, 1978), pp. 172–73.

47. Bade, *Femme Fatale,* pp. 30–31.

48. Hollander, *Seeing through Clothes,* pp. 151–56, 327–44.

49. Gus Kahn and Raymond B. Egan, "Ain't We Got Fun," 1921.

50. Georgina Howell, in *Vogue: Sixty Years of Celebrities and Fashion from British Vogue* (1975; New York; Penguin, 1978), pp. 19–37.

51. Howell, in *Vogue: Sixty Years,* pp. 9–11; Arlene Croce, *The Fred Astaire & Ginger Rogers Book* (New York: Galahad Books, 1972), p. 46.

52. Richard Griffith and Arthur Mayer, *The Movies: The Sixty Year Story of the World of Hollywood and Its Effect on America, from Pre-Nickelodeon Days to the Present* (New York: Simon and Schuster, 1957), p. 57.

53. Linda Nochlin, "Iconography Versus Ideology," personal communication.

54. Ephraim Katz, *The Film Encyclopedia* (New York: Thomas Y. Crowell, 1979), p. 464.

55. Hollander, *Seeing through Clothes,* pp. 345–49.

Chapter 8

1. George Bernard Shaw, *The Doctor's Dilemma* (Baltimore: Penguin Books, Inc., 1974), p. 68.

2. Peter Lindner, "Determining Competence in the Bariatric Physician," *Obesity and Bariatric Medicine* 9 (1980):105–107. Unless otherwise noted, descriptions of the ASBP and its members are based on observations and conversations at the Annual Obesity and Associated Conditions Symposium of the American Society of Bariatric Physicians, 25–28 September 1980, Aladdin Hotel, Las Vegas.

3. Blackburn, interview (22 August 1979).

4. *AMA Drug Evaluations,* 3rd ed. (Littleton, Mass.: Publishing Sciences Group, Inc., 1977), p. 487.

5. Lee, interview (28 September 1980).

6. Information on the history of the ASBP is from an interview with the society's Director of Professional Affairs, W. L. Asher, 25 September 1980.

7. Mark Lesses and Abraham Myerson, "Human Autonomic Pharmacology," *New England Journal of Medicine* 218 (1938):119–24.

8. Stanley Harris, A. C. Ivy, and Laureen Searle, "The Mechanism of Amphetamine-Induced Loss of Weight," *Journal of the American Medical Association* 134 (1947):1468–75.

9. Drug company statistics, unpublished, cited in Lester Grinspoon and Peter Hedblom, *The Speed Culture* (Cambridge, Mass.: Harvard University Press, 1975), p. 207; J. W. Finch, "The Overweight Obstetric Patient with Special Reference to the Use of Dexedrine Sulfate," *Journal of the Oklahoma State Medical Association* 40 (1947):119–22, cited ibid pp. 213–14.

10. U.S. Food and Drug Administration, "Anorectics Have Limited Use in Treatment of Obesity," *FDA Drug Bulletin,* December 1972.

11. Eliot Marshall, "FDA Bans Speed in Diet Pills," *Science* 205 (1979):474–75; "Cracking Down on Pep Pills," *Newsweek* 30 July 1979, p. 66; Einar Perman, "Speed in Sweden," *New England Journal of Medicine* 283 (1970):760–61. Information on street use of amphetaminelike drugs in the United States is from an interview with David Smith, medical director, Haight-Ashbury Free Medical Clinic, San Francisco, 3 December 1979.

12. Albert Simeons, "Chorionic Gonadotrophin in the Treatment of Obese Women," *American Journal of Clinical Nutrition* 13 (1963):197–98.

13. Rena Wing and Robert Jeffery, "Outpatient Treatments of Obesity," *International Journal of Obesity* 3 (1979):261–79.

14. Joel Gurin, "King of the California Diet Business," *San Francisco Magazine*, March 1980, pp. 51–54. Decision of the Fourth District Medical Review Committee adopted by the California Board of Medical Quality Assurance, 4 February 1981.

15. Thera-Thin ad in *San Francisco Chronicle/Examiner*, 12 November 1978; Maxi-Slim ad, ibid., 17 February 1980. See also "Delusions of Vigor," *Consumer Reports*, January 1979, pp. 50–54.

16. Pat Johnson Jacoby, "Fake Amphetamines Can Harm the Unaware," *University of California Clip Sheet*, 14 July 1981; Alan Richman, "Drug Buyer Beware," *Boston Globe* 20 May 1981.

17. "Fat Profits in Diet Aids," *San Francisco Chronicle*, 3 November 1980 (reprinted from *New York Times*); Albert Dietz, "Amphetamine-like Reactions to Phenylpropanolamine," *Journal of the American Medical Association* 245 (1981): 601–602.

18. J. Thomas Cooper with Paul Hagan, *Dr. Cooper's Fabulous Fructose Diet* (New York: M. Evans and Company, Inc., 1979); Advertisement, *New York Times* 3 April 1979, p. C11; J. Thomas Cooper, *Dr. Cooper's South American Diet* (Atlanta: Braswell Health Book Publishing Co., 1980).

19. Cooper, *South American Diet*, p. 15.

20. Cooper, interview at ASBP meeting (28 September 1980).

21. Theodore Berland and the Editors of Consumer Guide, *Rating the Diets* (New York: Signet, 1979); Frank Warren and Theodore Berland, *Lose Weight the Acupuncture Way* (1976; New York: Cornerstone Library, 1978).

22. *The Amazing Diet Secret of a Desperate Housewife*, cited in Berland, *Rating*, pp. 86–87; *Hollywood Emergency Diet* advertised in *Psychology Today*, October 1978, p. 83; Pritikin discussed in Berland, *Rating*, p. 150ff; Judy Mazel, *The Beverly Hills Diet* (New York: Macmillan Publishing Co., Inc., 1981), jacket copy and frontispiece.

23. Publishing history of *Calories Don't Count* is discussed in Peter Wyden, *The Overweight Society* (New York: William Morrow & Company, 1965), pp. 191–207; Robert Linn with Sandra Lee Stuart, *The Last Chance Diet* (1976; New York: Bantam, 1977); "Panacea for Obesity?" *Medical World News* 18 (22 August 1977):55.

24. Sidney Petrie with Robert Stone, *Fat Destroyer Foods* (1974; West Nyack, N.Y.: Parker Publishing Co., Inc., 1975), p. 48.

25. Edwin Bayrd, *The Thin Game* (New York: Newsweek Books, 1978), p. 53.

26. Mazel, *Beverly Hills*, p. 124.

27. *Ibid*, pp. xvii, 17.

28. Linn, *Last Chance Diet*.

29. Robert Atkins, *Dr. Atkins' Diet Revolution* (1972; New York: Bantam, 1973).

30. *Fasting* quoted in Berland, *Rating*, p. 19; Linn, *Last Chance Diet*, p. 78.

31. William Banting, *Letter on Corpulence Addressed to the Public,* 3rd ed. (London: Harrison, 1864), p. 17.

32. Herman Tarnower and Samm Sinclair Baker, *The Complete Scarsdale Medical Diet* (New York: Rawson, Wade Publishers, Inc., 1978).

33. Alfred Pennington, "Reorientation on Obesity," *New England Journal of Medicine* 248 (1953): 959–64.

34. Sidney C. Werner, "Comparison between Weight Reduction on a High-Calorie, High-Fat Diet and on an Isocaloric Regimen High in Carbohydrate," *New England Journal of Medicine* 252 (1955):661–65.

35. Herman Taller, *Calories Don't Count* (New York: Simon and Schuster, 1961).

36. Bayrd, *Thin Game,* pp. 57–60; Wyden, *Overweight Society,* pp. 202–206.

37. Laurance Kinsell et al., "Calories Do Count," *Metabolism* 13 (1964):195–204.

38. Theodore Van Itallie, "Dietary Fiber and Obesity," *American Journal of Clinical Nutrition* 31 (1978):S43–S52; James Anderson and Beverly Sieling, "High Fiber Diets for Obese Diabetic Patients," *Obesity and Bariatric Medicine* 9 (1980): 109–13; Olaf Mickelsen et al., "Effects of a High Fiber Bread Diet on Weight Loss in College-Age Males," *American Journal of Clinical Nutrition* 32 (1979): 1703–1709.

39. Atkins, *Diet Revolution,* p. 13.

40. Robert Sherwin et al., letter, *New England Journal of Medicine* 303 (1980):159.

41. Atkins, *Diet Revolution,* pp. 296–97.

42. Robert Atkins, *Dr. Atkins' Nutrition Breakthrough* (New York: William Morrow & Co., Inc., 1981). See Atkins, *Diet Revolution,* pp. 299–312.

43. Blackburn, interview (22 August 1979).

44. Saul Genuth, Jamie Castro, and Victor Vertes, "Weight Reduction in Obesity by Outpatient Semistarvation," *Journal of the American Medical Association* 230 (1974):987–91; Peter Lindner and George Blackburn, "Multidisciplinary Approach to Obesity Utilizing Fasting Modified by Protein-Sparing Therapy," *Obesity and Bariatric Medicine* 5 (1976):198–216; Victor Vertes, Saul Genuth, and Irene Hazelton, "Supplemented Fasting as a Large-Scale Outpatient Program," *Journal of the American Medical Association* 238 (1977):2151–53; Bruce Bistrian, "Clinical Use of a Protein-Sparing Modified Fast," ibid. 240 (1978):2299–302.

45. Genuth, Castro, and Vertes, "Weight Reduction in Obesity," p. 990.

46. Linn, *Last Chance Diet,* p. 91.

47. "Protein Warning," *Newsweek,* 26 February 1979, p. 20B; Linn, *Last Chance Diet,* p. 109; U.S. Food and Drug Administration, "Liquid Protein and Sudden Cardiac Deaths," *FDA Drug Bulletin* 8 (May–July 1978):18.

48. Julie Ann Miller, "Liquid Protein," *Science News* 114 (23 September 1978): 217.

49. Blackburn, interview (22 August 1979).

50. Rafael Lantigua et al., "Cardiac Arrhythmias Associated with a Liquid Protein Diet for the Treatment of Obesity," *New England Journal of Medicine* 303 (1980):735–38.

51. "Cardiac Arrhythmias during Liquid Protein Diet," Letters, *New England Journal of Medicine* 304 (1981):297–98.

52. Joseph DeHaven et al., "Nitrogen and Sodium Balance and Sympathetic-Nervous System Activity in Obese Subjects Treated with a Low-Calorie Protein or Mixed Diet," *New England Journal of Medicine* 302 (1980):477–82; Philip Felig,

"Four Questions about Protein Diets," ibid. 298 (1978):1025–26; Clifton Bogardus et al., "Comparison of Carbohydrate-Containing and Carbohydrate-Restricted Hypocaloric Diets in the Treatment of Obesity," *Journal of Clinical Investigation* 68 (1981):399–404.

53. Correspondence, *New England Journal of Medicine* 303 (1980):157–59; J. S. Garrow, *Energy Balance and Obesity in Man,* 2nd ed. (New York: Elsevier/North-Holland Biomedical Press, 1978), p. 167.

54. Julie Hatfield, "The Shrinking Woman," *Boston Globe,* 3 February 1981, p. 53.

55. Linda Dannenberg, "Beauty Treatments in the Paris Salons," *New York Times,* 24 January 1979.

56. "Tone-N-Trim," *Health and Diet Times,* September/October 1980, p. 47.

Chapter 9

1. Thomas Pickering, "Exercise and the Prevention of Coronary Heart Disease," *Cardiovascular Reviews and Reports* 2 (1981):227–29.

2. Eleanor Pao, "Nutrient Consumption Patterns of Individuals in 1977 and 1965," *Outlook '80,* U.S. Department of Agriculture, 6 November 1979; Sidney Abraham, *Weight by Height and Age for Adults 18–74 Years* (Hyattsville, Md.: U.S. Department of Health, Education and Welfare, 1979).

3. Ralph Paffenbarger and Wayne Hale, "Work Activity and Coronary Heart Mortality," *New England Journal of Medicine* 292 (1975):545–50.

4. George Gallup, "Motor Boating, Golf, and Bowling Decline as Participation Sports," *The Gallup Poll* (press release), 15 May 1980.

5. Cited in Richard Stuart and Barbara Davis, *Slim Chance in a Fat World* (Champaign, Ill.: Research Press, 1972), p. 172.

6. Frank Konishi, Judi Kesselman, and Franklynn Peterson, *The Eat Anything Exercise Diet* (New York: William Morrow & Co., Inc., 1979), as excerpted in *San Francisco Chronicle,* 30 January 1980, p. 36.

7. H. T. Edwards, A. Thorndike, and D. B. Dill, "The Energy Requirement in Strenuous Muscular Exercise," *New England Journal of Medicine* 213 (1935): 532–35.

8. Per Björntorp, "Exercise and Obesity," *Psychiatric Clinics of North America* 1 (1978):691–96.

9. Beverly Bullen, Robert Reed, and Jean Mayer, "Physical Activity of Obese and Nonobese Adolescent Girls Appraised by Motion Picture Sampling," *American Journal of Clinical Nutrition* 14 (1964):211–23.

10. Marjorie Waxman and Albert Stunkard, "Caloric Intake and Expenditure of Obese Boys," *Journal of Pediatrics* 2 (1980):187–93.

11. Anna-Marie Chirico and Albert Stunkard, "Physical Activity and Human Obesity," *New England Journal of Medicine* 263 (1960):935–40.

12. Bruce Harger, James Miller, and James Thomas, "The Caloric Cost of Running," *Journal of the American Medical Association* 228 (1974):482–83.

13. "How to Burn Up Fat Faster while Maintaining Muscle," *University of California Clip Sheet,* 20 May 1980; Stern, interview (7 May 1981); J. Skrobak-Kaczynski and K. Lange Andersen, "The Effect of a High Level of Habitual Physical Activity in the Regulation of Fatness During Aging," *International Archives of Occupational and Environmental Health* 36 (1975):41–46.

14. Grant Gwinup, "Effect of Exercise Alone on the Weight of Obese Women," *Archives of Internal Medicine* 135 (1975):676–80.

15. D. L. Moody, J. Kollias and E. R. Buskirk, "The Effect of a Moderate Exercise Program on Body Weight and Skinfold Thickness in Overweight College Women," *Medicine and Science in Sports* 1 (no.2, 1969):75–80; Arthur Leon et al., "Effects of a Vigorous Walking Program on Body Composition, and Carbohydrate and Lipid Metabolism of Obese Young Men," *American Journal of Clinical Nutrition* 32 (1979):1776–87.

16. Leonard Epstein and Rena Wing, "Aerobic Exercise and Weight," *Addictive Behaviors* 5 (1980):371–88; Erratum, ibid. 6 (1981):183.

17. Lawrence Oscai, "The Role of Exercise in Weight Control," in J. Wilmore, ed., *Exercise and Sports Review* (New York: Academic Press, 1973), 1:103–23; Herbert DeVries, *Physiology of Exercise for Physical Education and Athletics,* 2nd ed. (Dubuque, Iowa: Wm. C. Brown Co., Publishers, 1974), pp. 257–58.

18. W. C. Welham and A. R. Behnke, "The Specific Gravity of Healthy Men," *Journal of the American Medical Association* 118 (1942):498–501; "Heavy Duty for Heavyweights," *Newsweek,* 11 May 1981, p. 21.

19. Ullyot, interview (19 September 1980).

20. See Frank Katch and William McArdle, *Nutrition, Weight Control and Exercise* (Boston: Houghton Mifflin Co., 1977), pp. 39–68.

21. R. Margaria et al., "Energy Cost of Running," *Journal of Applied Physiology* 18 (1963): 367–70.

22. Knuttgen, interview (4 June 1980).

23. Ibid.

24. American College of Sports Medicine, "Position Statement, The Recommended Quantity and Quality of Exercise for Developing and Maintaining Fitness in Healthy Adults," *Medicine and Science in Sports* 10 (no. 3 1978):vii–x.

25. Epstein and Wing, "Aerobic Exercise and Weight."

26. Stephen Phinney et al., "Capacity for Moderate Exercise in Obese Subjects after Adaptation to a Hypocaloric Ketogenic Diet," *Journal of Clinical Investigation* 66 (1980):1152–61; Clifton Bogardus et al., "Comparison of Carbohydrate-Containing and Carbohydrate-Restricted Hypocaloric Diets in the Treatment of Obesity," ibid. 68 (1981):399–404; Phinney, interview (28 August 1981).

27. R. M. Kark, R. E. Johnson, and J. S. Lewis, "Defects of Pemmican as an Emergency Ration for Infantry Troops," *War Medicine* 7 (1945):345–52.

28. Grant Gwinup, Reg Chelvam, and Terry Steinberg, "Thickness of Subcutaneous Fat and Activity of Underlying Muscles," *Annals of Internal Medicine* 74 (1971):408–11.

29. Covert Bailey, *Fit or Fat?* (1977; Boston: Houghton Mifflin Co., 1978), pp. 54–55.

30. Maja Schade et al., "Spot Reducing in Overweight College Women," *Research Quarterly* 33 (1962):461–71.

31. Kathy Mackay, "Richard Simmons, the Sultan of Svelte, Applies both the Carrot and the Shtick," *People* 2 November 1981, pp. 93–100; *Richard Simmons' Never-Say-Diet Book* (New York: Warner, 1980), jacket and pp. 74, 76, 81.

32. Phil Gunby, "Losing Weight," *Journal of the American Medical Association* 239 (1978):1729–30.

33. Thomas Bassler, "Marathon Running and Immunity to Heart Disease,"

The Physician and Sportsmedicine 3 (April 1975):77–80; George Burch, "Of Jogging," *American Heart Journal* (1979)97:407; "Jogging Critic Retracts Claim," *San Francisco Chronicle*, 27 April 1979, p. 2; Barnard Quoted in "Grab Bag," *San Francisco Chronicle*, 30 June 1979.

34. Paul Thompson et al., "Death During Jogging or Running," *Journal of the American Medical Association* 242 (1979):1265–67; Jeffrey P. Koplan, "Cardiovascular Deaths While Running," ibid.:2578–79.

35. Paffenbarger and Hale, "Work Activity and Coronary Heart Mortality"; Ralph Paffenbarger, Alvin Wing, and Robert Hyde, "Physical Activity as an Index of Heart Attack Risk in College Alumni," *American Journal of Epidemiology* 108 (1978):161–75.

36. William Kannel and Paul Sorlie, "Some Health Benefits of Physical Activity," *Archives of Internal Medicine* 139 (1979):857–61; Thomas Royle Dawber, *The Framingham Study* (Cambridge, Mass.: Harvard University Press, 1980), pp. 157–71.

37. Tavia Gordon et al., "Diet and Its Relation to Coronary Heart Disease and Death in Three Populations," *Circulation* 63 (1981):500–515.

38. Michael Brown, Petri Kovanen, and Joseph Goldstein, "Regulation of Plasma Cholesterol by Lipoprotein Receptors," *Science* 212 (1981):628–35.

39. Peter Wood et al., "Plasma Lipoprotein Distributions in Male and Female Runners," *Annals of the New York Academy of Sciences*, 301 (1977):748–63; G. Harley Hartung et al., "Relation of Diet to High-Density-Lipoprotein Cholesterol in Middle-aged Marathon Runners, Joggers, and Inactive Men," *New England Journal of Medicine* 302 (1980):357–61; Jussi Huttunen et al., "Effect of Moderate Physical Exercise on Serum Lipoproteins," *Circulation* 60 (1979):1220–29.

40. Richard Christie, Hugh Bloore, and Robert Logan, "High-Density Lipoprotein (HDL) Cholesterol in Middle-aged Joggers," *New Zealand Medical Journal* 91 (1980):39–40; Aapo Lehtonen and Jorma Viikari, "Serum Lipids in Soccer and Ice-Hockey Players," *Metabolism* 29 (1980):36–39.

41. Roth, interview (2 October 1979); David Leff, "Receptors," *Medical World News* 20 (2 October 1978):70–81; Helena Wachslicht-Rodbard et al., "Increased Insulin Binding to Erythrocytes in Anorexia Nervosa," *New England Journal of Medicine* 300 (1979):882–87.

42. "Successful Diet and Exercise Therapy is Conducted in Vermont for 'Diabesity,'" *Journal of the American Medical Association* 243 (1980):519–20.

43. H. C. R. Simpson et al., "A High Carbohydrate Leguminous Diet Improves All Aspects of Diabetic Control," *Lancet* 1 (1981):1–5.

44. Kelly Brownell and Albert Stunkard, "Physical Activity in the Development and Control of Obesity," in Albert Stunkard, ed., *Obesity* (Philadelphia: W. B. Saunders Co., 1980), pp. 300–24.

45. Oluf Pedersen, Henning Beck-Nielsen, and Lise Heding, "Increased Insulin Receptors After Exercise in Patients with Insulin-Dependent Diabetes Mellitus," *New England Journal of Medicine* 302 (1980):886–92.

46. Elizabeth Rasche González, "Exercise Therapy 'Rediscovered' for Diabetes, But What Does It Do?" *Journal of the American Medical Association* 242 (1979): 1591–92.

47. Jeremiah Stamler et al., "Prevention and Control of Hypertension by Nutritional-Hygienic Means," *Journal of the American Medical Association* 243 (1980):1819–23.

48. Marcin Krotkiewski et al., "Effects of Long-Term Physical Training on

Body Fat, Metabolism, and Blood Pressure in Obesity," *Metabolism* 28 (1979): 650–58.

49. Ethan Sims, "Hypertension and Obesity," in Per Björntorp, ed., *Recent Advances in Obesity Research,* vol. 3 (London: John Libbey & Co., Ltd., in press).

50. Kahler, interview (31 May 1979).

Chapter 10

1. This is a minimum estimate, calculated from the revised ranges of desirable weight announced by the Society of Actuaries on April 12, 1979, and the population estimates published by the National Center for Health Statistics. It applies only to people aged forty to sixty-nine, the group covered by the society's tables released that day. The Society of Actuaries, "Are You of 'Average' Weight? Less Is Better, Study Finds" (press release, April 12, 1979); U.S. Department of Health, Education and Welfare, *Vital and Health Statistics: Series 11, Data from the National Health Survey,* no. 208 (DHEW Publication No. PHS 79-1656), 1979, pp. 17–23.

2. George Maddox and Veronica Liederman, "Overweight as a Social Disability with Medical Implications," *Journal of Medical Education* 44 (1969):214–20.

3. Bruce Hannon and Timothy Lohman, "The Energy Cost of Overweight in the United States," *American Journal of Public Health* 68 (1978):765–67.

4. Jack Germond and Jules Witcover, ". . . and Leaving the Smear Campaign Behind," *Boston Globe,* 7 August 1981, p. 17.

5. Margaret Mackenzie, *Fear of Fat: The Politics of Body Size* (New York: Columbia University Press, in press).

6. Jean Nidetch, *The Story of Weight Watchers* (1970; New York: Signet, 1979.)

7. Helen Canning and Jean Mayer, "Obesity—Its Possible Effect on College Acceptance," *New England Journal of Medicine* 275 (1966):1172–74; Albert Stunkard, "Presidential Address—1974," *Psychosomatic Medicine* 37 (1975):195–236; Stanley Garn et al., "Level of Education, Level of Income, and Level of Fatness in Adults," *American Journal of Clinical Nutrition* 30 (1977):721–25; David H. Tucker et al., "Report on the Study of Weight and Size Discrimination," State of Maryland Commission on Human Relations, 1980, p. 42.

8. "Fat Stewardess Sues to Get Rehired," *San Francisco Chronicle,* 26 June 1979; lawyer quoted in Chris Chase, *The Great American Waistline* (New York: Coward, McCann & Geoghegan, 1981), p. 196.

9. Toby Miller, Judith Coffman, and Ruth Linke, "Survey on Body Image, Weight, and Diet of College Students," *Journal of the American Dietetic Association* 77 (1980):561–66.

10. Susie Orbach, *Fat Is a Feminist Issue* (New York: Paddington Press, Ltd., 1978).

11. Wooley, interview (10 October 1979).

Index

acne, 190

Acton, William, *The Functions and Disorders of the Reproductive Organs,* 190, 192

actuarial tables, 108; development of, 123–28

Adams, Abigail, 185

adolescence: fat distribution in, 157–58; weight gain in, 36, 155

adrenaline, 37

age: weight gain with, 8, 137, 159

d'Agoult, Marie, 195

agriculture: and ability to get fat, 163–65; and epidemics, 166; hazards of, 143

"Ain't We Got Fun," 203

alcohol, 44–45, 129

Ali, Muhammad, 214

"alimentary orgasm," 26

American Academy of Psychoanalysis, 33, 58

American Medical Association, 211; on *Calories Don't Count,* 234

American Psychiatric Association, 32–33

American Society of Bariatric Physicians (ASBP), 212–18

amphetaminelike drugs, 220–21

amphetamines, 91–92; danger of, 219; discovery of, 218; regulation of, 217, 220–221; short-lived effect of, 219–20

Anderson, William, 163

androgyny, 191; and "It," 205

anorexia nervosa, 36; behavior modification's similarity to, 55; and restraint, 48

anxiety: eating to allay, 29–30, 39; of fat people, 32; with weight loss, 47

appetite: compensating for change in activity, 20–21; hormonal influence on, 77; and ketones, 233; two-day lag in, 21–23; *see also* hunger

appetite suppressants, 91–92, 218; over-the-counter, 223–25

Ariès, Philippe, 179

arthritis, and weight gain, 114

artificial sweeteners, 100, 280

atherosclerosis, 266

Atkins, Robert: *Diet Revolution,* 231, 235; *Dr. Atkins' Nutrition Breakthrough,* 236

aversion therapy, 53–54

Bailey, Covert, *Fit or Fat,* 259–60

Banting, William, *Letter on Corpulence,* 124, 232

Bara, Theda, 205

bariatricians, 212–14

Barnard, Christiaan, 263

Bassler, Thomas J., 263

beauty, standards of, 169–70

behavior modification, 49–58; effectiveness of, 56; similarity to anorexia nervosa, 55

di Belgiojoso, Cristina (Principessa, *née* Trivulzio), 194–97

di Belgiojoso, Emilio (Prince),194–95

benzocaine, 224

Berland, Theodore: *Rating the Diets,* 227; *Lose Weight the Acupuncture Way,* 227

Bernhardt, Sarah, 197–99, 201; figure of, 199; as Medea, 197; sculpture by, 198

Index

fashion, 168–209; current, 168; and liberation of women, 171–72; and slender figure, 204; and theater,200

fast: ketosis and, 235; protein-sparing modified (PSMF), 121, 237–40; and transcendence, 13

fat: automatic regulation of, 4; and beauty, 181; brown, 83–84; and child care, 154–155; deficiency of, 16; desire for, 63, 72; distribution of, 71–72; and euphemisms and synonyms for, *xiii–xiv*; as evidence of past hardship, 144; and fate, 3–23; and health hazards, 107–41; hunter-gatherers' preference for, 151; insulin's promotion of accumulation of, 119; lack of fossil evidence of, 144; natural tendency toward, 24; on older female, 159; and reproduction, 155–56; as signal of diabetes, 5; women's need for, in reproduction, 143; women's reserve of, 143; *see also* obesity

fatal man, 185–87

fat cells: chemical signals of, 76–77; number of, 70–71; setpoint and, 60–87; size of, 45

Fat is a Feminist Issue (Orbach), 27

fatness: and fertility, 173; and improved life expectancy, 139; of Polynesians, 162–63; pop psychology of, 25; predisposition to, 36; setpoint for, 42; symbolism of, 208; as term, *xiii*; treated as disease, 58; and tuberculosis, 123

fat people: activity of, 249–51; chronically starved, 41–42; as chronic dieters, 34; food intake of, 60–62; health of, 25, 107–21; mental health of, 30–33; setpoints of, 16; sexuality of, 27–28; stigmatization of, 272, 275, 278; stomach insensitivity of, 38–39; and suicide, 32; survival advantages of, 143–44, 146–47; "thin," 47–48

Fat Underground, 282

FDA (Food and Drug Administration): on amphetamines, 219–20; and phenylpropanolamine, 224

fear, and eating patterns, 38–39

Fee, Ingrid, 279

feminism: appearance of, 185; and fat, 27; and theater, 199

femme fatale, 193–99; comic version of, 205; domestication of, 201–2; return of, 206

fenfluramine, 91–92

Ferguson, James, 56

Ferriss, Alfred, 222–23

Ferster, Charles, 49–50, 54

fertile figure, 173–77, 180

fertility: and body weight, 155–56; excessive, 178–79; limitation of, 178–79, 193, 203; symbolization of, 174–75

flappers, 201, 205–6

Florodora girls, 201

Fonda, Jane, 208

food: crises of in agricultural society, 143; division of labor in gathering, 153; inappropriate use of, 35–36; obsession with, 15; preference for sweet and fatty, 151–52; as red herring, 60; reproduction as response to abundance of, 144; setpoint raised by tasty, 98–101; as tool in power struggle, 36

frame size, 137

Framingham study, 111–12, 264–65

free agent, figure of, 172, 205–8

Freud, Sigmund, 25

Frisch, Rose, 155–56

Functions and Disorders of the Reproductive Organs, The (Acton), 190

Gallup, George, 246

Garbo, Greta, 206

Garn, Stanley, 73–74

Garrow, J. S., 240

Gautier, Théophile, 186–87

genetics, 130–31

George III (King of England), 188

George VI (King of England), 188–89

Gibson, Charles Dana, 202

Gibson girls, 202

Index

jogging, 8; benefits and hazards of, 246
Jordan, Henry, 21–22, 28
Journal of Mathetics, 49
Joy of Sex, The (Comfort), 138
Justine (de Sade), 185

Kahler, Richard, 271
Kahn, Gus, 203
Kannel, William B., 124
Kaplan, Harold, 29–30
Kaplan, Helen Singer, 29–30
Keats, John, 187
Keesey, Richard, 86
Kempner, Walter, 68
Kesselman, Judi, 247
ketones: and claims of lowered appetite, 233, 235; detection of, 216; in protein-sparing modified fast, 237
Keys, Ancel, 11–13, 16–17, 19, 115–16
Kissileff, K. S., 55
Knuttgen, Howard, 257
Konishi, Frank, 247
!Kung San (Bushmen), 149; child care among, 154

Laetrile, 212
Lafayette, Marquis de, 195
Langer, William, 193
Lantigua, Rafael, 239
lazy-body hypothesis, 62
LDL's (low-density lipoproteins) 266
Le Boutillier, John, 276
Lee, Randall, 216–17
lemmings, 148
Leon, Arthur, 253
lethargy, obesity and, 19
Letter on Corpulence (Banting), 124, 232
Levitz, Leonard, 28
life expectancy: increase in, 109, 139; and weight loss, 134–35
life insurance industry, 108–10, 122; and development of actuarial tables, 123–38; unruly growth of, 125

Lindner, Peter, 212–13, 216
Linn, Robert, *Last Chance Diet,* 228, 238
liquid protein diet, 236–40
Liszt, Franz, 195
Lohman, Timothy, 275
Loos, Anita, 208
Luxuskonsumption (extra burning), 80–84

Mack, Debbie, 42–44
Mackarness, Richard, *Eat Fat and Grow Slim,* 228
MacKeen, Patricia, 262
Mackenzie, Margaret, *Fear of Fat: The Politics of Body Size,* 276–77
Mahoney, Michael, 55
Maoris, diet of, 163
marathon runners, 102
Marcus, Steven, 192
marijuana munchies, 45
Marks, Melody, 281
marriage, changes in, 177–78
masochism, 53–54; and exercise, 263
masturbation, Victorian view of, 190
maternal figure, 180–81
Mayer, Jean, 102–5, 248–49, 278
Mayer, Louis B., 206
Mazel, Judith, *The Beverly Hills Diet,* 228–30
McGovern, George, 236
megavitamin therapy, 212
men: anxiety over sexual liberation of women, 197–98; as hunters and fishers, 153–54; ideal body of, 191; leanness of, 156; Victorian, 189–90
Mendel, Gregor Johann, 130
mental health, of fat people, 30–33
metabolism: correcting for deviations from setpoint, 79–87; lowering of, 64; raised by exercise, 248–49; sluggish, 62; thrifty, 165–66
methylcellulose, 224
Metrecal, experimental use of, 21–22
Metropolitan Life Insurance Co., 129–30, 132, 134–36, 138; Welfare Bureau of, 129–30

310

Index